Ethnohistory

Volume 54, Number 1

Winter 2007

**Sexual Encounters/Sexual Collisions:
Alternative Sexualities in Colonial Mesoamerica**

Book Reviews

North America

Latin America

Editor's Introduction

Neil L. Whitehead, *University of Wisconsin–Madison*

This special issue on colonial sexualities demonstrates the importance of ethnohistory to the development of not just particular historiographies but also the theoretical frameworks that guide both historical and anthropological research. The guest editors and contributors have broached important new topics for ethnohistorical research, showing it to be a critical theoretical site for the analysis of the human condition, one that potentially informs all the humanistic and social science disciplines. Deriving from a panel session at the annual meetings of the American Society for Ethnohistory, the essays collected here open a new view on the colonial past in South America that is carefully researched and creatively developed, combining traditional historiographical approaches with the theoretical insights generated by the wider study of gender and sexualities during the last decade. This powerful combination of emerging theory and solid scholarship demonstrates the relevance of an inherently interdisciplinary approach, such as ethnohistory, and how the past, like other cultures, can be a potent source of knowing ourselves. Given the evident, if still often unexcavated, connections between sexuality, power, and desire and the way such relationships are expressed in regimes of bodily control and sexual expression and repression, the topic of sexuality could hardly be more important for ethnohistorians to consider. Current social policy debates in Europe and North America, as well as in postcolonial contexts where the globalized economy is creating dynamic social change, are connected to changing gender roles, emerging sexual economies, forms and

Ethnohistory 54:1 (Winter 2007) DOI 10.1215/00141801-2006-036

codes of representation of sexuality, no less than the status of "marriage" or the prevalence of "divorce." They would be well served by a better understanding of the nature of historical and cultural variation in human sexualities. This fine collection of articles begins that process.

Guest Editors' Introduction

Pete Sigal, *Duke University*
John F. Chuchiak IV, *Missouri State University*

This special issue of *Ethnohistory* presents new scholarship on colonial Mesoamerican sexualities. The contributions address a variety of common themes related to an "ethnohistory of sexuality" in parts of colonial Mesoamerica (Mexico and Guatemala). The authors address alternative and nonreproductive sexualities using a variety of methodologies and sources. From textual analysis to formal linguistic analysis of semantic categories of translation to traditional philology and the use of methodologies from social history, the contributors focus on the sexual experiences and ideologies of men and women, natives, Africans, mestizos, and Europeans, who came together in licit and illicit sexual encounters throughout the colonial period in Mesoamerica.

It is fitting that this special issue be published by *Ethnohistory*, a journal that has remained at the forefront of the field of colonial Latin American women's and gender history and that strives to promote the emerging field of studies in indigenous sexuality. In past issues, debates and presentations of similar emergent investigations have led to the creation of new fields of study into the ethnohistory of indigenous peoples. For instance, the impetus for new scholarly research on indigenous women and resistance began with a special issue of this journal ("Women, Power, and Resistance in Colonial Mesoamerica," vol. 42, no. 4 [1995]). Shortly thereafter, *Ethnohistory* published an issue presenting research on North American indigenous women's responses to colonization ("Native American Women's Responses to Christianity," vol. 43, no. 4 [1996]). A virtual explosion in the study of indigenous women's and gender history

Ethnohistory 54:1 (Winter 2007)   DOI 10.1215/00141801-2006-037

followed.[1] We offer our own special issue of the journal in the hope that
it, similarly, will spark scholarly interest in an ethnohistory of sexuality in
the Americas.

An Ethnohistory of Sexuality

What does it mean to develop an ethnohistory of sexuality? Since the history of sexuality itself is a relatively new field, having come to fruition in
the past generation, this endeavor may seem premature.[2] Further, to some
ethnohistorians (perhaps more than we think), the creation of a historical
field in which ethnohistorical research, or research into the relationship
between historical ethnicities and sexual desires and identities, may seem
frivolous. All of the contributors to this special issue agree that the time
has come to delineate the parameters of this emerging field. Thus we study
here the relationships between the creation of colonial societies; the interactions of indigenous, Hispanic, and African peoples; and the development of concepts of sexuality. This special issue of *Ethnohistory* is a first
attempt to analyze a new field of research, an effort many of the authors
plan to continue through their participation in a project designed to study
"ethnopornography."[3]

Having said this, we must hasten to add that most of the scholarship
reviewed for this issue remains oriented toward the peoples of central and
southeastern Mesoamerica, such as the Maya, but above all the Nahua
(and within this group the Mexica/Aztec), both before and after the conquest. Yet there is a perceptible shift in focus away from imperial capi-
tals, ceremonial centers, and ruling elites toward inquiries whose goal is
a better understanding of life in the appendages of empire, away from the
center, and gauging not only the influence of state systems on these places,
but also the impact of the "periphery" on the "core."

Still, research into the sexual cultures of indigenous peoples, as well as
of Africans and Europeans living in colonial Mesoamerica, is fraught with
problems and pitfalls for the researcher. Previously, the only sources for
understanding the sexual cultures of colonial peoples were the accounts of
colonial Spanish missionaries and conquistadors. Since the 1980s, however,
with the advent of the so-called New Philology, the textual analysis of the
rich indigenous-language resources has become available for the study of
Mesoamerican cultures. Scholars have explored the extant native-language
documentation of the Nahua, Maya, Mixtec, Purépecha, and other Mesoamerican groups. Nevertheless, many of these documents remain silent on
sexuality. There is still hope, however, as many of the articles in this special
issue prove. Through detailed examination and analysis of court records

(inquisitorial, episcopal, and civil), colonial correspondence and petitions, colonial dictionaries, confession manuals, and grammars, as well as other materials and testimonies, details and valuable information concerning sexuality can be rescued from historical oblivion. In the study of alternative sexualities, a wide documentary source base is essential. Archival research into distant provincial and regional archives holds promise for future scholarly attempts to create an ethnohistory of sexuality. As Zeb Tortorici posits in his contribution, "The reconstruction of sexuality and everyday culture in the colonial period is obviously not an impossible task, but it must lead historians to national and provincial archives in search of more systematic and conclusive evidence."

This Special Issue

The five essays and two commentaries presented here show both the intellectual diversity of the field and the set of issues at stake in the study of Mesoamerican sexuality. The methodologies used include microhistorical reconstruction, social history, Inquisition studies, cultural history, and literary analysis. None of the authors presents his or her case as a transparent study showing the realities of colonial sexual behavior. Rather, all problematize the archive as a site where power relations are omnipresent. Thus, just as Martha Few's doctor constructs bodies based on his notion of Enlightenment philosophy and science, the Maya of John F. Chuchiak IV use the concept of sexual sin to play a power game with the Franciscan friars. In colonial Mesoamerica the interactions that took place among the populations led to many conflicts over sexuality. Laura A. Lewis's actors play out scenarios based on the ways Spaniards related particular Mesoamerican ethnic groups to a type of gendered discourse, and Zeb Tortorici's Purépecha men find trouble when their desires and actions force them to interact with state institutions.

All of the authors show that an ethnohistory of colonial Mesoamerican sexualities allows the history of sexuality and Latin American history to make theoretical, methodological, and analytical advances. Pete Sigal's essay presents a tale in which he foregrounds method. By focusing on one, albeit extraordinary, text, Sigal shows that we can read the document to find its "authorial filters," the influences of European and indigenous discourse on its production. Sigal therefore pays close attention to translation, not just from one language to another but also, more deeply, from one system of meaning to another. In looking at filters and translations, Sigal offers a method for uncovering the cultural and intellectual genealogy of any text produced in a colonized environment.

Tortorici's microhistorical study of a criminal case in seventeenth-century Morelia challenges the conventional wisdom that Latin American male homosexualities have been structured around a system of domination and submission in which the dominant party always "tops" the submissive. Tortorici's analysis shows that, at least in Purépecha society, the sexual subculture was much more complex. Further, this case represents a significant historiographical advance, as Tortorici reveals sodomitical spaces and communities even in rural New Spain.

Chuchiak develops a method from social history, using a variety of documents that allege to signify social reality. Yet he goes beyond this method, showing how the Maya used various texts to assert strategic dominance over priests. Chuchiak finds that, while priests used the confessional and confession manuals to promote their own notions of sexual desire in Maya communities, Maya petitioners used the Spanish Inquisition to assert some control over the priests.

Lewis uses Inquisition and criminal sources to connect sodomy and witchcraft, thus working to resolve a debate between Richard Trexler and Michael Horswell in which Trexler asserts that indigenous societies degraded the passive male, while Horswell argues that they accepted, sometimes even celebrated, the passive. Lewis, based on her work on witchcraft, suggests the position of the "active pathic." She defines this position by suggesting that Hispanic and indigenous societies did indeed degrade the passive male, but through this degradation, the position of the passive asserted a certain amount of power in society. Through the symbols of dress, blood, and other elements, Lewis shows that there existed in Hispanic and indigenous societies a fear of contagion stemming from the passive male, a fear that alleged passive sodomites would destabilize social norms.

Few focuses on the case of a hermaphrodite in late colonial Guatemala, arguing that Enlightenment philosophy and science required a stable sex and gender system in which bodies equaled sexes, and in which there could only be two sexes or genders. Doctors and other public figures worked very hard to stabilize this system. The hermaphrodite challenged and threatened to destabilize it, and doctors found ways to place the hermaphrodite back in the appropriate structure. Few shows that the doctor who examined the "hermaphrodite" Juana La Larga staved off all alternative interpretations, whether from Maya or European popular notions, and instead worked to institute a singular scientific knowledge, one which sexed the body in a form that was to become standard in the modern world.

This ethnohistory of Mesoamerican sexuality is a challenge to anthropologists, art historians, and historians in our field. These articles show the vitality and importance of sexual behaviors, desires, and identities in the early Mesoamerican world. The topics broached here are just as important as political economy, social organization, ethnicity, and gender; topics that most scholars who study colonial Latin America agree are vital. Can we make the next leap and incorporate sexualities into the broader histories of this world?

Notes

1 A large number of scholarly studies quickly followed, leading to an explosion in indigenous women's studies in particular and gender studies in general. Most notable among the first wave were Steve J. Stern, *The Secret History of Gender: Women, Men, and Power in Late Colonial Mexico* (Chapel Hill, NC, 1995); Juutlje van der Valk, "Chastity as Legal Empowerment: The Province of Tetepango, Mexico, 1750-1800," in *The Legacy of the Disinherited: Popular Culture in Latin America: Modernity, Globalization, Hybridity and Authenticity*, ed. Ton Salman (Amsterdam, 1996), 93–111; and *Indian Women of Early Mexico*, ed. Susan Schroeder, Stephanie Wood, and Robert Haskett (Norman, OK, 1997). Several other articles and studies followed, including Elisa Sampson Vera Tudela, "Fashioning a *Cacique* Nun: From Saints' Lives to Indian Lives," *Gender History* 9.2 (1997): 171–200; Rebecca Overmyer-Velázquez, "Christian Morality Revealed in New Spain: The Inimical Nahua Woman in Book Ten of the Florentine Codex," *Journal of Women's History* 10.2 (1998): 9–38; Asunción Lavrin, "Indian Brides of Christ: Creating New Spaces for Indigenous Women in New Spain," *Mexican Studies* 15.2 (1999): 225–60; and Carmen Bohórquez, "La mujer indígena y la colonización de la erótica en América Latina," *Estudios: Filosofía, historia, letras* 2.2 (2001): 66–99. Several edited volumes and monographs continued the focus on gender, women, and colonialism, including Lyman L. Johnson and Sonya Lipsett-Rivera, eds., *The Faces of Honor: Sex, Shame, and Violence in Colonial Latin America* (Albuquerque, NM, 1998); Ann Twinam, *Public Lives, Private Secrets: Gender, Honor, Sexuality, and Illegitimacy in Colonial Spanish America* (Stanford, CA, 1999); and Juan Durán Luzio, *Entre la espada y el falo: La mujer americana bajo el conquistador europeo* (San José, Costa Rica, 1999).

2 Some key works that focus largely on sexuality in colonial Mesoamerica include Noemí Quezada, *Amor y magia amorosa entre los aztecas* (Mexico City, 1975); Quezada, *Sexualidad, amor y erotismo: México prehispánico y México colonial* (Mexico City, 1996); Solange Alberro et al., *Seis ensayos sobre el discurso colonial relativo a la comunidad domestica: Matrimonio, familia y sexualidad a través de los cronistas del siglo XVI, el Nuevo Testamento y el Santo Oficio de la Inquisición* (Mexico City, 1980); Alfredo López Austin, *Cuerpo humano e ideología* (Mexico City, 1980); Seminario de Historia de las Mentalidades, *Familia y sexualidad en Nueva España* (Mexico City, 1982); Seminario, *El placer de pecar y el afán de normar* (Mexico City, 1988); Seminario, *Del dicho al hecho: Transgresiones y pautas culturales en la Nueva España* (Mexico City, 1989); Seminario, *Vida cotidiana y cultura en el México virreinal: Antología* (Mexico City, 2000); Sergio Ortega,

ed., *De la santidad a la perversión, o de porqué no se cumplía la ley de Dios en la sociedad novohispana* (Mexico City, 1985); Ortega, ed., *Amor y desamor: Vivencias de parejas en la sociedad novohispano* (Mexico City, 1992); Louise M. Burkhart, *The Slippery Earth: Nahua-Christian Moral Dialogue in Sixteenth-Century Mexico* (Tucson, AZ, 1989); Ana María Atondo Rodríguez, *El amor venal y la condición feminina en el México colonial* (Mexico City, 1992); Rosemary A. Joyce, *Gender and Power in Prehispanic Mesoamerica* (Austin, TX, 2000); Pete Sigal, *From Moon Goddesses to Virgins: The Colonization of Yucatecan Maya Sexual Desire* (Austin, TX, 2000); Martha Few, *Women Who Live Evil Lives: Gender, Religion, and the Politics of Power in Colonial Guatemala, 1650–1750* (Austin, TX, 2002); Federico Garza Carvajal, *Butterflies Will Burn: Prosecuting Sodomites in Early Modern Spain and Mexico* (Austin, TX, 2003).

3 See the papers presented at the panels "Ethnopornography: Sexuality, Colonialism, and Anthropological Knowing," Conference of the American Society for Ethnohistory, Santa Fe, NM, November 2005.

Queer Nahuatl: Sahagún's Faggots and Sodomites, Lesbians and Hermaphrodites

Pete Sigal, *Duke University*

Abstract. This article provides a method for interpreting the place of sexuality in texts that defy analysis. The author uses one source, the *Florentine Codex*, a large and complex bilingual Nahuatl and Spanish document, to decipher some elements about cross-dressing individuals, homosexualities, and gender inversions in Nahua society at the time of the Spanish conquest. The methodology used combines close narrative analysis with intellectual genealogy. The author argues that decoding the texts in this way allows us to uncover a cross-dressing male who engaged in "passive" homosexual acts and had a degraded but institutionalized role to play.

Several years ago I first encountered a statement in the Spanish-language section of a document that read, "You, Tezcatlipoca, are a faggot" (*tu tezcatlipoca eres un puto*).[1] I had already read and retranslated the Nahuatl section of the same document (book 4 of the *Florentine Codex*), which has parallel Nahuatl and Spanish columns, and now I was looking at the Spanish translation. It struck me immediately that the Nahuatl text, which recounts a myth relating to the Nahua god Tezcatlipoca (see fig. 1), does not denigrate him in this way. The myth does state that not Tezcatlipoca, but a lesser god, one closely related to Tezcatlipoca, was a *cuiloni*, a term that I had loosely translated as "passive partner in the act of sodomy," but which one colonial dictionary had translated as *puto*.[2] Three things struck me at once. First, I asked myself, why did the Spanish-language text change the god in the myth from the lesser figure to Tezcatlipoca, one of the most powerful deities in the Nahua pantheon? Second, did *cuiloni* really appropriately translate as *puto*? Third, why would the Nahua have insulted a god

Ethnohistory 54:1 (Winter 2007) DOI 10.1215/00141801-2006-038
Copyright 2007 by American Society for Ethnohistory

by calling him a cuiloni? I knew that, in order to answer these questions, I would have to look at other sources related to Nahua homosexualities; I would have to uncover Nahua traditions, European backgrounds, and Spanish colonialist inventions; and I would have to analyze the filtering mechanisms and translations at play in the *Florentine Codex*.

In this article I microanalyze one brief statement. I thus use only one document (albeit a remarkable twelve-volume text) to derive particular conclusions. I will argue that a close analysis of this single source, focusing on text, translation, and authorial voice, is an important and necessary methodological innovation supported by the broader work that I have completed on Nahua sexuality.

The few other scholars who have analyzed this particular aspect of the *Florentine Codex* and other documents that relate to Nahua "homosexualities" have focused on answering the provocative and inappropriate question, "Were the Nahua at the time of the conquest homophobic?" Indeed, these scholars have answered this question in conflicting ways.[3] The question remains provocative because it plays into modern identity politics, challenging the masculinity of some who assert an unproblematized identification with Nahua warriors, and supporting the sexuality of others who assert an equally unproblematized identification with Nahua peoples who supported those with "two spirits."[4] The question remains inappropriate because it asserts transcultural, transhistorical continuities in presentations of sexual identity. One must focus on narration and discourse to understand how the texts perform sexualities in a context that the indigenous peoples understood. Thus we must ask, "How does this particular narration perform sex? For what purpose does it place sex in discourse?" By asking these questions, I argue that the text itself engages in a particular type of narration influenced by the circumstances of its production. Further, I will show that scholars have paid far too little attention to textual production and mediation—to the writing process itself.

The act of translation, both by the Franciscan friar who authorized and helped produce the *Florentine Codex* in the sixteenth century, and by modern interpreters, is a fundamentally political act. Bernardino de Sahagún, in using the term *puto*, ably associates a supreme Nahua god with unacceptable femininity. Modern translations assert particular concepts of identity politics, oversimplifying complex issues related to the ways the Nahua conceived of sexual behaviors and desires. Arthur Anderson and Charles Dibble, for example, translate *xochihua*, a term analyzed more extensively below, as "pervert."[5] Anderson and Dibble believe that the Nahua saw the xochihua as perverted, but they provide no evidence for

Figure 1. Tezcatlipoca, from the *Florentine Codex*

this translation. In fact, contemporary Western people (the audience for the translation) view perversion as opposed to normalcy. The concept is implicated in much psychological discourse as a particular type of disorder stemming from a disconnection with behaviors deemed normal.[6] Would the Nahua of the sixteenth century have understood such terminology?[7] Would they have seen the xochihua as existing in a binary opposition to a perceived norm? I will suggest that, once we place the term in the context of writing, we will have to answer "no."

Geoffrey Kimball translates the same term as "the one who is homosexual."[8] He also provides no evidence for his translation. The idea that a person *is* homosexual stems from a particular notion of an ingrained, unchanging sexual identity. In other words, such a definition suggests that a person's homosexuality comes from within that person. This is linked to concepts of nature and natural sexuality, concepts with which I will argue the Nahua were wholly unfamiliar.

No dictionaries or primary documents that I have found suggest either that the Nahua viewed the xochihua as "perverted" or that they asserted that this or any other person had an identity as a "homosexual" man (a term I take to mean that either the man in question or society defines this man's sexual identity based on a desire to have sex primarily with other men). Both Sahagún and the modern scholars repress any analysis of translation as a colonizing act.

Language and Text

This article focuses on text, translation, and authorial voice. I use written documents and images related to Nahua homosexualities to highlight my critical historical methodology, in which I seek to unearth the complex hidden network of authorial influences that together create the colonial narrative of sixteenth- and seventeenth-century Mexico. Elsewhere I have engaged in a more comprehensive analysis of Nahua homosexuality.[9] Here I highlight my methodological insights and suggest how current analysts of Nahua sexuality would benefit from a more critical reading of the texts.

I have shown previously that colonial Mesoamerican peoples related sexual behaviors and desires to state formation, the gods, human sacrifice, warfare, and sin—a hybrid cultural matrix in which traditional Meso-american concepts intermixed with Catholic ones.[10] This article emanates from my current work on sexuality among the early colonial Nahua. By using an ethnohistorical method and linguistic analysis, and sifting through the authorial filters of the texts, a method that I highlight here, I assert that the Nahua conception of sexual desire slowly and subtly changed.

The attempt at a sexual conquest through the confessional largely failed, instead producing a hybrid sexual system that survives today in many indigenous Mesoamerican societies. Though conscious efforts by Spaniards to alter Nahua ideas of sexuality did not succeed, much change did occur as the Nahua came into daily contact with Hispanized peoples, and by the early seventeenth century we witness in various archival sources (in both Nahuatl and Spanish) Nahua descriptions of sexual acts and categories that were largely consistent with views then common in Hispanic popular culture.[11] In the same time period, however, Nahua commoners still connected sexual desires with preconquest gods and goddesses, and both nobles and commoners had great difficulty understanding the clerical concept of sin.[12]

Having said this, I wish to emphasize the contingent nature of our knowledge of Nahua sexual desire and subjectivity, indeed of Nahua history and social reality in general. Nahua nobles on the eve of the Spanish conquest believed that the flower signified, among other things, excessive sexual desire. One hundred years later, some Nahua commoners believed that the existence of the scorpion showed them how the gods manipulated human sexual behavior. These two stories alone, related to Nahua metaphor and myth, show that indigenous understandings of sexuality were different from those of the Spanish colonizers, and that these concepts will remain at least partially unknowable to us. However, a careful analysis of the place of sex in the text will allow us to see how these myths and metaphors constructed particular relationships between Nahua culture and individual sexual desires and behaviors.

My scholarship utilizes a method designed to expose the multifaceted influences on the texts' authors. Here I respond to historian Eric Van Young's critique that many who study indigenous-language documents have insufficiently considered the work of interpretation done once the translations are complete.[13] Indeed, I show that many historians in my field need to answer Van Young's call for greater analysis of the power dynamics present in the creation of the texts. I argue that only by carefully uncovering European and indigenous (and later, African) influences can one envision the meanings that the Nahua gave to sexual acts and desires. In this way, and looking particularly closely at the intellectual connections between the individual texts and other, sometimes remote, sometimes close, historical forbearers, we can trace, although contingently, the colonization of the intimate.

The concept of the authorial filter allows me to access a particular mode of writing about sexual issues. Hence, I argue, we can never understand the writings that we use as unmediated sources in which we can hear/read authentic indigenous voices. Postconquest texts always contain voices mediated by a wide variety of influences, which often act as filters to make the voices heard in a framework that makes sense to the colonizing authorities. Thus Nahua voices seen as irrelevant to the colonial project are largely silenced. Still, an effective reader can uncover the mediation process by analyzing the authorial filter. We can discover the influences on any particular author by paying close attention to the writing process.

In this article I provide an example of my methodology in order to model a genealogical analysis in which I uncover one text's performance of sexuality.[14] Here I use the Nahuatl texts and images of the cross-dressing sodomite to illustrate my approach. Spaniards marginalized and maligned this individual, while the Nahua gave him an institutionalized but degraded role to play. I argue that, to understand the meaning of this person to society, we must employ a method that uncovers the filtering processes used to record and manufacture Nahua myths and metaphors in postconquest Nahuatl and Spanish documents.

Nahua Narratives of Homosexuality

In order to understand the process at work here, I find it necessary to recon-struct the authorial voice through a close textual analysis of the *Florentine Codex* and a few related texts that discuss the Nahua puto. The Spanish chronicles show that Spaniards found among the Nahua people whom they considered to be putos, or faggots. While certainly the Spaniards were attempting to "feminize" the "enemy" by calling him a faggot or a sod-omite, there seems little question that Nahuatl-speaking peoples found a role for an individual who, while biologically male, dressed as and per-formed some of the functions of a woman.[15] In order to contextualize the presence of the puto mentioned in the *Florentine Codex*, we must analyze a few contemporaneous Nahua texts that use the same or similar terms.

A sixteenth-century document of indigenous origin, the *Codex Bor-bonicus*, was written in traditional Nahua style, along with some Spanish glosses. Figure 2 relates to fertility and shows the goddess of maize. How-ever, the Spanish gloss accompanying the phallic figures says that "these puto priests did not leave the temple." This text, representing the puto as phallic, stands out from the other sources (indeed, the connection between the puto and fertility seems entirely unique) but still suggests the institu-tionalization of the pictured individual. A phallic puto would seem non-sensical in the Spanish framework. If the puto signifies femininity and the passive role in anal intercourse, his phallicism would be misplaced. How-ever, if we concede that the Spanish gloss may be a misrepresentation, we

Figure 2. Phallic "puto priests," from the *Codex Borbonicus*

can conjecture more about the nature of the cross-cultural translation at work.[16]

In the image the priests hold their hyperextended phalluses on the stage behind the central ceremony invoking the important goddess of maize. If we extended the image outward to cover the full page of the amate-bark manuscript, we would see more phallic priests approaching a sexualized Huastec goddess who appears pregnant.[17] Other descriptions of this ritual (Ochpaniztli) tell us that the priests are Huastecs and their phalluses are made from paper.[18] As Huastecs, outsiders (this ceremony takes place in the Valley of Mexico, while the Huastec emanate from the Gulf Coast), they signify an aggressive, penetrative masculinity. At the same time, the ritual process manipulates and controls their masculinity to assure fertility of both the earth and humans. Hence the painter of the image represents the Huastec phallus as a central ritual element, but he also keeps the phalluses and the priests themselves in the background. They play no role in the center of the image, which shows the top of the pyramid. Further, unlike the images of the priests in the center and the goddess of maize, the images of the Huastec priests do not contain any color. In the highly structured world of preconquest and early colonial Nahua writing, the positions and lack of color in the priests tell us that they do not have significant control over the ritual. Thus the Huastec position in the ritual remains ambiguous: they have the power to help maintain fertility, but they have no control over the ceremony that will ensure this fertility. This ambiguous position contrasts markedly with the Spanish text, which disempowers the priests by asserting them as the feminized Hispanic beings, putos.

Such translational problems are at the core of another anonymous sixteenth-century text, the *Codex Tudela*, which, while written in Spanish, was painted in the style of a traditional Nahua codex. It says, regarding the Mexica bathhouses (fig. 3):

> Temazcatl:[19] a bath of hot water in which they committed offenses against Our Lord. . . . In this bath there were many men and women. Thus there, with the heat, they illicitly used [each other]: men with women, women with men, and men with men. And in Mexico they had men dressed in women's clothes who were sodomites [*someticos*] and performed the offices of women, such as spinning and sewing. And some lords had one or two [of them] for their vices.[20]

The text uses the term *somético* to signify a cross-dressing figure, perhaps similar to the North American berdache, a person who, while biologically male, performed many of the functions of women.[21] But why would the narrative describe this person based on his engagement in a particular sexual act (sodomy was defined inconsistently, but it always referred to some sexual act), as opposed to his nonsexual behaviors? The text here moves in a rather confusing manner from sexual act (sodomy) to occupation (spinning and sewing) to sexual service performed for the leaders of society. The first description, *somético*, signifies the quasi-juridical identity of the late medieval and early modern man who engaged in sexual activity with other, primarily significantly younger, males. The term could refer also to the younger partners.[22] But did the Nahua cultural matrix form sexual identity in the same way, or were these concepts altered in translation from one social reality into another distinct and somewhat incompatible moral framework?

Puto and *somético* signify an element of Nahua discourse translated imprecisely into Spanish. The puto in Spanish popular culture signified the effeminate, the passive, the flamboyant man who flaunted his opposition to Spanish sexual and gender mores. He represented all that was degrading about a Spanish man who took a feminine role. He signified the one who played the passive role in sexual activity and the one who performed in a feminine manner in public. Popular literature and plays presented the puto as a decadent, unworthy figure. Yet he was tolerated in the major Spanish urban areas, and probably in rural areas as well.[23] The *somético* in Catholic religious discourse signified the man from Sodom and, more important, the sinner who engaged in the imprecisely defined act of sodomy.[24] He had sex with another man, ignoring the religious and legal consequences. He came into Spanish discourse through the confessional, theological literature, and in front of the Inquisition. The puto and the somético both had genealogies that stemmed from ancient and medieval Europe, in both religious discourse and popular culture.

Figure 3. A Nahua bathhouse, from the *Codex Tudela*

Why did the authors of the *Florentine Codex* use *puto* to signify a Nahua god, and why were both *puto* and *somético* used in early Nahua narratives? The above two texts suggest that the use of *puto* and *somético* surfaced in a world in which traditional Nahua moral discourse no longer served to describe elements unfamiliar to the conquerors. The rather confusing Spanish-language descriptions relate to the repression of translational ambiguity. The phallic priests, for example, do not fit into the Spanish concept of *puto*. They signify the fertility that will emanate from their copulation with the goddesses. Could the Spaniards have called these priests putos because the priests engaged in a ritual in which they simulated sexual intercourse with each other, calling on the goddesses to use their power to make the earth fertile? Although we have no direct evidence, this seems a likely interpretation since other ethnohistorical and ethnographic accounts show that ceremonies took place in which some priests dressed in the clothes and/or flayed skins of women who, while alive, had signified goddesses.[25] If so, Spaniards would have seen the priests as putos. And no doubt the term *puto*, partially unmoored from its Spanish context, could be used to stand in for many behaviors the Spaniards deemed sexually and otherwise inappropriate. Clearly the significance of the priestly sexual performance exceeded these categories. But the Spaniards, working inside their own framework, would have seen themselves as justified in using these concepts, as their imaginations only allowed them to see people who fit in their own system of categorization. The terms partially fit, after all, based on both the simulation of sexual activity among men and the feminine gendered performance of the priest dressed as a goddess. The meaning of the Nahua ceremony still left a remainder that could not be codified in the Spanish categories. That remainder (the ritualization, the connection with fertility) was repressed in the Spanish text. This repressive act was a central element of colonial power.

The Creation of the *Florentine Codex*

The *Florentine Codex* can tell us more about the figure being described alternately as *puto* and *somético*, but first we must understand something about the creation of the *Codex*. Bernardino de Sahagún, a Franciscan friar educated at the University of Salamanca, directed the project that produced the document now known as the *Florentine Codex*, a twelve-volume text with parallel Nahuatl and Spanish columns (see fig. 4). Sahagún had several Nahua aides trained to read and write in Latin, Spanish, and Nahuatl. They were educated at the Colegio de Santa Cruz, a college founded by the Franciscans in Tlatelolco in 1536 and designed to educate noble Nahua boys in the classical traditions, Christian theology, and the Latin and Spanish languages.[26]

The research that eventually became the bulk of the *Florentine Codex*, including all of the texts that I plan to discuss, took place between 1558 and 1569. In this project, Sahagún and his aides first went to Tepepolco, an indigenous community northeast of Tenochtitlán, in the modern state of Hidalgo. There, according to Sahagún, they went to the local *cabildo* and asked its members to support the project and recommend eight to ten older nobles who could remember the traditions as they had existed at the time of the conquest. Sahagún claims to have later done the same in Tlatelolco and then finally in Tenochtitlán.[27]

The manuscript for the *Florentine Codex* was completed in 1569. This document was intended to have three columns: the original Nahuatl text, a Spanish text that paraphrased the Nahuatl, and a third column of more polished Nahuatl. Unfortunately, the 1569 text has never been found. What we have in Florence is a text that was recopied from the 1569 manuscript, along with illustrations, between 1575 and 1580; this document has two columns, one Nahuatl and one Spanish. The fact that Sahagún had intended to but never did polish the Nahuatl suggests that the Nahuatl text we have, while recopied, is a version very close to the original.

There is significant dispute as to the roles of the aides, informants, and Sahagún himself in the whole project. By the time most of the research was done for the final text we have now, Sahagún had great difficulty writing, as he could not steady his hands. When the work was completed, he was probably eighty-one years old.[28] His Nahua aides wrote the overwhelming

no tenja deuocion a su signo,
nj hazia penjtencia a honrra
del. La razon: porque dezia:
que las quatro casas postreras,
de cada signo: eran bien afor
tunadas, es, porque dezian:
que aquellas quatro casas pos
treras, de todos los signos, se a
tribuyan a quatro dioses pros
peros. El primero de los qua
les: se llamaua tlauizcalpan
tecutli. Y el segundo: citlallicue.
Y el tercero: tonatiuh. Y el quar
to: tonacatecutli. Por esto dezian
los astrologos: que los que naci
an en estas casas, serian pros
peros, y tendrian larga vida:
si se baptizassen en la postrera.

quipaquiltia, iuh qujntzaccuiliaz, te
iiscali, auh oatl injc mjtoa, camaceoale,
tlacuopilhuiiani, camuchonian quj
caia, iuihquj inemactia mjzqujtla
mantli, njcan motoneoa. Noauh
quj maceoatl muchioaia in cioatl,
mocujltonoaia, momauizcohiaia, vel
motitiemqujani. Ramjc aquj njz tlaca
muchioarj, topan tlacoiarj. Et oc
auh in tlaca amo iuhquj ipan mo
chioaia, mjtoa: cacaiz coian, quevjia
conmo auj ,lia, y iuhmo tlacazth mjchibia
mjtonal: ipampa acacquel omonolь
acacomouel otlamaceuh, iuiuh ie
mjiecem omjto. Auh injc mjtoa: cen
ca qualian intonallzonco, injpan
matlaclomej oopmatli (ioan in oc
ceqvj ipan tonalzontli) injc vmpa
qujnqujac, qujmaltiaia in tlacatzin
injpan ia izqujtet tonalli omotoneuh
inqujxcentetocama, matlactli tochtli
ip ampa, mjtoa, qujlmach muchipa
navintin vncan, tlatoa: iehoan tla
camjlhujstilia, qujtlatlaltuja injtonal
zontli ito ca Tlauizcalpan tecutli,
ioan cittalliicue, njnam ic tonatiuh,
ioan tonaca tecutli: iehoatl injc quj
qualtitaia tonalzouhque, mjqujto
aia: cauel vncanca tlauilli, nemaclti,
ioon noqujtoaia, ouctoaia: in aqujn
vncan tlacatia, qujtoaia, qujtlamjz
monchijtiz, in tlaltiepac, tlamaujzos

bulk of the Nahuatl text, and while Sahagún almost certainly edited their writing, his energy clearly fluctuated from section to section.

The research methodology appears to have gone something like this. First, having gathered the informants, Sahagún and his aides interviewed them, asking them to describe specific cosmology, traditions, ceremonies, people, and natural phenomena. The aides apparently took many notes, few of which have been found, and quizzed the informants for details regarding a wide variety of topics. Second, Sahagún and the aides retreated and reorganized the notes. Third, they returned to their informants, reviewing the notes with them and making corrections along the way. Next, Sahagún created an outline for the final version of the manuscript, dividing every-thing into twelve books. Finally, Sahagún and his aides wrote the text. As this manuscript was being prepared, the final set of informants, those from Tenochtitlán, reviewed, modified, and amplified the text. All the while, Sahagún, with the assistance of either the aides or a Nahua copyist, trans-lated the text into Spanish, in some places rather freely.[29]

We need to understand the filtering process at work here: the aides questioned their informants, who were reaching back to their distant, often childhood, memories of preconquest times. The informants then told the aides something about those memories (one cannot assume that the infor-mants were always truthful), and the aides wrote down what they decided to record. It is quite clear that in some cases the aides wrote down verbatim what their informants told them, often without interruption. Where they wrote down extensive myths, we can see, based on comparative sources, internal consistency, and linguistic analysis, that the aides transcribed the myths quite directly from the mouths of the informants. At other points, particularly when discussing the book on "the people," which I will men-tion shortly, the aides clearly have asked a very specific question, perhaps given to them by Sahagún.

Sahagún's own filters came into play in organizing and translating the work as well as in preparing the questions. In the cases of the myths, gods, and traditional religious rituals, Sahagún made it clear in the prologues to the various books that his only goal was to destroy these practices.[30] However, others have emphasized what the tone of the *Florentine Codex* makes clear: the Nahua intrigued Sahagún to such an extent that he began to identify closely with them, if not with all of their ceremonies.

Sahagún and the other Franciscans trained the Nahua aides. We should note that these young men were children of the nobility, and in several cases they can be shown trying to restore the reputations of their parents and grandparents.[31] So their allegiances were complex. Finally, the informants were mostly elderly men, and they may have had limited memory of the preconquest past.

Given all of these filters, plus the fact that the original text has not been found, how can we make sense of the meanings of sexual acts and desires in the *Florentine Codex*? Many of my colleagues currently are involved in a debate regarding the *Codex*. At the extreme edges, that debate revolves around some scholars who have argued that the *Codex* gives us a clear window into Nahua culture and others who find that the text simply reproduces European ideology related to how a "savage" performs.[32] Instead of assuming either of these observations to be wholly accurate, I provide a methodology for interpretation of the *Codex*. I decipher many of the codes placed in the documents. First, I analyze the specific Nahuatl and Spanish texts, down to individual words and even in some cases syllables within words, in order to find the meanings hidden behind the translations. Second, I think about the various filters that all of the different authors of this text have, uncovering their filtering mechanisms as they appear. Third, I find a variety of documents that allow me to understand both the European and the indigenous contexts for the figures I mention. Fourth, with all of this analysis and context, I posit the various possible conclusions regarding sexual desires, behaviors, and identities.

Faggots and Hermaphrodites

Having said this, I will focus the remainder of this article on the meanings of three Nahuatl words, *xochihua*, *cuiloni*, and *patlachuia*, which I now will place in context. The *Florentine Codex* discusses the cross-dressing figure that I mentioned earlier. They call this figure the "xochihua" (which, although Anderson and Dibble translated it as "pervert," literally means "flower bearer"). The text of the flower bearer refers specifically to the cross-dressing figure. And the image accompanying the text shows the flower and signifies it as representing a cross-dressing person who performs various of the functions of women. The flower is a vital metaphor in the Nahua universe, where it is used to emphasize the importance of philosophy, poetry, and song; it is a general symbol of life's dualities.[33] But lest we think from this discussion that the Nahua viewed the flower bearer positively, I will quote from the Nahuatl text: "Xochihua: has women's speech, women's form of address, men's speech, men's form of address, . . . corrupts, confuses, and bewitches people, . . . uses flowers on someone [*texochihua*]."[34] And the following passage states: "Cuiloni: excrement, corruption, filth, filth sucker, little filth, corrupt, afflicted, frivolous, a joke,

Figure 5. The *Xochihua*, from the *Florentine Codex*

a mockery, annoying, makes people filthy, fills people's noses with filth, effeminate; . . . burns and is scorched; . . . talks like a woman and passes him- or herself off as a woman [see fig. 5]." [35]

In the Spanish section of the *Codex*, Sahagún maintains that the xochihua was one who enchanted or bewitched others.[36] Thus while Sahagún focused on the acts of the xochihua as a seducer, he missed the framework of the cross-dressing figure. However, other primary sources maintain with convincing regularity that the xochihua was a cross-dresser.[37]

The flower here and in other texts signifies both sexual desire and excess. The *Florentine Codex* and other documents show prostitutes dressed in clothing with flowers, and the prostitutes often carry flowers (see fig. 6). A goddess associated with both fertility and sexual excess, Xochiquetzal ("Quetzal Flower"), was connected closely with flowers.[38] The image shows what the flower bearer signified. Two figures, one dressed as a man, the other dressed as a woman, sit with a flower between them. They are shown talking to each other, with speech scrolls emanating from their mouths. The text states that the two figures are male, so the figure dressed as a woman must be a cross-dresser. One must remember here that the text written in the Roman alphabet is a postconquest innovation. Before the conquest, if their artists presented the Nahua with such a scene, the people would have seen the image with pictographs attached.[39] At the same time, they would have heard the words of an interpreter, a figure who would have told them the story. The interpreter and other Nahuas would have known that the figure was a cross-dressed male by identifying the significance of the flower, here thus a privileged signifier of a particular gendered performance incorporating transvestism.

The flower bearer is a complex metaphor related to the cross-dressing figure. The xochihua had an institutionalized, if degraded, role to play.

Nahua society prized masculinity, while the xochihua was seen as effeminate. However, the evidence shows that many high-level nobles kept xochihuas as dependents. They used them to perform household chores, to clean the temples, and to accompany warriors to war. When at war, the xochihuas provided the warriors with a variety of services, including sex. At other times, the xochihuas, some of whom were housed in the temples, were available for sexual favors and other chores to priests and other members of the high nobility.[40]

Figure 6. The Prostitute, from the *Florentine Codex*

The next term, *cuiloni*, which Sahagún and his aides translated as *puto*, was the word used to describe the deity mentioned earlier. But, if *puto* signified unacceptable femininity in a man, did *cuiloni* really signify the same thing? Or can we suggest that the terminological boundaries differed, and that the translation from one language to another obscured those boundaries?

We need to understand the process at work in the translations and the creation of the dictionaries. First, we must remember that the Spaniards found terms in Nahuatl, Quechua, and various Mayan languages to be equivalents of *puto*.[41] Were they accurately translating one social reality into another? The etymology of *cuiloni* refers specifically to a person taken from behind by another,[42] suggesting that the term was quite specific to the act of anal intercourse. As the cuiloni is a subcategory of the xochihua, it seems that, in many senses, this is a reference to effeminacy, and there is little question that this figure was denigrated. However, we must remember that for Spaniards, despite their daily tolerance for putos in their midst, the puto was not institutionalized. Further, in public discourse, both religious and secular, the puto was a symbol of the degradation of society, and he warranted only extreme marginalization or death.[43]

Was the same true for the cuiloni? Referring back to the above text and to figure 5, we note that the cuiloni was burned. The flames in the image signify either the penalty of death by fire or the afterlife in which the person burns in hell. I present two problems with these concepts. First, there is no primary evidence for any significant penalties against the cuiloni (or the xochihua) in preconquest Mesoamerica.[44] Second, the Nahua before the conquest did not have a concept of "hell." The Nahua viewed the afterlife not as a penalty for "sins" committed during one's lifetime but rather as a series of places where an individual would find him- or herself based primarily on position at birth and luck during life.[45] The image and text of the burned cuiloni have their origins in medieval Europe.[46]

If we examine the figure closely, we see that the artists present a dualistic image in which the left side shows the flower bearer in all his or her traditional garb, engaging in some sort of (sexual?) discussion with a man on the other side of the flower. The genealogy for this portion of the image comes from preconquest Nahua discourse. The right side, the image of the person burning over a fire made from long pieces of wood, emanates from European religious and juridical discourse. The two images together remind us that the *Florentine Codex* is a hybrid, postconquest text.

This discussion of the xochihua and the cuiloni comes from book 10 of the *Codex*, the one that discusses "the people." This book in many ways is the most contrived of the entire *Codex*. It simply lists various social categories of people and divides a wide variety of them into "good" and "evil," with the xochihua and cuiloni texts placed in the section on "evil men." The distinction between good and evil was a binary division asserted in the European framework, not in the Nahua moral universe, which tended to divide things instead into distinctions between order and chaos and moderation and excess. But even here we find elements of Nahua tradition. The ways we read the texts are most important. For, while book 10 of the *Florentine Codex* provides us with a set of largely European values, we see the Nahua informants peering back at us through the paper when we see a flower signifying a cross-dresser.

We can envision the Nahua in a more obscure way in another text that on the surface signifies a European moral framework: the one paragraph of book 10 that focuses on female homosexual desires and acts.

> Patlache: a filthy woman, a woman with a penis, possessor of an erect penis, a penis, and testicles; pairs up with a woman, befriends a woman, procures young women, and possesses young women; has a man's body; the top part of [the patlache's] body is that of a man; talks like a man and passes him- or herself off as a man; has a beard, body hair, and hair; does it to another woman [*tepatlachuia*], befriends a woman, never wants to marry, detests and never looks at men; is frightening. [See fig. 7.][47]

The term *patlache* relates to the more commonly found term *patlachuia*, both of which emanate from the stem *patlach-*, "a wide thing." As one can imagine, this definition perplexed Spanish friars, although we can have little

Figure 7. The *Patlache*, from the *Florentine Codex*

doubt that the Nahua knew what *patlachuia* meant. The term is defined in colonial dictionaries as "for one woman to do it with another."[48] This circumspection about female sexual activity led to many confused representations in the Nahuatl confession manuals and undoubtedly fueled ignorance among the priests hearing confession. The text from the *Florentine Codex* parallels early modern Europe's fascination with the hermaphrodite as a monstrous figure.[49] While the sense of monstrosity was unlikely to be lost on Sahagún's aides, to suggest that this text was completely a European creation would be problematic, as it is all about the misunderstood category *patlache* or *patlachuia*. Sahagún's attempt to understand the term leads to the notion of a hermaphrodite, similar to his own understanding of the monstrous European entity.

But the problem of translation again is repressed in Sahagún's account. The term *patlachuia* rarely appears in other texts. All of the texts that mention the term have a Hispanic provenance. Thus I will end this article suggesting the unknowability of the meanings, identities, and desires possessed by such a term. Witness the modern translations: Anderson and Dibble accept Sahagún's translation of "hermaphrodite."[50] Kimball, projecting modern sexual identities onto preconquest peoples, states that *patlache* properly means "homosexual woman" and *tepatlachuia* means "she has sexual relations with women."[51] Alfredo López Austin, as usual, is much more precise, but even he falls into the trap of modern identity politics when he says that *patlachuia* is, "according to . . . [Fray Alonso de Molina, author of the most important colonial Nahuatl/Spanish dictionary], 'for one woman to do it to another woman.' The correct meaning for *patlache* is 'the lesbian,' but through the description in the text one deduces there was confusion between the concept of lesbian and hermaphrodite." [52] By focusing on translation, we might suggest that the notion of patlachuia emanates not from confusion but rather from a particular gendered performance. The image (fig. 7) presents the woman standing in a sexualized manner, with her breasts exposed (a portrayal in preconquest Nahua iconography clearly intended to be sexually suggestive). [53] The standing figure is speaking to the seated woman. The image does not repeat the dual-gendered person signified by the text. Nor does she appear to be ambiguously gendered. [54] Rather, her image suggests sexual desire and potential. The erotic performance here remains unknowable to us, but nothing in it would allow us to assert any modern sexual identity.

Myths and Gods

Finally, I return to the text that shocked me when I read it. Tezcatlipoca, one of the most important gods in the Nahua universe, himself a paragon of masculinity, was, according to Sahagún, a puto.

The image of Tezcatlipoca in figure 1 comes from the *Florentine Codex*. He carries a shield and dresses as a very powerful warrior; he is among the most powerful gods. So we *might* presume that Sahagún's comment represents a colonial appropriation and denigration of Nahua masculinity. But in fact the reality is much more complex, as the history of Spanish colonialism intersects with preconquest Nahua notions of the places of homosexuality in ritual and myth.

Tezcatlipoca indeed is a complex figure who in many senses signifies both masculinity and femininity. The Nahua viewed him as a trickster with many identities and forms. [55] Cecelia Klein argues for the fundamental bisexuality of Tezcatlipoca. She states that his masculine comportment in Nahua ideology never conflicted with certain sexual ambiguities. Thus his masculine status as a warrior god was compatible with an "androgynous" beauty portrayed in certain rituals. [56] Nonetheless, the Nahua saw him as male and masculine, and they do not suggest that Tezcatlipoca had a sexual identity similar to that of the puto. The Nahuatl text says that Titlacauan (see fig. 8), not Tezcatlipoca, was a cuiloni. Some gods were simply more powerful than others, and Tezcatlipoca was among the most powerful warrior gods. Titlacauan was less powerful. He was one of Tezcatlipoca's many identities, and he was linked with the more powerful god.[57] Insulting him would not be the same thing as insulting Tezcatlipoca. In his picture in the *Florentine Codex*, Titlacauan is shown wearing only a loincloth, sandals, and an extensive knotted rope that appears to ensnare him. He carries a flower and he blows on what is intended to be a traditional Nahua flute. The flower signified his eroticism. The snare was connected with sexual transgressions and with the intestines, themselves associated with sodomy.[58] The flute, intentionally phallic, signified both penance and communication with the gods.

Perhaps most important, Titlacauan is not pictured as a warrior in the attire of someone like Tezcatlipoca. He is shown in the broader set of images as a helper, someone carrying things for the warriors. So Titlacauan himself is not seen in this image and other imagery as so powerful. Yet another myth presents Titlacauan as one who tricks others in order to seduce them.[59] Mythologically, therefore, to call Titlacauan a cuiloni would be seen as an insult but not one that was completely out of bounds. Moreover, in order for this insult to be performed in the Nahuatl text, the author had to discuss Titlacauan, not his more powerful counterpart. For Titlacauan himself was associated with excessive erotic activity, and the structure of the myth shows simply that the tables were turned on him.

So how does Tezcatlipoca become a puto? Sahagún transposes the names of the gods and then appropriates the term *puto* to stand in for *cuiloni*. This is entirely appropriate, given Sahagún's own filters. After all, Tezcatlipoca was a supreme Nahua god, one whom Sahagún calls *diablo* on several occasions. Why not denigrate him, perhaps even destroy him, by calling him a puto? Of course, it is hardly so clear as this, since the gods themselves overlapped, and Tezcatlipoca and Titlacauan could be two gods inside one body.[60]

Creating History from Myth and Metaphor

Just as the friars worked to reconceptualize indigenous religion as idolatry, the various homosexualities that had existed in preconquest Nahua society were to be categorized as sodomy and sin. Hence Sahagún was able to use his filters and his agenda to turn a myth into a tool that could aid in the eradication of indigenous religion. If a high-ranking god could be turned into a measly puto, Nahua cosmology would be in trouble. Of course we cannot say that the Nahua believed that Tezcatlipoca was a puto. Hence we have come to the crux of the problem for Sahagún: the spiritual conquest was failing.

Nonetheless, by reading the *Florentine Codex* in a new way, we can

Figure 8. Titlacauan, from the *Florentine Codex*

uncover the preconquest Nahua institutionalization of the xochihua and
the presence of the cuiloni in mythology. While we find precious few details
about the concept behind the term *patlachuia*, the inclusion of the category
in the *Codex* remains intriguing. By using an innovative methodology and
sifting through authorial filters, we will learn more about pre- and postconquest Nahua sexualities.

  To return to questions of translation, we need to understand the translations proffered by modern scholars as interpretations based on notions
of sexual politics. When Anderson and Dibble translate *xochihua* as "pervert," they promote a particular psychological notion, differentiating normalcy from perversion. We find no evidence that the Nahua viewed the

xochihua as a deviation from a norm. Quite the contrary: no norm is asserted in these texts with regard to sexual desires. When Kimball translates the same term as "the homosexual," and then proceeds to translate *patlache* as "homosexual woman," he promotes a modern sexual identity (and a notion of male linguistic superiority) that does not appear to have any place in Nahua discourse. The evidence presents *xochihua* as related to cross-dressing and to the signifier of the flower, and *patlachuia* as a sexual performance that we cannot comprehend from the documents. Translation is a political project and, unless modern interpreters take great care, they will assert a transcultural and transhistorical continuity that does epistemic violence to the conceptual universe of the Nahua.

The phallic faggot of the *Codex Borbonicus*, the cross-dressed sodomite of the *Codex Tudela*, and the various presences in the *Florentine Codex* all signify the violent and often unconscious mixture of moral frameworks promoted by the hybrid colonial discourse. Indeed, the colonialist maneuver represses difference in order to recategorize the very existences of the colonized peoples. Still, we can detect and decode this act, and we find that the ways the Nahua performed gender and sexuality do not fit into the categories constructed in the Spanish language. To make sense of these figures, we must decode the texts, focusing on the marginalia, the remainders not incorporated in the Spanish descriptions, discovering the ways the Nahua performed sex and gender. We must present Sahagún's restructuring of Tezcatlipoca as a puto along with the gendered performance of the cross-dressed figure discussing sex with a man over a flower. And we must show the radical incongruity of a set of priests with phalluses about to penetrate a goddess in order to make the earth fertile at the same time as their identities are constructed as those who will engage in sexual activity only as the passive partners to other men.

Still, as this article is more about text than sex, it also serves as a challenge to the ethnohistorians and philologists and perhaps all historians in my field. We must go back to our sources and unmask the face behind the obscured authorial voice. How did those mysterious scribes, litigious petitioners, and verbose friars enter into their own discourse? Can we follow the webs of meaning, spun by those long dead, coming from Salamanca and Seville, perhaps Rome and Athens, extending across a wide ocean, and coming also from Tenochtitlán and Tlatelolco, perhaps Aztlán and Teotihuacán, moving through Mexico City and Florence, still ensnaring our imaginations today? Ethnohistorians and all historians must try, always reminding ourselves of the contingent nature of our narrative constructions.

Indeed, as always, we must recall the context of the Nahua struggles of the sixteenth century. The great empire had crumbled and a new world order would be built on the rubble. Our present work provides a glimpse into that process; a look at the ways people brought in the old and the new, mixing them together in an often unconscious manner, searching for meaning, and finding it in the hybrid culture of sixteenth-century Mexico.

Notes

1 Bernardino de Sahagún, *Códice Florentino* (*Florentine Codex*) (Mexico City, 1979, facsimile edition [hereafter *FC*]), book 4, chap. 9, fol. 24r.

2 Alonso de Molina, *Vocabulario en lengua castellana y mexicana y mexicana y castellana*, 2 vols. (Mexico City, 1992), vol. 1, fol. 100v.

3 See Noemí Quezada, *Amor y magia amorosa entre los aztecas* (Mexico City, 1975), 139–40; Alfredo López Austin, *The Human Body and Ideology: Concepts of the Ancient Nahuas*, 2 vols., trans. Thelma Ortiz de Montellano and Bernard Ortiz de Montellano (Salt Lake City, UT, 1988), 1:305; Geoffrey Kimball, "Aztec Homosexuality: The Textual Evidence," *Journal of Homosexuality* 26.1 (1993): 20; Araceli Barbosa Sánchez, *Sexo y conquista* (Mexico City, 1994), 130–32; Cecelia F. Klein, "None of the Above: Gender Ambiguity in Nahua Ideology," in *Gender in Pre-Hispanic America: A Symposium at Dumbarton Oaks*, ed. Cecelia F. Klein (Washington, DC, 2001), 192; Richard C. Trexler, "Gender Subordination and Political Hierarchy in Pre-Hispanic America," in *Infamous Desire: Male Homosexuality in Colonial Latin America*, ed. Pete Sigal (Chicago, 2003), 80. Indeed, López Austin, always one of the most rigorous of scholars, admits later that, having viewed more sources, he can no longer argue that the Nahua "exalted the sexual life"; López Austin, *Tamoanchan, Tlalocan: Places of Mist*, trans. Bernard Ortiz de Montellano and Thelma Ortiz de Montellano (Niwot, CO, 1997), 275.

4 In California today, a variety of groups support a Nahua warrior motif that rejects all forms of femininity in men. Some Chicano political movements, tattoo artists, and the Monty Montezuma mascot at San Diego State University have conflicting investments in Nahua masculinity. The support for a "two-spirit" identity is a form in which some activists suggest that all native societies supported a ritualized alignment of masculinity and femininity that would come together in a cross-dressing figure. There even exists a gay tourist Web site that promotes this concept through its reading of Mexican history ("Gay Chronicles," www.geocities.com/gueroperro/Chron-Mex.htm [accessed 24 October 2004]). See also Gabriel S. Estrada, "The 'Macho' Body as Social Malinche," in *Velvet Barrios: Popular Culture and Chicana/o Sexualities*, ed. Alicia Gaspar de Alba (New York, 2003), 41–48.

5 Bernardino de Sahagún, *Florentine Codex: General History of the Things of New Spain*, ed. Arthur J. O. Anderson and Charles E. Dibble, 12 vols. (Santa Fe, NM, 1950–1982 [hereafter Anderson and Dibble, *Florentine Codex*]), 10:37.

6 For a critique of this modern discourse from a Lacanian perspective, see Bruce Fink, *A Clinical Introduction to Lacanian Psychoanalysis: Theory and Technique* (Cambridge, MA, 1997).

7 One can ask the same question of the Spaniards. Would they have understood the puto as "perverted"? The answer to this question also appears to be "no." See Rafael Carrasco, *Inquisición y represión sexual en Valencia: Historia de los sodomitas, 1565–1785* (Barcelona, 1985).

8 Kimball, "Aztec Homosexuality," 10.

9 See Pete Sigal, "The *Cuiloni*, the *Patlache*, and the Abominable Sin: Homosexualities in Early Colonial Nahua Society," *Hispanic American Historical Review* 85 (2005): 555–94.

10 Pete Sigal, *From Moon Goddesses to Virgins: The Colonization of Yucatecan Maya Sexual Desire* (Austin, TX, 2000).

11 In one of many examples, representatives of an urban community of Nahuas from Puebla state that a mulatto "gave people powders, by means of which he took advantage of small children"; from *The Puebla Annals*, Museo Nacional de Antropología e Historia, Archivo Histórico, Colección Gómez Orozco (hereafter GO 184), fol. 29r. The text goes on to call the mulatto a puto and says that he was executed by fire. Hispanic popular culture connected mulattoes with both witchcraft and pederasty. See Doris Mathilde Namala, "Chimalpahin in His Time: An Analysis of the Writings of a Nahua Annalist of Seventeenth-Century Mexico Concerning His Own Lifetime," PhD diss., University of California, Los Angeles, 2002. Also see Susan Kellogg, *Law and the Transformation of Aztec Culture, 1500–1700* (Norman, OK, 1995); Steve J. Stern, *The Secret History of Gender: Women, Men, and Power in Late Colonial Mexico* (Chapel Hill, NC, 1995); Lisa Sousa, "Women in Native Societies and Cultures of Colonial Mexico," PhD diss., University of California, Los Angeles, 1998.

12 Louise M. Burkhart, *The Slippery Earth: Nahua-Christian Moral Dialogue in Sixteenth-Century Mexico* (Tucson, AZ, 1989); Noemí Quezada, *Sexualidad, amor y erotismo: México prehispánico y México colonial* (Mexico City, 1996); Rosemary A. Joyce, *Gender and Power in Prehispanic Mesoamerica* (Austin, TX, 2000).

13 Eric Van Young, "The New Cultural History Comes to Old Mexico," *Hispanic American Historical Review* 79 (1999): 211–47.

14 I use the term *genealogy*, following Michel Foucault, to show that a particular text has hidden influences that need to be uncovered if we are to understand the meanings and uses of the narrative. As such, a genealogy seeks to uncover the ways in which the text fits into particular intellectual traditions. I use the term *performance* to evoke Judith Butler, who argues that both gender and sexuality are repeatedly performed. Both genealogy and performativity are amply demonstrated in the Nahuatl text discussed here. See Foucault, "Nietzsche, Genealogy, History," in *Language, Counter-Memory, Practice* (Oxford, 1977); Judith Butler, *Gender Trouble: Feminism and the Subversion of Identity* (New York, 1990).

15 Here I am avoiding all discussion of the gender and sexual roles of this individual. I comment extensively on this issue elsewhere, and such a discussion would distract from the methodological focus of this article. See Pete Sigal, "(Homo)Sexual Desire and Masculine Power in Colonial Latin America: Notes toward an Integrated Analysis," in *Infamous Desire: Male Homosexuality in Colonial Latin America*, ed. Pete Sigal (Chicago, 2003). On the broader issue, see Michael Horswell, "Toward an Andean Theory of Ritual Same-Sex Sexuality and Third-Gender Subjectivity," in Sigal, *Infamous Desire*; Richard C.

Trexler, *Sex and Conquest: Gendered Violence, Political Order, and the European Conquest of the Americas* (Ithaca, NY, 1995).

16 We may think that the priests could signify another possible interpretation of the term *puto*, which in current usage can also represent a man who engages in excessive sex, deemed illegitimate by the speakers of the word. For example, in Mexico I have heard a wife call her husband a puto for engaging in an adulterous relationship with a woman. However, I have never seen the term used in this manner in relation to Nahua documents or even among colonial Spaniards, so this interpretation seems unlikely.

17 This goddess, Tlazolteotl, is sexualized in all preconquest Nahua images of her. She signifies fertility and all sexual acts, both those intended for procreation and those not so intended. See Patrice Giasson, "Tlazolteotl, deidad del abono: Una propuesta," *Estudios de cultura náhuatl* 32 (2001): 137–57. See also my discussion of Tlazolteotl in chap. 1 of *The Flower and the Scorpion: Sexuality in Early Nahua Culture and Society* (Durham, NC, forthcoming).

18 Diego Durán, *Book of the Gods and Rites and the Ancient Calendar*, ed. and trans. Fernando Horcasitas and Doris Heyden (Norman, OK, 1971), 229–37.

19 This should be *temazcalli*.

20 "Temazcatl horno o baño de agua caliente donde se hazian ofensas a Nro Sr . . . . en este baño muchos onbres e mujeres, y alla dentro, con la calor, onbres con mujeres e mujeres con onbres e onbres con onbres, yliçitamente husavan y en mexco avia onbres vestidos en ábito de mujeres y estos eran sométicos y hazian los oficios de mujeres, como es texer y hilar, y algunos señores tenían uno y dos para sus viçios" (*Códice Tudela* [Madrid, 1980, facsimile edition], fol. 62r).

21 See Trexler, *Sex and Conquest*; Will Roscoe, *Changing Ones: Third and Fourth Genders in Native North America* (New York, 1998).

22 See Michael Rocke, *Forbidden Friendships: Homosexuality and Male Culture in Renaissance Florence* (New York, 1996); Mark Jordan, *The Invention of Sodomy in Christian Theology* (Chicago, 1997); Helmut Puff, *Sodomy in Reformation Germany and Switzerland, 1400–1600* (Chicago, 2003).

23 Rafael Carrasco, *Inquisición y represión sexual*.

24 While "sodomy" theoretically could include anal intercourse with women and intercourse with animals, in practice judges and confessors almost universally considered sodomy to signify only anal intercourse between men.

25 See Klein, "None of the Above"; Davíd Carrasco, "The Sacrifice of Women in the *Florentine Codex*: The Hearts of Plants and Players in War Games," in *Representing Aztec Ritual: Performance, Text, and Image in the Work of Sahagún*, ed. Eloise Quiñones Keber (Boulder, CO, 2002).

26 Arthur J. O. Anderson, "Sahagún in His Times," in *Sixteenth-Century Mexico: The Work of Sahagún*, ed. Munro S. Edmonson (Albuquerque, NM, 1974), 20–21; Luis Nicolau D'Olwer, *Fray Bernardino de Sahagún*, trans. Mauricio J. Mixco (Salt Lake City, UT, 1987), 13–23; Miguel León-Portilla, *Bernardino de Sahagún: First Anthropologist*, trans. Mauricio J. Mixco (Norman, OK, 2002), 95–99.

27 Bernardino de Sahagún, *Florentine Codex, General History of the Things of New Spain: Introduction and Indexes*, ed. Arthur J. O. Anderson and Charles E. Dibble (Santa Fe, NM, 1982 [hereafter Anderson and Dibble, *Introduction and Indexes*), 53–56.

28 León-Portilla, *Bernardino de Sahagún*, 175.

29 On Sahagún's research method, see Alfredo López Austin, "The Research Method of Fray Bernardino de Sahagún: The Questionnaires," in *Sixteenth-Century Mexico*; D'Olwer, *Fray Bernardino de Sahagún*, 32–58; James Lockhart, *We People Here: Nahuatl Accounts of the Conquest of Mexico* (Berkeley, CA, 1993); León-Portilla, *Bernardino de Sahagún*, 132–64.

30 Anderson and Dibble, *Introduction and Indexes*, 45–46, 53–56, 59–60, 67–68.

31 See Lockhart, *We People Here*.

32 For a critique of these views, see Walden Browne, *Sahagún and the Transition to Modernity* (Norman, OK, 2000).

33 See Sigal, *From Moon Goddesses to Virgins*, 45–52.

34 "SUCHIOA: in suchioa cioatlatole, cioanotzale, oquichtlatole, oquichnotzale, . . . teiollocuepani, teiolmalacachoani, tenanacauiani, . . . tesuchiuia, teixmalacachoa, teiolcuepa" (*FC*, book 10, chap. 11, fol. 25r–v; Anderson and Dibble, *Florentine Codex*, 10:37–38).

35 "CUILONI: chimouhqui, cuitzotl itlacauhqui, tlahelli, tlahelchichi, tlahelpul, tlacamiqui, teupoliuhqui auilli, camanalli, netopeoalli, tequalani, tetlahelti, teuiqueh, teiacapitztlahelti, cioaciuhqui, mocioanenequini, tlatiloni, tlatlani, chichinoloni, tlatla, chichinolo, cihcioatlatoa, mocioanenequi" (ibid.).

36 Sahagún's translation of the entire passage is "Embaucadores: El embaucador, o la embaucadora, tiene estas propiedades, que sabe ciertas palabras con que embauca a las mujeres, y ellas por el contrario con que engañan a los hombres, y así cada una de estas hacen a los hombre y a las mujeres andar elevados o embelesados, o enhechizados, vanos y locos, atónitos y desvanecidos" (*FC*, book 10, chap. 11, fol. 25r–v).

37 See the sources I have cited in Sigal, "The *Cuiloni*, the *Patlache*, and the Abominable Sin." The secondary sources also support this view. Anderson and Dibble and Kimball, despite their modern biases with regard to sexual desires and identities, locate the xochihua as a cross-dressing figure. Sousa sees the xochihua as a sort of transgender being.

38 See Geoffrey G. McCafferty and Sharisse D. McCafferty, "The Metamorphosis of Xochiquetzal: A Window on Womanhood in Pre- and Post-Conquest Mexico," in *Manifesting Power: Gender and the Interpretation of Power in Archaeology*, ed. Tracy Sweely (New York: Routledge, 1999).

39 On preconquest writing, see Elizabeth Hill Boone, *Stories in Red and Black: Pictorial Histories of the Aztecs and Mixtecs* (Austin, TX, 2000).

40 See Sigal, "The *Cuiloni*, the *Patlache*, and the Abominable Sin"; and Trexler, *Sex and Conquest*.

41 On the Maya, see Sigal, *From Moon Goddesses to Virgins*. On the Quechua-speaking peoples, see Horswell, "Toward an Andean Theory." See also Ana Mariella Bacigalupo, "The Struggle for Mapuche Shamans' Masculinity: Colonial Politics of Gender, Sexuality, and Power in Southern Chile," *Ethnohistory* 51 (2004): 489–533.

42 *Cuiloni* derives from *cui*, "to take." The *-loni* ending signifies a passive form of the verb and the creation of an agentive noun. *Cuiloni* also relates to the "rectum" (*cuilchilli*). *Cuiloni* derives from "someone/something taken," and clearly related to the anus, thus one taken from behind. While the answer will have to remain speculative, the use of *tecuilonti* certainly leads us to the conclusion that *cuiloni* referred to the "passive" position in sodomy. *Tecuilonti* is a

preterit agentive noun. This suggests that *tecuilonti* is based on *cuiloni*, showing Molina's Spanish translation to be correct. *Tecuilonti* refers to the "active," *cuiloni* to the "passive."

43 Rafael Carrasco, *Inquisición y represión sexual.*

44 Trexler ("Gender Subordination," 80) argues convincingly that no penalties existed. The only sources that suggest penalties for "sodomy" are those that have significant Hispanic influence. All other sources that mention the topic state that no penalty existed, but that the people who engaged in such activities were degraded.

45 See López Austin, *Tamoanchan, Tlalocan.*

46 See Sigal, "The *Cuiloni*, the *Patlache*, and the Abominable Sin."

47 "PATLACHE: In patlache: ca tlahelcioatl, cioatl xipine tepule, choneoa, mioa, ateoa, mocioapotiani, mocioaicniuhtiani, mocicioapiltiani, cicioapile, oquich-nacaio, oquichtlaque, ôoquichtlatoa, ôoquichnenemi, tetentzone, tomio, tzô-tzoio, tepatlachuia, mocioaicniuhtia, aic monamictiznequi, cenca quinco-colia aiel quimittaz in oquichti, tlatetzauia" (*FC*, book 10, chap. 15, fol. 40v; Anderson and Dibble, *Florentine Codex*, 10:56).

48 Molina, *Vocabulario*, vol. 2, fol. 80r.

49 For the literature on hermaphrodites in early modern Europe, see Sigal, "The *Cuiloni*, the *Patlache*, and the Abominable Sin."

50 Anderson and Dibble, *Florentine Codex*, 10:56.

51 Kimball, "Aztec Homosexuality," 16.

52 López Austin, *Human Body*, 2:279.

53 See Thelma D. Sullivan, "Tlazolteotl-Ixcuina: The Great Spinner and Weaver," in *The Art and Iconography of Late Post-Classic Mexico*, ed. Elizabeth Hill Boone (Washington, DC, 1982).

54 Klein ("None of the Above") shows that ambiguously gendered and dual-gendered people had significant ritual roles to play.

55 Klein, "None of the Above," 219-32; Guilhem Olivier, "The Hidden King and the Broken Flutes: Mythical and Royal Dimensions of the Feast of Tezcatlipoca in Toxcatl," in *Representing Aztec Ritual: Performance, Text, and Image in the Work of Sahagún*, ed. Eloise Quiñones Keber (Boulder, CO, 2002), 107-42.

56 See Klein, "None of the Above"; and Klein, "The Aztec Sacrifice of Tezcatlipoca and Its Implications for Christ Crucified," in *Festschrift in Honor of Richard C. Trexler*, ed. Peter Arnade and Michael Rocke (Toronto, forthcoming).

57 Nahua gods often changed forms and identities. It was only through his iden-tification with Titlacauan that Tezcatlipoca was portrayed as a god who might engage in sodomy. Titlacauan was closely linked with Tezcatlipoca, but was always viewed as a more generic equivalent, a sort of everyday god of the people. See Guilhem Olivier, *Mockeries and Metamorphoses of an Aztec God: Tezcatlipoca, "Lord of the Smoking Mirror,"* trans. Michel Besson (Boulder, CO, 2003).

58 Cecilia Klein, "Snares and Entrails: Mesoamerican Symbols of Sin and Punish-ment," *Res* 19-20 (1990-91): 81-103.

59 *FC*, book 3, fol. 8r.

60 See my discussion of Tezcatlipoca in *The Flower and the Scorpion*, chap. 3.

"Heran Todos Putos": Sodomitical Subcultures and Disordered Desire in Early Colonial Mexico

Zeb Tortorici, *University of California, Los Angeles*

Abstract. This essay focuses on a 1604 document from Morelia's criminal archive dealing initially with the prosecution of two Purépecha men accused of committing sodomy in a *temascal*. Attention is paid to individual testimonies and details surrounding sexual acts between the men in the temascal and between other Purépecha men from Uruapan, Tzintzuntzan, and surrounding pueblos. This criminal case offers strong evidence that sodomitical subcultures—social networks of men who knew when and where to seek out sex with other men—existed outside of urban areas in colonial Mexico. The document further demonstrates how Spaniards conceptualized sodomy in the highly gendered terms of activity and passivity that suggested domination and submission, and how this model of male-male sexual relations is inadequate and problematic for understanding historical realities.

The Details of a 1604 Sodomy Case in Valladolid, Michoacán

At around 2:00 p.m. on 15 August 1604, the day of the local Fiesta de la Virgen in Valladolid (now Morelia), Michoacán, two indigenous Purépecha men later identified as Simpliciano Cuyne and Pedro Quini were caught in flagrante delicto committing the *pecado nefando*—the nefarious sin of sodomy—in a *temascal* on the property of the priest Juan Velázquez Rangel.[1] It was Padre Velázquez's fourteen-year-old nephew who discovered the two men in their compromising position, "the one on top of the other with their pants undone *as if they were man and woman.*"[2] In his testimony, the nephew relates how he was searching for a lost horse that had escaped from his uncle's corrals when through the walls of the temascal he saw what he thought were "a man and a woman that were there committing some-

Ethnohistory 54:1 (Winter 2007) DOI 10.1215/00141801-2006-039

thing carnal."[3] He said that he heard some noises coming from the man on top and he saw that he was thrusting (*dando rrempuzones*) as if he were on top of a woman. Juan soon realized, however, that the person on the bottom also appeared to be a man.[4] The nephew rushed to call his uncle's young Nahuatl-speaking indigenous servant, Gaspar, to verify if he really was witnessing two men committing the *pecado nefando contra natura*—the nefarious sin against nature. Once the young servant confirmed what was taking place, the nephew ran to the nearby central plaza to alert the first two Spanish men he saw, García Maldonado and Juan Hernández.

The Spanish men returned with the two boys to the temascal and witnessed what was going on between Cuyne and Quini. Once the Purépecha men realized that they had been discovered, the man who was on top, Cuyne, fled to the Church of San Agustín from which he was later forcibly removed, against the wishes of the priest, by local authorities and brought to prison. This priestly intervention, power, and influence ultimately saved Cuyne from being prosecuted for the crime of sodomy. Quini, though he argued and tried to escape, was more quickly apprehended in his "white underwear wet with fresh blood" by one of the Spanish men who understood the Purépecha language and ascertained from Quini that Cuyne was drunk.[5] The most interesting details of the case of course come directly from the testimonies of Cuyne, Quini, and later, the other men implicated in this criminal case.

Both Cuyne and Quini testified through interpreters who translated from the men's native Purépecha (referred to as *tarasca* in the document) into Spanish. Unfortunately for the ethnohistorian, these written records include none of the original Purépecha language that Cuyne, Quini, and the other indigenous men used to confess and testify. Similarly, there is no inclusion of the Nahuatl that Gaspar, the indigenous servant of Padre Velázquez, would have used in his testimony. None of the native peoples involved in this case wrote Spanish or spoke enough of it to make their formal confessions and declarations to colonial authorities in that language. Because the entire criminal case was recorded in Spanish, we must rely on what can only be imperfect and imprecise translations. Despite these colonial filters and the problems associated with the complicated processes of translation and interpretation, these testimonies nonetheless offer important details that shed light on aspects of sexuality and its regulation in early colonial Michoacán.

In his testimony taken on 16 August, Simpliciano Cuyne asserted that he was twenty years old and married to a Purépecha woman in San Agustín, Vitoria, and made no attempt to deny that he and another man (unknown to him by name but later identified as Pedro Quini) were found together with their legs intertwined (*juntos y entrepernados*) in the temascal. He said that on that day he was at a house near the convent of San Agustín with some other Purépecha friends when two *negros*—either African slaves or their descendants—whom they did not know came to sell them wine and *pulque*.[6] They had already been drinking when an unknown Purépecha man, Quini, came to them attempting to sell a blue piece of clothing (*una rropilla de paño azul*). Though Cuyne and his friends soon left the house and headed toward the corrals behind the church, this man followed them, begging the others to buy the blue cloth. According to Cuyne, he eventually went with the man because he was tired of his begging and felt "defeated by his pleas."[7] On leaving his friends' company, Cuyne told the man with the blue cloth that he wanted to sleep, whereupon the man suggested they go to a nearby temascal where, according to the testimony, the following took place: "He went with him to the said temascal and this witness [Cuyne] entered first. He threw himself on the floor [to sleep] and then the said *yndio* who is now in prison [Quini], and whose name he does not know, came up to this witness and began to hug him and to kiss him and he put his hand inside the fly of his pants."[8] After Quini put his hand in the fly of Cuyne's pants, Cuyne purportedly objected, whereby Quini told him that he had much desire (*que el tenia mucho deseo*) and that he would give him the blue cloth if he continued.[9] Despite Cuyne's attempt to prove to criminal authorities that he was without desire and therefore without agency in the initiation of the sexual acts, in his testimony there is a clear mention of desire and intimacy (in the form of hugging, kissing, and caressing initiated by Quini) between the two men. This detailed reference to sexual desire and intimacy between men is fairly rare even in criminal or Inquisition cases dealing with sodomy.

By turning to sexual desire as a category of historical analysis, historians might better understand the reasons upon which people based some of their everyday decisions. As seen in this document, sexual desire can blur the boundaries between order and disorder. Although both Cuyne and Quini were married to Purépecha women and without children, the orderly and potentially procreative sexual desire that would have taken place within the bonds of matrimony functioned alongside the male-male sexual desire that colonial authorities deemed unnatural, disorderly, and in need of regulation. In terms of historicizing desire, we see that women and men of colonial Mexico oscillated between being desiring subjects and desired objects. They desired women and/or men on physical, sexual, emotional, and spiritual planes. Whereas on a religious plane most women and men desired salvation, on a more physical one they desired potential partners for marriage, their spouses, and others who fell outside of

marriage as in the case of Pedro Quini. For the women and men of colonial Mexico, desire in its many quotidian physical, sexual, emotional, and
spiritual manifestations was omnipresent. It continually influenced the
decisions, acts, and beliefs of individuals who were often merely trying to
live in accordance with conflicting desires, church dogma, and everyday
pressures. It was this desire that Quini felt for Cuyne that led him to initiate sexual contact. Cuyne eventually said that he no longer wanted the
blue cloth but that after the unflagging persistence on the part of Quini,

> the said yndio [Quini] removed the belt of the confessant's [Cuyne's]
> pants and then untied them. He then untied his own pants and stretched
> out on the floor, and being lifted upward, this witness [Cuyne] threw
> himself on top of the said [Pedro Quini] and placed his virile member
> in Quini's anus, and having it inside as if he were with a woman he
> completed [the sexual act, i.e., ejaculated] and had carnal copulation
> through this part [the anus] with the said yndio.[10]

It was precisely at this moment, "when Cuyne finished having the said
carnal copulation and ejaculated in the anus of the said [Quini]," that
Cuyne turned his head toward the door, saw the observers, and fled to
the nearby church.[11] Later in his testimony Cuyne asserted that this was
the only time that he had ever committed sodomy. In response to specific
questions in the course of the interrogation, he also stated that he did not
know where the large quantity of blood on the white underpants came
from and that, in the end, the blue cloth was not given in exchange for sex
because he bought it from Quini. There was a genuine concern on the part
of the authorities that this instance involved male-male prostitution as well
as sodomy, though it appears that this was not the case.

Quini's testimony yields even more interesting details regarding his
sexual activity with other males. In the first testimony, also taken on 16
August, Quini said that he was from Tzintzuntzan and was married to the
yndia María. He states that he doesn't know his age, but according to the
criminal authorities looks about twenty-five. Quini verified that he was
found with another indigenous man in the temascal but that they had only
gone there temporarily to hide because they had been drinking pulque
and were afraid of being caught by judicial authorities. Quini said that he
sold the other man a piece of blue cloth for a small sum, and denied that
anything more than what he had said took place. Asked if he began at any
point to kiss, hug, or touch the other man, Quini denied the allegations,
stating that he had been drunk and therefore did not remember exactly
what he had done. In a second testimony taken on 18 August, face-to-face
with Cuyne in the *careo*, Quini changed his story dramatically.[12] He not

only admitted to the events in the temascal but also told how he had committed the pecado nefando with a number of other men—termed *putos*—in and around Valladolid.[13] This was merely the beginning of a criminal trial that began to investigate a possible network of men accustomed to committing the pecado nefando in colonial Valladolid and the towns surrounding Lake Pátzcuaro.

A Historically Complicated Web of Sodomy
Accusations in Colonial Michoacán

In order to historically locate and better discuss the 1604 sodomy case from Michoacán, it is necessary to briefly discuss the early history of Michoacán alongside the infamous 1530 criminal trial and execution of Tzintzincha Tangaxoan, El Caltzontzin, the noble indigenous ruler of the Purépecha peoples in Michoacán. While the conquest of Michoacán began shortly after the conquest of Mexico City—Tenochtitlán—in 1521, Spanish power was not consolidated until 1529–30, when the expedition of conquistador Nuño de Guzmán, the president of the first *audiencia* of New Spain, passed through the region toward the town of Tzintzuntzan with Spanish soldiers and indigenous allies.[14] Among these allies was El Caltzontzin, known also by his Spanish name don Francisco, who was accused of grave crimes on 26 January 1530 by a Spanish *encomienda* owner from Uruapan, Francisco de Villegas, who was also traveling with the campaign.[15] The most serious among these charges were that El Caltzontzin had repeatedly ordered Spaniards to be killed in Michoacán and that he had committed acts of sodomy over a long period.[16] It also became known early in the trial that El Caltzontzin had previously been formally tried for sodomy by the Spaniard Pedro Sánchez Farfán, then acting as *visitador* of the province of Michoacán, sometime in the late 1520s. According to Francisco de Villegas, Farfán "held a trial against the said Caltzontzin for sodomy in which he found a large amount of information."[17] For these crimes, Guzmán pronounced the death sentence—by means of garrote, strangulation, with the corpse to be burned to ashes—on El Caltzontzin on 14 February 1530.

While some historians have discussed this 1530 *proceso* in detail, the representations of sodomy in it have yet to be thoroughly examined or linked to other sodomy trials in early colonial Mexico. Perhaps the best discussion of El Caltzontzin's trial in recent historiography is offered by James Krippner-Martínez, who shows how a reading of the trial "against the grain" debunks any myth of indigenous passivity to the violence and encroachments of Spanish colonialism in Michoacán. While it became clear throughout the trial that El Caltzontzin did in fact order Spaniards to be killed on numerous occasions, what the trial records tell us about sodomy is less concrete. Although many of the witnesses had heard of the earlier sodomy trial by Farfán against El Caltzontzin, the only detailed description in the entire proceeding of any male-male sexuality is in the testimony of a Purépecha man named Cuaraque, who was questioned as to whether or not he knew El Caltzontzin to have committed the "abominable sin of sodomy," and as to whether or not he maintained *indios* with whom he fornicated and committed the abominable sin.[18] To this, Cuaraque asserted

> that he knows that [El Caltzontzin] has [male] indios with whom he sleeps.[19] One is named Juanico, who is in Apascuaro and will arrive soon. The other one [Cuaraque] knew, who is now deceased,[20] is named Guysacaro. And this is what he has heard spoken and is notorious among all the indigenous servants of the said Cazonzi [El Caltzontzin]. And when the said Cazonzi is drunk, he has seen him put his tongue in the said Juanillo's [Juanico's] mouth and kiss him. And that since he was little the said Cazonzi has been accustomed to having those [male indios] for such use. It is notorious that he has them for that [use] and thus they themselves are used.[21]

While this text, like all colonial texts, must be treated with a degree of skepticism, the many rumors about El Caltzontzin's sodomitical proclivities and the detailed account offered by Cuaraque make it likely there was some truth in Cuaraque's eyewitness testimony. Most important, according to this testimony, El Caltzontzin had long been notorious for having same-sex interactions and relationships.

Why was El Caltzontzin not condemned after the earlier sodomy trial by Farfán (of which no written records have surfaced)? This is perhaps due to a lack of information or, more likely, because El Caltzontzin's wealth and status protected him. Indeed, Francisco de Villegas tells us in his original complaint against El Caltzontzin, despite the many earlier trials and executions of indigenous nobles in Michoacán for grave crimes and idolatries, "the said Caltzontzin with his crafty skills and large quantities of gold and silver exempted himself from [i.e., bought his way out of] the punishments that he deserved."[22] El Caltzontzin clearly gave certain Spaniards gold and silver in exchange for his freedom. Ultimately, no matter how it is analyzed, the 1530 trial against El Caltzontzin offers limited information on the regulation of sodomy and sexuality in early colonial Michoacán. Clearly a highly gendered and sexualized discourse of "othering," central to the Spanish colonial projects in the Americas, was also at work here. Krippner-Martínez notes that the inclusion of the questions relating to sodomy by Nuño de Guzmán "demonstrates the construction of an image of the Cazonzi [El Caltzontzin] as a 'perverse other' in the eyes of the Spanish interrogators. This was an essential step in creating the necessary distance, between victor and victim, for what was to ensue."[23] But given Cuaraque's detailed testimony and El Caltzontzin's earlier trial specifically for sodomy by Farfán, which he escaped only through bribes, the inclusion of sodomy in the charges against El Caltzontzin in 1530 was not merely a way to construct him as a "perverse other" in the eyes of the Spanish authorities.

While the information we have on El Caltzontzin's 1530 trial might tell us more about the nature of rumor and how sodomy accusations played out than about the historical realities of sodomites in early colonial Michoacán, this trial offers a good historical introduction to the 1604 sodomy case from Valladolid examined here. All in all, in 1604 thirteen men were implicated in what started out as a criminal investigation of two men caught having sex in a temascal.[24] This web of sodomy accusations began with Quini's second confession on 18 August 1604, in which he not only admitted to having had sexual relations with Cuyne a few days earlier in the temascal, but also inculpated the indigenous servant of Andrés Guesore, Joaquín Ziziqui. When asked about why he was relating information about the other putos that he knew, Quini replied that "now . . . God wants him to declare and reveal the truth."[25] He stated that the two of them had sex twice and that Ziziqui "served him both times as a woman [i.e., on bottom]" because he had inserted his penis in Ziziqui's anus and ejaculated both times. He also asserted that "when he committed the sin with him [Ziziqui] he always presumed that the said Joaquín was accustomed to committing this sin."[26]

Quini then stated that the first time he had committed the pecado nefando with another man was about four years before with Ziziqui, and that it took place in the company of two other indigenous men: the already deceased cook (later identified as Marcos) of the Spanish treasurer Pedro de Aguaya and a young painter from Uruapan (later identified as Miguel) who was *de buen cuerpo y buen parecer*—with a good body and good looks. According to Quini, these men were putos and he himself had heard from Ziziqui that "*heran todos putos*—they were all putos who were accustomed to committing to nefarious sin."[27] What initially seems like a string of false accusations starts to make more sense as the story continues. While Ziziqui from Uruapan was eventually caught by authorities and also tried for the sin of sodomy, the young painter from Uruapan was never located. Quini's testimony is completely corroborated by Ziziqui's confession, in which he admitted to having had sex with and being penetrated by Quini

twice. Ziziqui in the course of his confession did however say that he really
did not know if the young painter and the already deceased cook from
Uruapan were putos or not.[28] While Ziziqui, who was unmarried and did
not know his age but looked about twenty-five, admitted to having committed sodomy with Quini, he also tried to negate his own agency in the
act and exculpate himself by saying that "he is a Christian and that about
six years ago, [when Ziziqui was] only a boy living in the neighborhood
of San Francisco, the said *yndio* Pedro Quini committed and persuaded
him to commit the nefarious sin. And that being a young boy not knowing
what he was doing, he fell into the nefarious sin."[29] Although his tactic did
not work, Ziziqui interestingly used religion, his youth and naïveté, and
a lack of individual agency in an attempt to deflect his own culpability in
sodomy.

The next to be implicated in this trial was a Purépecha baker named
Francisco Capiche with whom Pedro Quini had had sex about eleven days
earlier. According to Quini, that night Capiche invited him to sleep at the
house of don Francisco Muñoz, where he worked. Around midnight the
two entered the house with a large oven where Capiche started to beg Quini
"that he do it," at which point Quini "copulated with him" by placing
his penis in Capiche's anus and ejaculating inside him.[30] Quini then discussed with his interrogators his relationship with an yndio from Cuisco
named Miguel, with whom he had sex a month before at five o'clock in
the afternoon behind a black cloak. Miguel had invited Quini to enter the
colegio (most likely the place where a community of religious men would
have been studying and possibly living) where he worked washing clothes,
through some side walls so that nobody would see him enter. As Quini
secretly entered the colegio he found Miguel waiting for him and the two
promptly "entered to sleep in the kitchen and lying there the said Miguel
began to insist that Pedro try to put his penis [*miembro genital*] inside of
him," and as he did this, "the said Miguel served him as a woman."[31]
Quini stated that this was the only time that he had sex with Miguel and
that he did not know if Miguel had had sex with other men. While Francisco Capiche was eventually caught and tried for the pecado nefando,
Miguel from Cuisco was never found or mentioned again. At first Capiche
flatly denied any sexual involvement with Quini, but once the instruments
of torture were introduced, Capiche admitted to everything. Although it
is not exactly clear whether Capiche was actually physically tortured at
any point, or whether he confessed upon being threatened with torture, it
appears that the latter took place.[32]

In the single most interesting denunciation, Quini accused Francisco
Conduyi, a baker and single man in his mid-thirties from Tzintzuntzan,

of being a puto and possibly a male prostitute. It was at Conduyi's house, next to Tzintzuntzan's church and just past a small bridge, where a few years prior to 1604 Quini first learned how to commit the pecado nefando. Quini stated that he knew that Conduyi was "a puto and that he has committed the nefarious sin and the former in the occupation of committing sodomy because he has seen him do it about three years ago and he also saw him numerous times serve as a woman [i.e., be penetrated in the act of sodomy]."[33] Quini asserted that Conduyi's father was dead, his mother was named Ysabel, and that an indigenous man named Ticata lived with him (que bibe junto deste d[ic]ho Franco yndio).[34] Quini, only slightly later in this testimony, also made a rather vague reference to "the other yndio [this may or may not have been Ticata] who served the said Francisco Conduyi as if he were his woman."[35] Given how Quini described him, this might even have been someone biologically male who lived and served as a woman in terms of dress, traditional tasks and chores, and sex over a long period. There is a striking semantic difference between the verb tenses and the terminology Quini used here to describe this man who served, in the long-term and habitual, imperfect conjugation of the Spanish verb servir, as if he were a woman over a long period of time (servía como si fuese muger) and any other man who in a single instance of sodomy was sexually penetrated and therefore served, in the short-term, preterit tense of the verb, as a woman (sirvió de muger). Because Quini was speaking Purépecha and not Spanish, however, we cannot know if he made this same imperfect-preterit distinction in his original testimony or if this temporal distinction was imposed by Spanish grammar through the act of translation. Especially fascinating in this testimony is that Quini saw Conduyi repeatedly serve "as a woman" in the act of sodomy while at the same time Conduyi had this indigenous man who served him as if he were his woman.

Even more interesting than the fact that Conduyi's home served as a meeting place for men seeking out sexual activity with other men (and possibly as a place for male-male prostitution) is that, as Quini related, about three years earlier local authorities in Tzintzuntzan had tried to imprison Conduyi for supposedly committing the pecado nefando with other men. Authorities never caught him because Conduyi fled town, later secretly returning to the pueblo. Fortunately for Conduyi, he fled again in 1604, most likely after hearing that Quini was imprisoned for sodomy. That Conduyi's house served as a meeting point for men who sought out sex with other men brings up numerous unanswerable questions about privacy and local levels of tolerance. How could Conduyi hide his activities from his neighbors? Did his neighbors know about the men who had sex in his house, about the man named Ticata who lived with him, or about the indigenous man who over a seemingly long period "served [him] as if he were his woman"? How did legal authorities in Tzintzuntzan years prior to 1604 come to find out about Conduyi's sodomitical activities? In terms of local levels of tolerance, we might also ask how Quini was able to hide his sodomitical proclivities from his wife, María—if he did indeed hide them—for such a long time. Some of these questions might have been resolved had Conduyi ever made a statement or a confession to the court. The authorities' repeated attempts to locate him failed, and Conduyi dropped out of the historical record.

In a final string of accusations, Quini mentioned two men, Pedro Zinzo and Joachinque, both from Tzintzuntzan, that he saw have sex once. Neither was ever found by colonial authorities. Lastly, Quini mentioned a boy identified only as the fifteen-year-old Juan, the indigenous servant of Francisco Ruiz, with whom, according to Quini, he had never had sex despite the boy's pleas on two separate occasions that they do so. Though it might have something to do with Juan's young age, it is unclear why after such detailed accounts of the people Quini had had sex with— names, sexual positions, times, dates, and places—here when discussing Juan yndio, Quini denied having had sex with him. It was not until a few days later, when asked about his relationship with Quini, that Juan gave a very detailed account of how about two weeks before Quini had gone to the butcher's shop where Juan worked to buy some meat. Upon arriving, Quini began to chat and eventually beg Juan to go with him to the pasture (*sacatal*) behind the corrals of the butcher's shop. It was about nine in the morning when the two went to the pasture, and there Juan stripped his underwear to allow Quini to enter him and ejaculate inside his anus.[36] Again we see attempts by both Quini and Juan to deflect the agency of the sexual act. While Quini asserted that is was Juan who begged him to have sex, Juan reported the opposite. Although Juan said that this was the only time he had had sex with Quini, his story does not stop here.

About a week before this meeting with Quini, Juan stated, he had sex with another yndio, Miguel Hidalgo.[37] Juan asserted that in the *barrancas* of the corrals near the hacienda where Hidalgo worked, he was pressured by Hidalgo to have sex. He also said that he had served Hidalgo as "the woman," while Hidalgo served as "the man."[38] Hidalgo, in his confession taken later, said that he did not even know Juan, but unfortunately for him various witnesses attested that they did indeed work together in the same house for a time, and that they were friends and had been seen talking repeatedly to one another. Although Juan later denied that these stories were true, most likely acting on the advice of his legal defense, it helped little given that Quini in his careo with Juan on 23 August admitted to having had sexual relations with him. Interestingly, perhaps due to Juan's young age, Quini stated that initially he was too scared to tell the truth about what had happened with him. Juan much later, and only under threat of torture, admitted again that these stories were in fact true. Although in total thirteen men are implicated in this criminal trial, in the end Juan yndio, Joaquín Ziziqui, Miguel Hidalgo, and Francisco Capiche were tried along with Pedro Quini and Simpliciano Cuyne for having committed the pecado nefando — "such an abominable crime and such a great offense to God."[39] In this complicated web of sodomy accusations, there is clearly an attempt to deflect the charges from oneself onto others. However, there is a simultaneous attempt by some men to hide and limit information in order to protect themselves, their friends, and their acquaintances. Unfortunately for the men, this criminal trial had a grim outcome for nearly all involved.

Language and the Inapplicability of the Active/Passive Model

Decidedly one of the major problems with using official documents to examine the intimate lives of individuals is the way the formulaic language used in criminal and Inquisition trials obscures the realities of popular conceptions of eroticism and sexuality. This obviously holds true for cases from colonial Mexico. Unfortunately much of the original language and terms most probably used to describe certain situations are lost through official discourse. It is highly unlikely that the fourteen-year-old nephew of Padre Rangel or the even younger indigenous servant Gaspar would have described what they saw as the *pecado nefando contra natura* — the nefarious sin against nature. Other terms including *sodomía* (sodomy), *acceso carnal* (carnal access), *cópula* (copulation), and *abominable delito* (the abominable crime) continually recur in the official discourse and clearly relate to theological categories and concepts of sodomy put forth in Spanish laws.[40] Though all of these terms are constructed through colonial discourse, it becomes difficult to tell which might have been used by the witnesses and defendants and which were imposed on them by judges and prosecutors asking specific questions. We do see, however, other more common terms used to describe what happened between Quini and Cuyne that day in the temascal. The word *puto*, for example, is often used to describe those accused by Quini to refer not simply to someone who has committed sodomy, but rather to someone who is accustomed to having sodomitical relations. The adjectives *ensima* (on top), *abaxo* (on bottom), and *boca abaxo* (face down) are also commonly employed to describe positions in sexual acts between men. These terms, however, highlight an even larger problem in understanding the realities and meanings of sodomy in early colonial Mexico: the problematic *como si fueran hombre y muger* — "as if they were man and woman" — model of understanding sexual acts between men.

Martin Nesvig, in his historiographical essay "The Complicated Terrain of Latin American Homosexuality" (2001), discusses the evolution of the treatment of Latin American "homosexuality" in historical and anthropological scholarly literature since the early 1980s. Nesvig's main concern is that much of the scholarship on sexuality in Latin America is tainted by assumptions of patriarchy and male-dominated sexuality. Nesvig asserts that the male-active-penetrator and female-passive-penetrated paradigms, reiterated by Octavio Paz's *hijos de la chingada* model, also have been grafted onto conceptions of male-male sexual encounters. In colonial historiography and in contemporary anthropological work on same-sex sexuality, a dominant-submissive dichotomy, which obscures the complexities of reality, is often assumed and left unchallenged. This 1604 criminal sodomy case from Michoacán further challenges associations between male-active-penetrator and female-passive-penetrated. Due to the inherent problems of linguistic, cultural, and ideological translation, we cannot be sure if the notion that the penetrated bottom served as *muger* — woman (and hence being "passive") or the idea that the top served as *hombre* — man (and hence being "active") were concepts that came from the Purépecha speakers, witnesses, and participants themselves. It is possible that these were solely categories imposed by the Spanish religious and cultural ways of viewing the world in order to classify and denigrate sexual relations between men.[41]

What we see upon closer inspection is that the "as if they were man and woman" model of explaining male same-sex sexual activity does not correspond necessarily to masculinity, femininity, activity, or passivity.[42] Table 1 summarizes the names, ages, and occupations of the thirteen men accused of committing sodomy as well as the locations, times, and positions of the sexual acts. It also demonstrates that at least in this small group most men typically assumed either a top or bottom role in all of their sexual encounters with other men. Quini almost always assumed the role of the top. From the rich yet incomplete information that the document provides, only Quini and possibly Conduyi assumed both top and bottom roles in sodomy with other men. While Quini repeatedly saw Conduyi at his house with a variety of men playing the role of the bottom, he also said Conduyi had a man who served him as if he were his woman. The young Juan yndio in his two experiences with slightly older men always served as a bottom. In none of the testimonies, however, are tops described as being more masculine or bottoms as more feminine.

Table 1. Thirteen sodomy accusations: Circumstances, names, occupations, ages, dates, and locations

(1, 2) Pedro Quini, ~25 (bottom) with Simpliciano Cuyne, ~20 (top), sacristan. 15 August 1604, 2:00 p.m. in the temascal. Quini is immediately caught and Cuyne flees to the church where he is later apprehended. Both admit (in careo) to being caught in flagrante delicto.	(3) Pedro Quini, ~25 (top) with Joaquín Ziziqui, ~25 (bottom), from Uruapan, baker and servant of Andrés Guesore. Sodomy took place two times between 1598 and 1600. Both admit. This was Quini's first sexual experience with a male.	(4, 5) Pedro Quini accuses Marcos the already deceased cook of the Spanish treasurer Pedro de Aguaya and Miguel the young painter from Uruapan of being putos, but no sexual acts take place. Neither is caught.
(6) Pedro Quini, ~25 (top) with Francisco Capiche, ~25 (bottom), baker in the house of Francisco Muñoz. August 1604 (eleven days before the temascal incident), 12:00 midnight. Francisco Capiche admits only under threat of torture.	(7) Pedro Quini, ~25 (top) with Miguel of Cuisco (bottom). Sunday, July 1604, 5:00 p.m., underneath a black cloak in the kitchen of the colegio. Miguel of Cuisco is never caught.	(8, 9) Pedro Quini accuses Francisco Conduyi, mid-thirties (bottom), from Tzintzuntzan, of being a puto. It was at his house that Quini first learned how to commit the pecado nefando. Conduyi flees town for the second time and is never caught. Quini also refers to a man who "served as if he were [Conduyi's] woman."
(10, 11) According to Pedro Quini's testimony, Pedro Zinzo (bottom) with Joachinque (top). Neither of the men is caught despite repeated attempts by authorities, who imprison the wrong man, Pedro Ziziqui, for a short time thinking that he is either Pedro Zinzo or Joachinque.	(12) Pedro Quini, ~25 (top) with Juan yndio, ~15 (bottom), servant in butcher's shop. August 1604, 9:00 a.m., in the pastures behind the corrals of the butcher's shop. Juan admits, then changes his story. Quini denies, then changes his story. Both eventually admit (after Juan is threatened with torture).	(13) Juan yndio, ~15 (bottom) with Miguel Hidalgo, ~20 (top), laborer. July 1604 near the corrals of the house where he worked. Hidalgo denied that he knew Juan, but witnesses show that the two worked in the same house. Juan admits, then denies, then later admits again.

Where the male-active-penetrator and female-passive-penetrated paradigms and the "as if they were man and woman" model fall short, however, is in their corresponding notions of activity and passivity. While there is definitely penile penetration of the anus, I would argue that there is a sort of "penetrational ambiguity" present throughout the texts. While it is clear which bodily orifices are being penetrated, it often remains unclear who is penetrating whom for what motives and reasons.[43] The one who initiates the sexual activity with another man (who might typically be seen as the "aggressor") is often not the one on top or the person who penetrates. We see this in Quini's drunken seduction of Cuyne, as well as in Capiche's seduction of Quini. In both instances, the one who assumed the bottom role in anal sex was the one who initiated sexual activity. It is also important to note that we do not see much age stratification here, as there possibly was in the case of El Caltzontzin, in relation to activity or passivity, top or bottom. While it was most common for older men to pressure younger men into performing various sexual acts, the older man is clearly not always the top, "active," or more "masculine" partner in the sexual relationship. All this complicates the "as if they were man and woman" model of understanding sexual acts between men as well as its typically associated notions of activity, passivity, dominance, and submission.

There also appears to be a historiographical debate as to whether the top or the bottom (usually phrased as "active" and "passive") in sodomy cases was punished more harshly, and as to why this is the case. Nesvig argues that the active/passive dichotomy in understanding sexual acts between males obscures the reality of the cases, because the active partner has not always escaped condemnation. Mary Elizabeth Perry's research on early modern Spain, however, upholds this dichotomy. While Perry rightly asserts that heterosexual sodomy was never seen by authorities as being as serious a crime as same-sex sodomy, she asserts that "this implies that the real crime of sodomy was not in ejaculating nonprocreatively, nor in the use of the anus, but in requiring a male to play the passive 'female' role and in violating the physical integrity of the male recipient body."[44] Rafael Carrasco's study of sodomy in Valencia between 1565 and 1785 shows that in Spain the "active" participants in anal sex were punished more harshly than "passive" participants.

Lee Penyak's research into sodomy cases in his 1993 dissertation "Criminal Sexuality in Central Mexico, 1750–1850," however, tells a different story. Penyak's research shows that "willing participants convicted of sodomy [clearly excluding rape victims] could expect to receive the same penalty whatever sexual position they used."[45] As Nesvig asserts, "The Inquisition did not distinguish between homosexuals or heterosexuals in this matter. All who committed this act [sodomy] were guilty before the Holy Office."[46] In early colonial Michoacán, criminal authorities in meting out their punishments also failed to distinguish between top/bottom, active/passive, or putatively male/female roles in sodomy cases. This 1604 criminal case upholds the notion that in early colonial Mexico both top ("active") and bottom ("passive") in male sodomy cases were punished aggressively.

In Valladolid on 26 August 1604, an order was given to confiscate all the goods of the men charged with sodomy.[47] In a strange twist of events, however, it appears that Cuyne was granted immunity from the judicial process due to his having fled after the temascal incident and entered the nearby church where he served as sacristan, and because he was forcibly removed by local authorities against the wishes of the priests. The priests of the Iglesia de San Agustín successfully petitioned for Cuyne "as an obedient son of the Holy Church"; as far as we know, he was never punished for sodomy.[48] This is in spite of the advice of the *alcalde ordinario*, who argued that due to the severity of Cuyne's crime and the fact that he confessed under oath to everything, he should be prosecuted to the full extent of the law. That priestly power ultimately protected Cuyne seems to support the conclusions of Lee Penyak, Pete Sigal, and David Higgs that for the most part early modern priests were not greatly concerned with sodomy. While there was considerable debate as to whether or not Cuyne should be granted immunity, in the end, despite the gravity of his crime, he was spared from punishment and conversely, in what appears to be punishment for having forcibly removed Cuyne from the church against the priests' wishes, the *alcalde* (mayor) was forced to pay "two pounds of wax for the *santissima sacramento*" and the *alguacil* (constable) was fined one *marco* of silver.[49]

On 20 September 1604, Miguel Hidalgo, the only one of the remaining five convicted of sodomy who had yet to confess his crime, was sentenced to be publicly tortured by garrote and ropes (*cordeles*). On that same day, Pedro Quini, Joaquín Ziziqui, Francisco Capiche, and Juan yndio were sentenced to

> be taken from the prison where they are being held on horseback, with their necks, feet, and hands tied with ropes, and with a town crier who proclaims their crime. They shall be carried through the public streets to the place where they will be executed according to the form of justice. And there they will be given the garrote in the usual manner until they die naturally, and, once dead, their bodies shall be burned in the flames of fire until they are turned into ashes. Lastly, I declare

that all of the belongings of the said [men] that are found shall be confiscated for the Supreme Council of Your Majesty.[50]

That four of the six men tried for sodomy received the death penalty had absolutely nothing to do with their being either top or bottom, "active" or "passive," married or single, or with this being their first, second, or third time committing the sin of sodomy with another man. Despite the fact that Miguel never confessed, he would be tortured by the garrote and with ropes, but apparently he was not put to death. Neither was Cuyne because he had been granted immunity by the church. Although this final sentence was passed on 20 September 1604, a final appeal by the defense to the Court of the Real Audiencia of Mexico was rejected on 15 October 1604. We can only assume that the executions were carried out later that year in Valladolid.

Sodomitical Subcultures and the Historiographical Pursuit of "Homosexuality"

Currently, there is an important historiographical debate about the existence of sodomitical subcultures—social networks of men who knew when and where to have sex with other men—in colonial Latin America. Historians of colonial Brazil and Latin America have been more or less at odds with one another regarding the issue of "homosexual" subcultures in the colonial period. While some historians have employed an essentialist viewpoint to assert the existence of "gay" individuals in the colonial period, other historians have flatly denied the existence of same-sex sexual subcultures. Yet others have grappled with the scarcity of sources dealing with the topic. Nesvig speaks, perhaps most aptly, of the potential existence of sodomitical subcultures in certain geographic locations. The category of a sodomitical subculture, although imperfect, can describe men who sought out and knew where to find sex with other men.

Serge Gruzinski's groundbreaking essay "Las cenizas del deseo" (1985) addressed the absolute lack of historical research on men who engaged in sexual relationships with other men in colonial Latin America. Using incomplete documents found in Seville's Archivo de las Indias, specifically, a few letters from 1658, a list of fourteen men executed for committing sodomy, and a summary of the judicial investigation (the original case is lost), Gruzinski was able to reconstruct details of the lives of some 123 men—mostly mestizos, indigenous, Spanish, blacks, and mulattoes from Puebla and Mexico City—who were accused of engaging in the pecado nefando in Mexico City. Testimonies allowed Gruzinski to reconstruct the affiliations and links among many of the accused men, showing that at least in colonial Puebla and Mexico City, there was likely a clandestine community of men who sought out other men for sex. These sexual activities between men were not isolated cases; rather, as Gruzinski asserted, the documents reveal "a subculture [with] its own secret geography, its own network of information and informants, [and] its own language and codes."[51] In Gruzinski's discussion, however, this subculture is limited to the urban spaces of Puebla and Mexico City.

The documents also demonstrate the great frequency of sexual activities between men that took place in various locations: primarily in individual homes, *pulquerías*, and temascales. Gruzinski reached three important conclusions that have served as starting points for much of the subsequent research on same-sex sexual activity in colonial Latin America: (1) that urban networks of men who sought out other men for sexual relationships did exist in the colonial period; (2) that these men did not live in fear, despite occasional yet harsh repression by the church; and (3) that these men's activities operated at the threshold of social and religious tolerance. Gruzinski also intimated that there was often a tacit acceptance of this behavior so long as it was kept private and discreet. This is something that has been continually affirmed by other historians studying gender, honor, and sexuality in colonial Latin America.[52]

In what has thus far been the most cogent and comprehensive examination of sodomy cases in colonial Mexico, Penyak, in his chapter "Sodomy, Bestiality, and Female Deviant Sexuality," used approximately forty late-colonial cases to illustrate the nature of sodomy as well as cases of male-male solicitation in the confessional. He asserted that although formidable subcultures of men who sought out sex with other men have been amply documented in places like Venice, Italy, and Valencia, Spain, there is not enough evidence to make similar conclusions about colonial Mexico.[53] It is true that the simple existence of sodomitical subcultures in early modern Europe does not allow us to infer a similar phenomenon in colonial Mexico. In light of recent scholarship and archival evidence revealed since 1993, we can now reevaluate Penyak's assertion that "there are no indications that homosexuals [in Mexico] established their own sub-culture or that they ever felt safe enough to form friendships with like-minded persons with whom they might espouse a particular vision of the world or simply feel comfortable."[54] Historical analyses of sexuality in colonial Mexico are now limited less by a lack of sources and documentation than by a collective need to find, put together, and analyze more of the pertinent archival documents in conjunction with one another.

As this 1604 criminal document from colonial Valladolid is most likely the largest and most richly detailed extant document dealing with sodomy in colonial Mexico, especially when analyzed in conjunction with other cases, it has the potential to alter some of the previously held beliefs about the nature of sodomy in colonial Mexico. While I agree with Penyak that the sodomitical subcultures found in early modern Europe were more substantial and formidable than anything found in colonial Mexico, the growing evidence relating to sodomy and same-sex sexual relations in colonial Mexico attests to the undeniable existence of sodomitical subcultures in rural as well as urban spaces, in the church, and even on the ships that traveled between Spain and the Americas. Federico Garza Carjaval asserts that even the "men and boys likewise traveling to and from the Indies demonstrated an awareness of sodomitical subculture."[55]

While Gruzinski asserts that sodomitical subcultures existed only in urban areas like Puebla and Mexico City, this document intimates that even in rural areas there were tightly knit communities of men accustomed to committing the pecado nefando.[56] The research here does support some of Gruzinski's conclusions, namely, that networks of men who sought out sex with other men did exist, and that local levels of tolerance allowed them to live in other than absolute fear. One interesting difference between the group of men persecuted in Mexico City in 1658 for sodomy and those punished in Valladolid in 1604 is that the Mexico City group was multi-ethnic, made up of mestizos, natives, blacks, mulattoes, and Spaniards, whereas the group in Michoacán was made up entirely of Purépecha men. This 1604 document proves that networks, however small, of men who sought out sex with other men existed in both rural and urban areas of colonial Mexico.

Sites, Symbols, and Markers of Social Disorder

Another primary concern in analyzing this case is the false dichotomy between order and disorder. We must examine the applicability to disordered gender and sexuality of William B. Taylor's assertion that "the pulquería was a 'time-out' setting where the rules outside did not necessarily apply."[57] According to a 1692 letter by Joseph Vidal de Figueroa, many indios in the taverns of Mexico City, "in order to satisfy their sordid appetite, . . . dress in the clothes of women at night, and they sleep among the clients in a drunken state and . . . provoke among them the vile act [sodomy]."[58] According to Ana María Rodríguez Atondo, in the later colonial period "some of the places most frequented by women of 'mala vida' during the [eighteenth-century] period of the Enlightenment were the stands that sold alcoholic beverages: the pulquerías and *vinaterías*."[59]

Garza Carvajal, in his *Butterflies Will Burn* (2003), uses archival cases and the writings of friars, chroniclers, conquistadores, and historiographers like Bernardino de Sahagún, Tomás de Torquemada, Fernando de Alva Ixtlilxóchitl, Bartolomé de Alva, Toribio Motolinia, Hernán Cortés, and Christopher Columbus to demonstrate that in Spain sodomites were typically associated with the foreign, whereas in New Spain "colonial officials, jurists, theologians, and other writers associated signifiers like the diabolic, anthropophagy, inebriation, and effeminacy with perceptions of the pecado nefando."[60] Alcohol, inebriation, and sodomy functioned symbiotically in the minds of colonial authorities as symbols of disorder, and the 1604 sodomy case from Michoacán analyzed here bears out Garza Carvajal's conclusion that in New Spain sodomy was seen as linked to alcohol consumption.

It is interesting to note how much same-sex sexuality, transvestism, and prostitution took place inside some pulquerías and temascales; yet, while it is easy to characterize these dark places distanced from the public gaze as inherently disorderly given the amount of crime and illicit sexual activity that occurred there, they were hardly the only sites of "social disorder." To refer to the places where male same-sex sexual activity took place as "sites of disorder" is not to say that sodomy or other nonreproductive sexual acts were inherently disorderly; indeed, the entire fabric of colonial life was characterized by simultaneous order and disorder. Given that unsanctioned sexual activity also took place in the home, rural fields, the colegio, the church, or workplaces such as the bakery or the corrals behind the butcher's shop, these physical spaces represent (dis)order to the same extent that the pulquería or the temascal do.

If taverns and other places set aside for the consumption of alcohol functioned, at least in the mind of the Spaniards, as physical and ideological spaces for disorderly activities, then a hot temascal where bathers disrobed and alcohol was consumed, as in this 1604 case, could only have been worse. That the temascal is so central to the narrative of the 1604 sodomy case discussed here comes as no surprise: it was imagined by many Spaniards as inherently a space of unsanctioned sexual activity.[61] Recent research on the temascal also provides a fascinating peek into the supposed sources of disorder in colonial life. The sixteenth-century *Codex Tudela*, heavily influenced by Christian morality, defines the temascal—using the Nahuatl word *temazacatl*—as a

> bath of hot water where offenses to our Lord are committed, because if someone became sick, he would come to bathe in this hot place that held water inside. And it happened that many men and women would

enter this bath, and there inside, with such heat, men with women, and women with men, and men with men used each other in illicit ways. And in Mexico there were men dressed in the habit of women and these were the sodomites and they took on the offices of women, such as weaving and sewing, and some elite men even had one or two [of these transvested men] for their vices.[62]

The ambiguities of the temascal as a culturally liminal space between ritual cleanliness—certainly in pre-Hispanic times—and pollution—as imagined by the Spanish—must not be lost here. The temascal confounded and complicated the relationship between order and disorder, cleanliness and defilement.

In addition to featuring physical sites of social disorder, the 1604 sodomy trial also includes many social and ideological markers of disorder. Interestingly, the case starts out with the disrupting influence of blacks, who sell wine and pulque to Simpliciano Cuyne and his friends. As Cuyne related, on 15 August 1604, he "came to the house with his other Indian friends from the *obra* of the said convent [of San Agustín] to drink pulque because there in a room of the said house two *negros* [most likely mulattoes or enslaved Africans] that he did not know sold them wine and pulque."[63] While it is difficult to tell the exact racial composition of colonial Michoacán in the early 1600s, there were clearly many indigenous inhabitants, a much smaller number of Spaniards, members of the racially mixed *castas*, and an increasingly large black population that resulted from the rapid expansion of slavery in Michoacán that began around 1600.[64]

While places like Michoacán did not have the ethnic and racial heterogeneity of Mexico City, the expansion of slavery, in particular, made rural regions of colonial Michoacán quite diverse. Only a few years later, in 1625, the racial and cultural *mestizaje* in the province of Michoacán was described by one Spaniard in the following account: "Among them there are mestizos and mulattoes, children of Spaniards, blacks, mulattoes, and others from this country. Those who are mestizos and mulattoes, being born from Indian women and raised with them and among Indian men, live in accordance with the customs natural to the mothers, speaking their Indian language."[65] This portrayal of life in colonial Michoacán is given by a Spaniard who was ultimately denouncing a black for counterfeit visions of the Virgin Mary. The denouncer also blamed native culture, specifically indigenous women, for the fact that racially mixed children ate meat on days prohibited by the church. In this account from the files of the Inquisition, mestizos, mulattoes, blacks, and indigenous women functioned as markers of social disorder, a seemingly unbridled cultural and linguistic mestizaje in early colonial Michoacán. Much as in the 1604 criminal sodomy case, both black and indigenous communities were envisioned by the Spanish as inherently disorderly and as racially, religiously, and sexually impure, and therefore in need of paternal edification and punishment.

Sexual desire itself functioned as a marker of disorder in religious discourse and legal codes. In terms of disorderly desire, the 1726 *Diccionario de la lengua castellana* defines the word *luxuria*—the capital sin of luxury under which the sin of sodomy would have fallen—as "the disordered appetite, or the excessive use of sensuality or carnality."[66] Sodomy (alongside bestiality) epitomized the disordered sexual desire that fell outside of both the proper vaginal vessel and the bonds of matrimony. Martín Navarro de Azpilcueta, also thinking about disorderly sexual activity in his 1556 *Manual de Confessores*, defined the sin of luxury as the "vice of the soul that inclines one to want the disordered sensual pleasure of carnal copulation or the actions and stimulations leading up to it [copulation] . . . and all sensual pleasure that is born from carnal copulation, or the stimulations leading up to it, is disordered except marital copulation. For this, every craving, desire, or enjoyment of sensual pleasure, except that which is marital, is a sin."[67] While it was all too easy for religious discourse to characterize sexual desire outside of the bonds of matrimony or ejaculation outside of the "proper vessel" as inherently disorderly, historical realities demonstrate that "disorderly" sexual activity functioned alongside and often in conjunction with "orderly" sexual activity.[68] Some of the men prosecuted in this sodomy trial were married and even attempted to use this fact as a mitigating factor in their crime.

Specific body parts also signified disorder to colonial authorities. In her 1966 anthropological discussion of the concepts of pollution, cleanliness, and taboo, Mary Douglas wrote that "sometimes bodily orifices seem to represent points of entry or exit to social units."[69] Bodily markers of disorder in this 1604 sodomy case demonstrate the slippery boundaries between order and disorder. Throughout the case the anus (*sieso*) functions as a physiological, sexual, and ideological entry point to social networks, sexual subcultures, and colonial regulatory processes. The ejaculation of semen into the anus represents the ultimate achievement of the sodomitical act, and, at least according to Catholic religious discourse, the anus as a vessel and receptacle disorders procreative sexuality. Throughout this case, Purépecha men, sexual desire between men, nonprocreative ejaculation in the anus, the temascal, alcohol, and black men selling wine and pulque all function as disruptive symbols and markers of social disorder in colonial Michoacán.

Conclusion: Researching Nonreproductive
Sexualities in Colonial Mexico

I have reproduced the details of this document not merely to highlight the important intersections of ethnicity, sexuality, order and disorder, and colonialism in early seventeenth-century Michoacán, but also to demonstrate that a document like this is now fair game for legitimate historical research and inquiry into the past. In evaluating some of the historiographical contributions and methods used by historians to examine sodomy and so-called deviant sexuality in colonial Latin America, I have sought to show that facile consensus among historians should never be reached. The value of historiographical dialogue lies in the contentions, disagreements, and contradictory conclusions that highlight the complexity and ambiguity of colonial spaces and situations. As this 1604 criminal case demonstrates, the historical study of sexuality can illuminate quotidian realities, relationship dynamics, shifting notions of tolerance and (dis)order, conceptions of privacy and intimacy, and regulatory processes in colonial Mexico. While scholars have been increasingly turning their attention toward sodomy and other nonreproductive sexualities in colonial Latin American history, much work has yet to be done in this nascent field.[70]

Despite the relatively little research on sodomy in colonial Latin America, it is sometimes assumed that the pecado nefando was "the worst of all vices in the New World."[71] Historical evidence does not support this claim unreservedly. As Lee Penyak, Pete Sigal, Gregory Spurling, David Higgs, and Ronaldo Vainfas demonstrate, there was often a higher degree of tolerance for members of the clergy accused of sodomy or sexual acts with other males. Even in this 1604 criminal case from Michoacán, it is priestly power—pointing to local levels of tolerance—that protects Cuyne. Regarding the punishments meted out to those accused of sodomy in late colonial Mexico, Penyak asserted that "whereas laymen were sent to prisons, to public works programs and occasionally whipped, priests were forced to pray."[72] This definitely allows for the possibility that the church, while simultaneously punishing sodomy, maintained some form of a small but undeniably present sodomitical subculture among certain priests. The 1604 criminal trial from Michoacán allows us to relocate this discussion of sodomitical subcultures from urban settings and the church to the rural communities of colonial Mexico.

It is clear that Pedro Quini, Joaquín Ziziqui, Francisco Conduyi, and the other men termed putos were part of a formidable subculture of men in and around colonial Valladolid who knew where to seek out sex with other men. Their sodomitical acts and the physical spaces where they chose to perform them show that the entire fabric of colonial life was characterized by simultaneous order and disorder. The rupture of the order/disorder binary and the existence of local levels of tolerance alongside severe but sporadic repression and regulation in turn underscore the contradictions and complexities of colonial culture. Some of these contradictions of colonialism are evident in the legal and ideological defenses of the men accused of sodomy used by the judges, prosecutors, and lawyers in this case. In its attempt to exculpate Quini of his acts, his defense refers to him as an "incapable Indian without any understanding who neither knows nor understands the gravity and abomination [of sodomy]."[73] This view of indigenous peoples as absolutely incapable of understanding the abominable reveals a clear association between the Spanish conceptions of sin, sodomy, lack of reason, and indigenousness. Similarly Joaquín Ziziqui, Francisco Capuche, and Juan yndio are referred to as "ignorant Indians of little reason or understanding," which was why, at least according to their defenses, they supposedly confessed to crimes which they did not commit.[74] While these defenses sought to free these Purépecha men of culpability for their acts, the reliance on such tropes of native ignorance and inability to understand the abominable ultimately reinscribed the men's position in a colonial hierarchy while simultaneously pushing them into a space where the completion of the colonial process was ideologically unattainable.

We also see some of the ambiguities of colonialism in the confusion of religious and secular jurisdiction over sodomy. Jorge Bracamonte, in his "Los nefandos placeres de la carne" (1998), explores the secularization of sexual sin throughout the colonial period and, more specifically, the transformation of the pecado nefando—the *sin* of sodomy—into a criminal act through the course of the eighteenth century. While Bracamonte rightly highlights the prolonged jurisdictional dispute between the church and the state over the regulation and punishment of so-called deviant sexual practices, I am somewhat skeptical of this overall shift and of the idea that sodomy was transformed from sin to crime during the colonial period.[75] Sodomy in this early 1604 criminal trial is treated jurisdictionally as an abominable crime—*tan abominable delito*—but ideologically as a sin—*en tan gran ofensa de dios*—"in such a great offense to God."[76] While in 1604 four of the Purépecha men accused of sodomy were executed for their crimes, in the eighteenth century men found guilty of sodomy were never executed for their crimes.[77] Although those termed yndios from native communities were outside of the jurisdiction of the Inquisition because of their relatively recent conversion and introduction to Christianity, they were not outside of criminal jurisdiction for similar crimes, like sodomy, that were seen as mortal sins and bordered on heresy. Throughout the colonial period sodomy was irregularly, sporadically, and unequally prosecuted as much as it was either reluctantly tolerated or blatantly ignored by ecclesiastical and secular colonial authorities.

Ultimately the colonial process was ambiguous, contradictory, and disorderly, but it did successfully establish regulatory processes at certain levels. More research on sodomy as well as other types of unnatural and nonreproductive sexualities such as bestiality, male-male solicitation by priests, oral sex, masturbation and sexual caresses, sexual witchcraft, abortion, erotic visions by religious women (*beatas*), sexually explicit paintings and drawings, and illicit statements will only give a more nuanced understanding of the thoughts, behaviors, and conceptions of (dis)order of those who lived in colonial Mexico. While the 1604 trial record provides many valuable details of and glimpses into colonial life, and clearly demonstrates that at least in early colonial Michoacán there existed a rural network of men who had sex with other men, any historical analysis of documents such as this one is possible only because other historians have created historiographical space and dialogue to examine sexuality in colonial Latin America. The reconstruction of sexuality and everyday culture in the colonial period is obviously not an impossible task, but it must lead historians to national and provincial archives in search of more systematic and conclusive evidence.

Appendix

Table 2. Rural sodomy network in early colonial Michoacán

1604	Simpliciano Cuyne (top)—Pedro Quini (bottom)
1598–1600	Pedro Quini (top)—Joaquín Ziziqui (bottom)
1598–1600	Pedro Quini accuses Marcos and Miguel of being putos
1604	Pedro Quini (top)—Miguel of Cuisco (bottom)
1604	Pedro Quini accuses Francisco Conduyi of being a puto
Late 1590s, early 1600s	Francisco Conduyi (bottom)—numerous men
Late 1590s, early 1600s	Francisco Conduyi lives with Ticata
Late 1590s, early 1600s	Francisco Conduyi —man who serves as woman
1604	Pedro Quini (top)—Juan yndio (bottom)
1604	Juan yndio (bottom)—Miguel Hidalgo (top)
????	According to Pedro Quini, Pedro Zinzo (bottom)— Joachinque (bottom)

Notes

I offer special thanks to Kevin Terraciano, Pete Sigal, Martin Nesvig, and Lee Penyak for their support, valuable feedback, and continual encouragement. I also wish to thank the two anonymous reviewers of this article for their critical and helpful comments, Bendte Fagge at Duke University Press for her suggestions, and the friendly staff of the Archivo Histórico Municipal in Morelia, Michoacán. Finally, I am grateful to the UCLA Department of History and Graduate Division for the funding that made this research possible.

1 Archivo Histórico Municipal de Morelia, Michoacán (hereafter AHMM), box 30, exp. 20. The temascal was a type of enclosed pre-Hispanic steam bath or sauna that typically had ritualistic, ceremonial, and therapeutic effects. The Purépecha were the dominant indigenous group in the region of Michoacán. The main pre-Hispanic center was the town of Tzintzuntzan, located on the eastern shore of Lake Pátzcuaro. The Spaniards referred to the Purépecha as the *tarasco* (Tarascan) and the Nahua referred to them in Nahuatl, and in clear reference to Lake Pátzcuaro, as the *michoaque* (those who possessed fish, i.e., those who fished).

2 AHMM, box 30, exp. 20, fol. 4: "El uno ensima del otro desatacados los calzones como si fueran hombre y muger." In quotations throughout this essay I rely on seventeenth-century Spanish orthography and direct archival transcriptions in order to preserve the documents' original linguistic flavor.

3 AHMM, box 30, exp. 20, fol. 3: "Entendio que heran hombre y muger y que estavam alli cometiendo algo carnal porque oyó los asesidos del yndio que estava ensima y le vio que estava dando rrempuzones como si estubiera ensima de alguna muger."

4 AHMM, box 30, exp. 20, fol. 3: "Le paresio que heran hombres y que estavan cometiendo el pecado nefando contra natura."

5 AHMM, box 30, exp. 20, fol. 3: According to Gaspar, the Nahuatl-speaking servant of Padre Velázquez, "Tiene por cierto que ambos a dos estavan cometiendo el dicho pecado y de mas de lo que tiene dicho, vido al dicho yndio [Quini] q primero de prendio que tenia unos calzones blancos mojados de sangre fresca y que lo que tiene dicho es la verdad." According to the testimony of one of the Spanish men, García Maldonado, Quini "le rrespondio en su lengua que este testigo entiende que estava borracho el dicho Simpliciano."

6 Pulque is a thick fermented alcoholic beverage made in Mexico from various species of the maguey or agave plant. It is defined in the Real Academia's *Diccionario de la lengua castellana* (1737) as "the juice or liquor of the maguey, made by cutting its trunk when it is ready to be opened and leaving a large cavity, where it is then distilled. This drink is highly esteemed in New Spain, where they add certain ingredients to give it greater punch." For an interesting discussion of alcohol and language as they related to evangelization in Mexico throughout the colonial period, see Sonia Corcuera de Mancera, *Del amor al temor: Borrachez, catequesis y control en la Nueva España (1555-1771)* (Mexico City, 1994).

7 AHMM, box 30, exp. 20, fol. 9: "[Quini] le rrogo y persuadio que le comprase la dicha rropilla y este ql [Cuyne] se le cansava dello y tanto se le rrogo y que se

bolbiese que bebieran y dormiria y que este ql vensido de sus ruegos vino com el solo a la dicha casa [with the temascal] aparte de donde avían bebido."

8 AHMM, box 30, exp. 20, fol. 9: "Se fue con el al dicho temascal y este testigo [Cuyne] entro del primero y se le echo al suelo para dormir y luego el dicho yndio que era preso [Pedro Quini] que no save como se llama se llego a este testigo y le comenzo a abrasar y a besar y le metio la mano que abia puesta en la bragueta."

9 AHMM, box 30, exp. 20, fol. 10: "[Quini] le dixo a este ql [Cuyne] que el tenia mucho deseo que se lo hiziese y que le daria la rropilla y este ql le rrespondio que no queria al fin."

10 AHMM, box 30, exp. 20, fol. 10: "El dicho yndio quito a este confesante la sinta de los calzones y los desataco y se desataco ellos suyos y se tendio en el suelo y estando arremangado este testigo se echo ensima del susodicho y le metio su miembro beril por el sieso y teniendo lo dentro como si estubiera con una muger cumplio con el y tubo copula carnal por esta parte con el dicho yndio." *Calzones* are trousers of unbleached, coarse cotton cloth introduced by the Spaniards to the Indians. See Woodrow Borah, *Justice by Insurance: The General Indian Court of Colonial Mexico and the Legal Aides of the Half-Real* (Berkeley, CA, 1983), 440.

11 AHMM, box 30, exp. 20, fol. 10: "Quando acabo de aver tenydo la dicha copula carnal y despranando en el sieso del susodicho." The verb *despranar* appears to be an older version or a corruption of the verb *desplazar*, meaning to ejaculate, or literally to take something from one person or place and deposit it in another.

12 The careo was a juridical process whereby conflicting testimonies were resolved by placing two individuals side by side in a court in order to corroborate their statements.

13 The *Diccionario de la lengua castellana* (1737) defines the word *puto* simply as "el hombre que comete el pecado nefando," that is, a man who commits the nefarious sin (of sodomy).

14 See James Krippner-Martínez, *Rereading the Conquest: Power, Politics, and the History of Early Colonial Michoacán, Mexico, 1521-1565* (University Park, PA, 2001), 9–45, for the interpretation that the execution of El Caltzontzin demonstrated both the consolidation of Spanish authority and intense political rivalry in the region.

15 France V. Scholes and Eleanor B. Adams, *Proceso contra Tzintzicha Tangaxoan el Caltzontzín, formado por Nuño de Guzmán, año 1530* (Mexico City, 1952), 7.

16 Ibid., 14.

17 Armando M. Escobar Olmedo, *Proceso, tormento y muerte del Cazonci, último Gran Señor de los Tarascos, por Nuño de Guzmán, 1530* (Mexico City, 1997), 40. According to the accusations made by Francisco de Villegas, the sixth question to be asked to the witnesses during the trial was "Yten, si saben, vieron, oyeron dezir que Pero Sánchez Farfán hizo proçeso contra el dicho Cazonzi de sodomía, de lo qual halló bastante informaçión." Unfortunately the written records of the sodomy trial by Farfán have not yet surfaced, if they still exist.

18 Scholes and Adams, *Proceso contra Tzintzicha Tangaxoan el Caltzontzín*: "Preguntado si sabe que el dicho Cazonzi comete e use el pecado abominable de la sodomía, teniendo consigo indios con quien fornique e comete el dicho pecado" (90).

19 The Spanish verb *echarse* is used as a synonym for *acostarse*—to lie down (with someone).

20 Although Adams and Scholes published the first transcription of *Proceso* in 1952, the transcription I use here is that provided by Escobar Olmedo, *Proceso, tormento y muerte* (1997), because it is a more direct and careful copy of the text. Here Escobar Olmedo reads this word as an abbreviation for *muerto*, "dead," whereas Scholes and Adams read the word as *mozo*, "young boy." I unfortunately do not know which transcription is correct.

21 Escobar Olmedo, *Proceso, tormento y muerte*: "Que sabe que tiene indios con quien se echa, que se llama el uno Juanico, que está en Apascuaro que verná agora, e otro que conosció, que es muerto [mozo?], que se llama Guysacaro. E esto que lo a oido dezir e que es notorio a todos los indios criados del dicho Cazonzi, e que quando está borracho el dicho Cazonzi, le a visto meter la lengua en la boca e besar al dicho Juanillo, e que desde chequito tiene por costumbre el dicho Cazonzi de tener aquellos para aquel efeto, e que así es notorio que los tiene para aquello e por tales son avidos e tenidos entre ellos" (90). See also Scholes and Adams, *Proceso*, 47, for a slightly different transcription.

22 Escobar Olmedo, *Proceso, tormento y muerte*: "E aunque han venido a esta Provinçia muchos juezes por mandado de los que han governado la tierra para hacer justiçia sobre ello, e han hecho muchas informaçiones e procesos contra él [El Caltzontzin] e contra otros muchos prençipales por los quales han mereçido muchas muertes, el dicho Cazonzi, e con sus mañas e con mucha copia de oro e plata se a esemido [exhimido] de las penas que a mereçido" (25, 36).

23 Krippner-Martínez, *Rereading the Conquest*, 30.

24 See table 1 on page 47 and table 2 in the appendix for a more concise breakdown of the thirteen accusations, the people involved, their ages and occupations, and the dates and locations of the sexual acts.

25 AHMM, box 30, exp. 20, fol. 16: "Ya que dios a querido declarar y descubrir la verdad."

26 Ibid.: "El dho Joaquin le sirvio de muger ambas a dos beces, y el ql fue el hombre y ambas a dos le metio su miembro veril por el sieso y desprano y tubo copula carnal com el y q quando cometio el pecado com el siempre presumio que el dho Joaquin hera acostumbrado a cometer este pecado."

27 Ibid.: "le ha dho que heran todos putos y que acostumbravan a cometer el pecado nefando."

28 AHMM, box 30, exp. 20, fol. 27.

29 Ibid.: "dixo que es cristiano y que puede aver seis años poco mas o menos que siendo este ql muchacho bibiendo en el barrio de San Franco el dho Pedro Quini yndio a cometido a este ql y persuadio que cometiesse el pecado nefando y este ql como muchacho no saviendo lo que hazia vino el ello."

30 AHMM, box 30, exp. 20, fol. 16: "Lo convido a dormir con el [Francisco Capiche] y le dixo que se lo hiziese y este ql [Pedro Quini] se quedo a dormir com el dho yndio em la dha casa em donde está un forno y estando alli echados el dho Franco Capiche le rrogo que se lo hiziese y siendo como a medianoche y estando juntos, este ql tubo copula com el y le metio su miembro beril por el sieso y tubo aceso com el dho Franco Capiche despranando."

31 AHMM, box 30, exp. 20, fol. 17: "Entraron a dormir en la cosina y estando echados el dho Miguel yndio comenzo a insistir a este y atentarle su miembro genital y se convinieron y el dho Miguel yndio le sirvio de muger."

32 AHMM, box 30, exp. 20, fol. 28.

33 AHMM, box 30, exp. 20, fol. 17: "Es puto y que a cometido el pecado nefando y el antiguo en el ofisio de cometerlo porque se lo a visto cometer puede aver tres años y le vido muchas vezes servir de muger . . . en su casa lo tenia por costumbre q se lo hizieses . . . y de alli aprendio este ql a cometer el pecado nefando."

34 Ibid.: "Y un yndio llamado Ticata por sobrenome bibe junto deste dho Franco yndio."

35 Ibid.: "El otro yndio le servía al dho Franco Conduyi como si fuese su muger."

36 AHMM, box 30, exp. 20, fol. 30: Quini "le rrogo que comitiese el pecado nefando y se fueron a un sacatal que esta detras de los corrales de la dha carne-seria . . . a las nueve antes de mediodia y estando alli este ql desataco sus cal-zones y se tendio al suelo . . . y [Quini] despranado como si estuviera con una muger lo qual sintio este ql."

37 This is a different Miguel than the one mentioned by Quini earlier in his testimony.

38 AHMM, box 30, exp. 20, fol. 30.

39 AHMM, box 30, exp. 20, fol. 2: "Tan abominable delito y en tan gran ofensa de dios."

40 In the Spanish *Siete Partidas*, Partida 7, Title 21, Laws 1 and 2 required the death penalty for all sins against nature; Mary Elizabeth Perry, *Gender and Disorder in Early Modern Seville* (Princeton, NJ, 1990), 123. The *Diccionario de la langua castellana* (1737) defines sodomy (*sodomía*) as "cohabitation between people of the same sex, or in the improper vessel [i.e., the anus]."

41 Both Louise M. Burkhart, *The Slippery Earth: Nahua Christian Moral Dialogue in Sixteenth-Century Mexico* (Tucson, AZ, 1989), and Vicente Rafael, *Contracting Colonialism: Translation and Christian Conversion in Tagalog Society under Early Spanish Rule* (Durham, NC, 1993), demonstrate that cultural, ideological, religious, and linguistic mistranslations characterized all aspects of colonialism and conversion.

42 This point is further evident in a 1691 Inquisition sodomy case from Mérida in which an evidently feminine mulatto is caught sexually penetrating an indigenous man originally from Valladolid; Archivo General de la Nación, Mexico City (hereafter AGN), Inquisición, vol. 498, exp. 16. The male-active-penetrator and female-passive-penetrated paradigms fall completely short in explaining how a "feminine" man could penetrate an indigenous man who is not described in any way as being feminine. See Laura A. Lewis, *Hall of Mirrors: Power, Witchcraft, and Caste in Colonial Mexico* (Durham, NC, 2003), 112–14, and her essay in this issue for a different interpretation of this case. Lewis asserts that the indigenous man emerges as the more effeminate of the two because of his status as an "yndio," because he is coupled with a mulatto, and finally because he is paternalistically protected by the law from the Inquisition's jurisdiction.

43 For yet another example of "penetrational ambiguity," see a 1742 criminal sodomy case from Morelia dealing with a seventy-year-old "yndio" who attempted to seduce a twenty-year-old man in the quarry (*canteras*) where he worked (AHMM, box 156, exp. 18). Although some sexual activity clearly took place, authorities were not sure which activities occurred. It appears that the

actual act of anal sex did not take place, but authorities nonetheless assumed that the "old yndio" (who undeniably initiated physical contact between the two) served as the bottom and hence passive (*paciente*) since he was caught with his underwear down around his legs and the backside of his *calzones* were wet. The young man fled the scene only to be caught later by authorities. Despite both men's denial of all charges, they were imprisoned for at least seven years as their case was pending. The historical record stops tracing this case in 1749 when the boy escaped his prison in the Valle de Santiago during an uprising. For a rather different application of this concept of penetrational ambiguity, see Zeb Tortorici, "Queering Pornography: Desiring Youth, Race, and Fantasy in Gay Male Porn," in *Queer Youth Cultures*, ed. Susan Driver (Albany, NY, forthcoming).

44 Perry, *Gender and Disorder*, 125.

45 Lee Penyak, "Criminal Sexuality in Central Mexico, 1750-1850," PhD diss., University of Connecticut, 1993, 279.

46 Martin Nesvig, "The Complicated Terrain of Latin American Homosexuality," *Hispanic American Historical Review* 81 (2001): 706.

47 AHMM, box 30, exp. 20, fol. 41.

48 AHMM, box 30, exp. 20, fol. 22: "como hijo obediente de la santa yglessia."

49 AHMM, box 30, exp. 20, fol. 23. One *marco* was equivalent to 136 pesos.

50 AHMM, box 30, exp. 20, fol. 75: "Que sean sacados de la carcel y prission en que estan en bestias de albarda con sogas a las gargantas atados los pies y manos y voz de pregonero que manifieste su delito y llevados por las calles publicas al lugar donde suelen executarse semejantes justicias. Y alli se les da garrote en la forma acostumbrada hasta que mueran naturalmente y muertos los cuerpos sean quemados en llama de fuego y hechos ceniça y declaro todos sus bienes que de los susodichos se hallaren por perdidos y por de la camara de su magestad."

51 "La existencia de una subcultura que tiene su geografía secreta, su red de información e informantes, su lenguaje y sus códigos"; Serge Gruzinski, "Las cenizas del deseo: Homosexuales novohispanos a mediados del siglo XVII," in *De la santidad a la perversión, o de porqué no se cumplía la ley de Dios en la sociedad novohispana*, ed. Sergio Ortega (Mexico City, 1985), 278. An English translation of the essay can be found in Pete Sigal, ed., *Infamous Desire: Male Homosexuality in Colonial Latin America* (Chicago, 2003).

52 Since the publication of Gruzinski's study, Brazilian historians and other Latin Americanists have provided extraordinary scholarship on sodomy and other nonreproductive sexualities in colonial Brazil and Latin America. Luiz Mott, *O sexo proibido: Escravos, gays e virgens nas garras da Inquisição* (São Paulo, 1988), reconstructs the history of Luiz Delgado, a Portuguese tobacco merchant in his early twenties who was repeatedly questioned by the Inquisition and eventually exiled for having committed sexual acts with a twelve-year-old boy among many others. Ligia Bellini, *A coisa obscura: Mulher, sodomia, e Inquisição no Brasil colonial* (São Paulo, 1987), makes a valuable contribution to colonial Latin American historiography, using ten Inquisition cases from late-sixteenth-century Brazil to trace fragments of the lives of twenty-nine women prosecuted for *sodomia foeminarum* (sexual relations between women including anal or vaginal insertion of objects). Ronaldo Vainfas, *Trópico dos pecados:*

Moral, sexualidade e Inquisição no Brasil (Rio de Janeiro, 1997), uses some 160 sodomy cases from the Lisbon's Arquivo Nacional da Torre do Tombo to conclude that, unlike in Rome, Lisbon, Paris, Puebla, and Mexico City, where there were formidable subcultures of men who sought out sex with other men, colonial Brazil had nothing of the sort. Regarding sodomy prosecutions in the Audiencia of Charcas, Geoffrey Spurling, "Honor, Sexuality, and the Colonial Church: The Sins of Dr. González, Cathedral Canon," in *The Faces of Honor: Sex, Shame, and Violence in Colonial Latin America*, ed. Lyman L. Johnson and Sonya Lipsett-Rivera (Albuquerque, NM, 1998), explores how sodomy accusations were often mitigated by race and class. Using two trials from 1595, Spurling demonstrates that despite González's affectionate behavior with various male lovers (publicly embracing, kissing, and even feeding each other), the doctor escaped the garrote and the stake, unlike one of his less influential lovers, because of his wealth and social standing. Carolina Giraldo Botero, in her *Deseo y Represión: Homoeroticidad en la Nueva Granada (1559–1822)* (Bogota, 2002), mines the Archivo General de la Nación in Colombia for twelve criminal cases in which some forty-six men and women were prosecuted for sodomy. Giraldo Botero asserts that in Nueva Granada, in contrast to colonial Mexico, sexual acts between persons of the same sex almost never took place in public spaces.

53 See Rafael Carrasco, *Inquisición y represión sexual en Valencia* (Barcelona, 1985), and Guido Ruggiero, *The Boundaries of Eros: Sex Crime and Sexuality in Renaissance Venice* (New York, 1985) for discussions of early modern Valencia and Venice.

54 Penyak, "Criminal Sexuality," 249. See Sigal, *Moon Goddesses to Virgins*; Nesvig, "Complicated Terrain"; Federico Garza Carvajal, *Butterflies Will Burn: Prosecuting Sodomites in Early Modern Spain and Mexico* (Austin, TX, 2003); Lewis, *Hall of Mirrors*; José Guillermo de Los Reyes, "Sodomy and Society: Sexuality, Gender, Race, and Class in Colonial Mexico," PhD diss., University of Pennsylvania, 2004; and Jorge Bracamonte, "Los nefandos placeres de la carne: La Iglesia y el Estado frente a la sodomía en la Nueva España, 1721–1820," *Debate feminista* 18 (1998): 393–415. Regarding some of the most recent scholarship, Sigal's groundbreaking *From Moon Goddesses to Virgins: The Colonization of Yucatecan Maya Sexual Desire* (Austin, TX, 2000) offers a sophisticated philological analysis of esoteric Maya language texts that shows how Maya idealized and symbolic conceptions of sodomy changed as Catholic discourse on sin influenced and altered Maya sexual desires and behaviors. Sigal, ed., *Infamous Desire: Male Homosexuality in Colonial Latin America* (Chicago, 2003), is an equally important contribution that seeks dialogue between historians and a historical location of sodomy and male same-sex sexual acts in relation to desire, power, and colonialism. In both works Sigal rightly argues that the cultural, political, and social history of early Latin America cannot be understood without studying how sexual acts and desires were created, manipulated, and changed.

55 Garza Carvajal, *Butterflies Will Burn*, 128.

56 The essay by Laura Lewis in this issue also points to the existence of sodomitical subcultures in rural colonial Mexico (specifically in Mérida, Yucatán).

57 William B. Taylor, *Drinking, Homicide, and Rebellion in Colonial Mexican Villages* (Stanford, CA, 1979), 66. A pulquería was any tavern that sold pulque.

58 This letter is cited in Gruzinski, *De la santidad a la perversión*, 278: "Para sasiar su torpe apetito se visten en traje de mujeres de noches y se acuestan entre ellos embriagados y los provocan al acto torpe."

59 "Algunos de los lugares mas frecuentados por las mujeres [and possibly men] de 'mala vida' en la época de la Ilustración fueron los puestos de bebidas alcohólicas: las pulquerías y las vinaterías"; Ana María Rodríguez Atondo, *El amor venal y la condición femenina en el México colonial* (Mexico City, 1992), 221.

60 Garza Carvajal, *Butterflies Will Burn*, 132. The sole archival case that he uses in relation to New Spain is the same one previously examined by Gruzinski. As Garza Carvajal states in the introduction, however, his focus is "on those discourses that reflected Spain's perceptions of manliness and not necessarily on the historical reality of sodomites" (2).

61 See also Archivo Histórico del Estado de Tlaxcala, San Pablo de Apetatitlán, box 20, exp. 65. In this 1701 judicial case (in Nahuatl and Spanish) a Nahua man, Francisco Martín, is accused of witchcraft by two other Nahua men. One of the major offenses takes place when in a temascal Martín slaps one of the men's buttocks (*nalgas*), which subsequently causes the man's thighs and lower body to become sick. There are definite sexual undertones throughout the document, as Martín is also said to appear naked one night in the bed of one of the accusers. I wish to thank Mark Morris of Indiana University for showing me this document in the archives and for giving me a transcription of the Nahuatl. Penyak ("Criminal Sexuality," 250–51) also cites the temascal as a site where colonial authorities feared that illicit sexual activities took place in a 1791 case from Mexico City involving pulque consumption. In this instance, authorities ultimately mandated not only that men and women bathe separately, but that no two men and no two women bathe together at the same time.

62 *Códice Tudela*, fol. 62: "Temazcatl[:] horno o baño de agua caliente donde se hazian ofensas a Nro Sr, porq si alguno estaba enfermo se venia a bañar en este horno q avia agua dentro. y aconteçía meterse en este baño munchos onbres e mujeres, y alla dentro, con la calor, onbres con mujeres e mujeres con onbres e onbres con onbres, yliçitamente husavan y en mexco avia onbres vestidos en ábito de mujeres y estos eran sométicos y hazian los oficios de mujeres, como es texer y hilar, y algunos señores tenían uno y dos para sus vícios." I thank Pete Sigal for giving me the reference to this document and providing me with the transcription. A manuscript of the *Codex* can be found in the UCLA Young Research Library Special Collections.

63 Ibid., fol. 9: "Vino a la dicha casa con otros compañeros suyos yndios della obra del dicho convento a beber pulque porque allí en un aposento dela dicha casa dos negros que no los conoce les vendieron vino y pulque."

64 For a discussion of slavery in Michoacán from the latter half of the sixteenth century to 1650, see María Guadalupe Chávez Carbajal, *Propietarios y esclavos negros en Valladolid de Michoacán, 1600-1650* (Morelia, Mexico, 1994).

65 AGN, Inq., vol. 510, exp. 29., fol. 79: "Entre ellos ay mestizos y mulatos, hijos de españoles, negros, mulatos, y otros deste paez [parte/país (?)]. Los quales mestizos y mulatos, siendo nacidos de yndias y criadas com ellas y entre yndios, siguen em todo el natural de las madres, hablando su lengua yndiana."

66 The 1726 *Diccionario de la lengua castellana* (vol. 4) defines *luxuria* as "el apetito desordenado, o excesivo uso de la sensualidad o carnalidad."

67 "La luxuria es vicio del alma, que la inclina à querer deléite desordenado de
    cópula carnal, ò de preparatórios de ella . . . y como todo deléite que nace de
    cópula carnal ò de sus preparatívos es desordenado, excepto el de la *cópula*
    marital, por esto todo querer, deséo, ò gozo de deléite de *cópula*, excepto el de
    la marital, es pecado" (Martín Navarro de Azpilcueta, *Manual de Confessores*
    [Madrid, 1556]). This passage is cited as an example in the 1729 *Diccionario de
    la lengua castellana* under the definition of *copula*.
68 For an example of disordered sexual desire within the bonds of matrimony, see
    AGN, Inq., vol. 510, exp. 127, for the 1625 denunciation of Andrés Arias, who
    locked his wife, Beatris de Las Cassas, in a room, bound her hands, tied her
    up, and forced her to have anal sex with him. While she did not go straight to
    the Inquisition, she confessed the act to her local priest, who said it was valid
    grounds for divorce. She also talked about it with a female friend, who told
    a man who eventually denounced this story to the Inquisition. When called
    before the Inquisition, Las Cassas asserted that the story was completely true
    but that there were no eyewitnesses. The Inquisition never tried Arias, and it
    seemed to care less about the violent acts against Las Cassas than about Arias's
    assertion that the pecado nefando with one's wife was not a sin. We do not
    know if Las Cassas ever divorced Arias. See also AGN, Inq., vol. 370, exp. 6,
    for the 1630 denunciation of Pedro de Gimelena, who repeatedly attempted to
    commit the pecado nefando with his wife. Though she never consented to anal
    sex, one time he felt so frustrated and angry that he broke a small statue of
    Jesus on the crucifix and cursed God. While the Holy Office of the Inquisition
    took formal denunciations from a few people and ratified them, it never held
    trials against either Gimelena or Arias. For an example of disordered sexual
    desire functioning alongside ordered desire, see AGN Criminal 62, exp. 20,
    fol. 472; in this 1801 criminal trial, eighteen-year-old mestizo Ysidro Boni-
    facio tried to mitigate being caught having drunken sex with a donkey by
    recounting his previous three-week illicit friendship with a young woman.
    Though he clearly hoped that this relationship would reduce his ultimate sen-
    tence, it does not appear to have mollified the court: he was sentenced to three-
    years' confinement in a fort (*presidio*) without hard labor. While all of these
    cases involve clear force and coercion, they demonstrate in ways different from
    the 1604 sodomy case how seemingly ordered sexuality—heterosexual desire
    and sex within marriage—could sometimes be disordered in violent and vio-
    lating ways.
69 Mary Douglas, *Purity and Danger: An Analysis of the Concepts of Pollution and
    Taboo* (London, 1966), 4.
70 While I have discussed nonreproductive sexuality here solely in terms of sodomy,
    other manifestations of unsanctioned sexuality that should be explored include
    masturbation, bestiality, male-male solicitation by priests, oral sex, sexual
    caresses, sexual witchcraft, abortion, erotic religious visions, sexually explicit
    paintings and drawings, and possibly even illicit statements and conversations.
    I will further explore the regulation of nonreproductive and unsanctioned sexu-
    alities in colonial Mexico in my dissertation, tentatively titled "The Appearance
    of Colonial Order: Sin, Crime, Tolerance, and the Regulation of 'Unnatural'
    Sexuality in Colonial Mexico, 1600–1800." For some of the few historical ana-
    lyses of bestiality in colonial Latin America, see Penyak, "Criminal Sexuality,"
    chap. 5; Leonardo Alberto Vega Umbasia, *Pecado y delito en la colonia: La bes-*

tialidad como una forma de contravención sexual, 1740-1808 (Bogotá, 1994); and Zeb Tortorici, "Animals, Indians, and the Category of the 'Unnatural' in Late Colonial Mexico" (paper presented at the American Society for Ethnohistory conference, Sante Fe, NM, 16–20 November 2005).

71 Regina Harrison, "The Theology of Concupiscence: Spanish-Quechua Confessional Manuals in the Andes" in *Coded Encounters: Writing, Gender, and Ethnicity in Colonial Latin America*, ed. Francisco Javier Cevallos-Candau, Jeffrey A. Cole, Nina M. Scott, and Nicomedes Suárez-Araúz (Amherst, MA, 1994), 149.

72 Penyak, "Criminal Sexuality," 271. David Higgs comes to similar conclusions, using a rich case from the mid-1600s to show the sordid details of Padre Frei António Soares's mutual masturbation and anal sex with other priests, novitiates, and prison inmates; Higgs, "Tales of Two Carmelites: Inquisitorial Narratives from Portugal and Brazil," in *Infamous Desire: Male Homosexuality in Colonial Latin America*, ed. Pete Sigal (Chicago, 2003). A Portuguese priest accused of engaging in sodomy with dozens of men, Soares was exiled to Brazil for a few years, where he amassed a fortune and continued his lascivious lifestyle before returning to Portugal.

73 AHMM, box 30, exp. 20, fol. 39: "Yndio yncapaz sin entendimiento, sin saber ni entender la grabedad y abominacion."

74 AHMM, box 30, exp. 20, fol. 38: "Yndios ignorantes de poco rrazon y entendimiento."

75 Penyak, "Criminal Sexuality" (253), citing Carrasco, *Inquisición y represión*, asserts that "Ferdinand the Catholic placed sodomy cases under the jurisdiction of the Inquisition in 1505, but placed it under the auspices of criminal authorities in 1509." But this did little to alter popular conceptions of sodomy and other unsanctioned sexual acts as sinful, and therefore worthy of being denounced to the Inquisition, as they were throughout the colonial period. Clearly the concepts of illicit sexuality, heresy, sin, and criminality intermixed and indistinctly overlapped in the minds of the Inquisitors, secular authorities, and popular levels of society.

76 AHMM, box 30, exp. 20, fol. 2.

77 Gruzinski, *De la santidad a la perversión*; Penyak, "Criminal Sexuality," 245–80. Jorge Bracamonte ("Nefandos placeres," 393) accurately highlights the reduced severity of punishments given to those accused of sodomy in the context of the secularization of colonial Mexican society.

The Sins of the Fathers: Franciscan Friars, Parish Priests, and the Sexual Conquest of the Yucatec Maya, 1545–1808

John F. Chuchiak IV, *Missouri State University*

Abstract. Differing from the rapid political, economic, and social conquests, the conquest of indigenous sexuality was often a long and deeply contested arena of indigenous-Spanish encounters. The roots of what can be called the "sexual conquest" of the Yucatec Maya began with the initial missions of the Franciscan friars. The earliest friars produced vocabularies, grammars, sermons, and confession manuals as tools for their missionary effort. By analyzing these missionary creations, we can approach an understanding of the friars' views of Maya sexuality. The Maya, however, often took the missionary teachings concerning proper and improper sexual activities, and through the lens of their own cultural concepts of sexuality and sexual relations they manipulated them for their own purposes. This paper will examine how the knowledge of the "sins of the fathers" served both the missionaries and the Maya in their struggle for control over the complex nature of evolving colonial sexuality.

> *In that time there will be lies and madness, and also lust and fornication.*
> —Chilam Balam of Chumayel

On 6 July 1609, Francisco Ek and his son Clemente traveled from the Maya town of Hocaba to the city of Mérida to appear before Fray Hernando de Nava, the commissary of the Holy Office of the Inquisition in the province of Yucatán. Francisco Ek presented a petition that the interpreter, Fray Rodrigo Tinoco, translated from the Maya. Francisco pleaded, "We come before your Excellency . . . in order to tell you and let you know how it is that Padre Cristóbal de Valencia perverts the good Christian doctrine of the town of Hocaba."[1]

Ethnohistory 54:1 (Winter 2007)   DOI 10.1215/00141801-2006-040
Copyright 2007 by American Society for Ethnohistory

The Eks told a terrible tale, one filled with sexual violence and clerical misconduct. According to the Maya, Father Cristóbal de Valencia called Clemente to a confession in his sacristy. The priest suddenly appeared naked, telling Clemente: "Come and take my private parts in your hands and play with them because this is the service of God and it is the office of the saints who are in heaven. . . . and if you do not comply with this and play with my private parts, go and bring me your wife, because she has a large vagina and has slept with the entire village."[2] Clemente responded in shock, "Why do you say this, Father, this is a very shameful thing. . . . look here is the sacred chalice and you say this in front of it." The priest retorted, "Don't you come here and preach to me. . . . I will have my way with you without anyone ever knowing it and if not I will kill you tonight!"[3] According to Clemente, the priest cursed and attacked him. He then pulled down Clemente's breeches and grabbed his penis, squeezing it until blood ran. He then mockingly challenged Clemente, "Go and complain about this to the bishop or the inquisitor. . . . I have the power to burn you alive and I am not afraid. . . . even if four hundred bishops come here I will not dirty my pants out of fear. . . . I am the bishop here."[4]

Following this sexual violation, Clemente Ek and his father went to denounce the priest before the Inquisition. The horrified commissary of the Inquisition ordered the priest's arrest and an immediate investigation.[5] Following the graphic accusations of these two Maya men, Padre Cristóbal de Valencia lost his post as the parish priest of Hocaba and faced a trial that lasted for several years.

Trial testimony revealed that Valencia was a well-known pervert and a pederast.[6] By all accounts, he had taken sexual advantage of virtually all members of his parish, either in private or in the sanctity of the confessional. Testimony and accusations poured into the investigator's office as Mayas from the towns of Hocaba, Sanlahcat, Yaxcaba, and Hoctun came forward to denounce the priest for sexual abuse.[7] The ecclesiastical authorities considered the accusation that Valencia abused the sacrament of confession to be the most abhorrent and damning. Charges of sexually molesting parishioners or living in open concubinage with Indian women seldom led to serious sanction.[8] Accusations of impropriety in the confessional or solicitation of sex during confession, in contrast, ended a clergyman's career.[9]

Things, however, were not always as they seemed. Valencia claimed that the Mayas falsely accused him because he had punished them for drunkenness and idolatry. The priest stated that

> both this native and other natives testify falsely against him out of the
> hatred that they have for his having punished them for their crimes

against God and their other vices and sins which he preached against publicly. He refers the Inquisitor to the testimony and opinions of the other parish priests who have served in the province of Hocaba who know and can tell him how it is public knowledge that the Mayas from the town of Hocaba have a common practice of raising false testimony against their priests in order to get rid of them.[10]

This leaves the historian with the question of whom to believe, the Mayas or the priest. The overwhelming number of Mayas who testified against the priest suggests either a high level of sexual depravity on the part of the clergyman or an impressive ability of the Maya to conspire to remove their priest. Whatever the answer, the trial against Padre Valencia reveals the intricate nature of sexual relations and sexual morality in colonial Yucatán.

The Maya, following the conquest, found themselves threatened by an alien culture that sought to impose an entirely new code of sexuality and morality over long-standing traditions and beliefs. The Maya quickly learned that Spain's cultural codes could be manipulated and turned against their conquerors who sought to impose their religion and morality on them. The historian Guido Ruggerio argues that in fourteenth- and fifteenth-century Europe two very different worlds of sexuality emerged: the world of marriage and procreation, and the libertine world in which women were raped, prostitutes used, nuns seduced, and boys sodomized.[11] When the Spaniards conquered the province of Yucatán, they encountered a third world of traditional Maya sexual customs and practices. The Maya, in turn, were caught in a confusing sexual universe, where Spanish libertines raped and abused them while simultaneously preaching the values of marriage and chastity, and the sins inherent in sexuality.[12] The Yucatec Maya, however, quickly learned how to use the Europeans' contradictory attitude toward sexuality and morality for their own purposes. Accusations of sexual misconduct, especially against priests and friars, became potent weapons for the colonial Maya, otherwise powerless to defend themselves against the economic and/or sexual abuses of their priests and friars. The use of Europe's sexual morality to defend Maya culture is a metaphor for the Maya's ability, despite oppressive adversity, to protect themselves during the centuries of colonial rule.

This case against Padre Cristóbal de Valencia is but one of many formal accusations of sexual misconduct and solicitation of sex in the confessional in colonial Yucatán (see table 3 in the appendix). Cases such as this one are pivotal in understanding both how Spanish Catholicism attempted to regulate the sexuality of Europeans and their colonial subjects, and how individual Mayas responded to and reacted against these attempts.[13]

Maya accusations of fornication and sexual misconduct are widespread in colonial documents. Their denunciations of and petitions against Catholic clergymen reveal the intricate layers of sexual morality and sexuality that existed in New Spain.[14] They illustrate how the Maya and Spanish Christian concepts of sexuality and sexual perversion diverged, intermingled, and collided. The encounters and collisions between these different cultural concepts are most evident in the accusations against clergymen found guilty of *solicitación*.[15] The conflicting views of sexual normalcy and perversity indicate that in the early colonial period there had been an attempt at a "sexual conquest."[16] This conquest proved incomplete and must be seen as a metaphor for how the Maya used Spain's culture as a political weapon to defend their own civilization. The Spanish tried to "conquer" the sexuality and morals of the Yucatec Maya by imposing their own values forcibly on the region. At the same time, as they attempted to impose their moral first world of sexuality on the Maya, they also brought the Maya into the second world of Spanish libertine sexuality and abuse. The Maya exploited these contradictions, creating a universe where they defended their traditional third world of Maya sex and sexuality from the Spaniards by pitting the colonizers' first world of morality against the second world of libertine sexuality. The astute Maya shrewdly used accusations of sexual misconduct to defend their unique culture, including its sexual mores, against their Spanish overlords, administrators, and priests. This Maya struggle to maintain their traditions against the Spaniards, however, also transformed their own views of sexuality as these three worlds collided.

Although a majority of Yucatec Maya undoubtedly suffered real sexual abuse, a significant number of them cleverly manipulated European sexual morality to subvert the colonial system. The many worlds of sexual exploitation, abuse, and accusation illustrate how the politics of culture, morality, and sexuality helped to shape colonial Yucatán as the Maya skillfully maneuvered the two worlds of Spanish sexuality against each other, all the while struggling to maintain their own view of sex and sexuality, which had little to do with either the strict chastity of Spanish Catholicism or the passionate sexuality of the Renaissance libertine.

Pre-Columbian Maya Attitudes and Sexual Morality

Sex and concepts of sexuality have played a major role in determining how people respond to their environment.[17] When two different cultures come into contact, their concepts of sex and sexuality inevitably clash and conflict. Maya concepts of sexuality differed markedly from those held by the Spanish colonizers. As Pete Sigal has argued, "For the preconquest Maya,

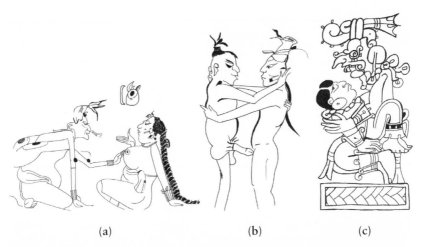

Figure 1. Images of Maya gods and goddesses copulating. (a) Detail of a female goddess in a "copulation" scene with a Maya god. Redrawn from a Maya ceramic vase, provenience unknown, ca. AD 600–1000, Justin Kerr Collection, Kerr #1339. (b) Detail of a painting showing sexual relations between a Maya man and a youth. Detail from a Naj Tunich cave painting, ca. AD 700–900, El Petén, Guatemala. (c) Detail of the Maya rain god Chac in a "copulation" scene with a Maya goddess. Redrawn from the Maya *Dresden Codex* (D 19c), ca. AD 1200–1500. Drawings by Argelia Segovia Liga

sexuality was a part of a greater ritual discourse and performance, and all sex acts were understood in terms of their power to create, maintain, and destroy society." As Sigal argues, the Maya adapted to life under colonial rule, but they neither fully abandoned their earlier views concerning sexuality nor completely adopted the formulation of sexuality prescribed by Spanish Catholicism. Instead, as Sigal concludes, "they evolved hybridized notions of sexual desire."[18] Nevertheless, the Maya's contacts with Spaniards, both religious and secular, would greatly impact their own conceptions and worldviews.

According to surviving historical and ethnohistorical evidence, the preconquest Maya knew of and participated in a large variety of sexual relations and sexual contact including vaginal and anal intercourse, oral sex, masturbation, pederasty (with boys and girls), bestiality, and unspecified sexual acts between women.[19] Unlike Europeans, the Maya also conceived of engaging in ritualized sexual acts with gods and animals.[20] In fact, in several instances, images of Maya gods and goddesses in copulation have survived in the iconography of Maya art (see fig. 1). In the pre-Hispanic codices, however, female deities are occasionally shown engaging

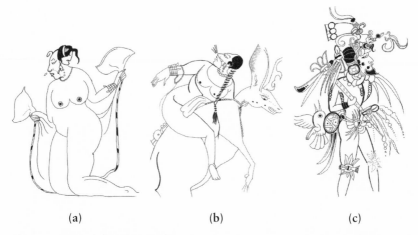

(a)   (b)   (c)

Figure 2. Images of explicit nudity in pre-Hispanic Maya art. (a) Detail of a naked female goddess. Redrawn from a Maya ceramic vase, provenience unknown, ca. AD 600–1000, Justin Kerr Collection, Kerr #1339. (b) Detail of a nude Maya goddess mounted on a mythical deer. Redrawn from a Maya ceramic vase, provenience unknown, ca. AD 600–1000, Justin Kerr Collection, Kerr #1339. (c) Detail of one of the male Maya figures "bleeding" his penis from the Maya murals of San Bartolo, Guatemala. Drawings by Argelia Segovia Liga

in sexual intercourse, but the images are far from explicit. With the exception of the goddesses caressing the face of their male counterpart, and their naked revealed breast, no graphic displays of Maya sexuality exist to compare with the explicit images of sexual relations portrayed in the Moche pottery of pre-Hispanic Peru.

In Classic Maya representations of art and iconography, images of naked women are rare, with only a few examples existing (see fig. 2).

However, it is documented that before the conquest, Maya men and women went about seminude, with the women covered only from their waists down, especially in the coastal regions, and the men wearing only loincloths that revealed more than they covered (see fig. 3).[21]

Preconquest Maya sexuality, however, reveals a few unexplainable paradoxes that confuse the otherwise simplistic description of categories of sexual conduct. Even among the preconquest Maya, there was a dichotomy between the norm and the reality of sexual conduct. According to most sources, all Maya but the highest nobles were supposed to practice monogamy.[22] However, according to a few early colonial sources, even the common Maya could easily "divorce" their spouses and engage in a type of serial monogamy. The Spaniard Alonso Julián, writing shortly after

(a)   (b)

Figure 3. Images of typical male and female Maya dress. (a) Image of Maya man wearing typical "ex" or loincloth. Redrawn from a Maya ceramic vase, provenience unknown, ca. AD 600–1000, Justin Kerr Collection, Kerr #2357. (b) Image of a bare-breasted Maya woman wearing a typical Maya skirt. Detail of a figure from the Maya *Dresden Codex* (17a), ca. AD 1200–1500. Drawings by Argelia Segovia Liga

the conquest, stated that the large populations the Europeans had earlier encountered existed because of the "many women that each Indian man had."[23] Martín de Palomar corrected this error, adding that "they did not commonly live with more than one woman, but for the most trivial of things they could leave their wives, and they married again with another woman, and there were among them men who had married ten or twelve times, and others more or less, and this same liberty also belonged to the women, who could leave their husbands and take other men."[24]

Polygamy was the rule for Maya kings, but apparently higher and even mid-level nobles could take a large number of concubines. Juan Gutiérrez Picón, encomendero of Ekbalam, observed that although the lords and rich principal men were each "assigned one woman, this did not stop them from having female slaves for concubines."[25] The earliest conquerors also commented on aspects of Maya sexuality that they considered strange or different. In terms of Maya concepts of virginity, a Spanish observer in the Maya town of Motul remarked that one rite of passage involved a red colored stone as a symbol of a young Maya girl's virginity:

> The mothers of the little girls placed a red colored stone tied to a string that they let hang over the little girls' shameful parts, and this served as a sign that the girl was a virgin, and when they had their type of baptism ceremony, they cut off this string and they took away the stone, and from that point on they could be married. . . . but if the young girls were not still virgins, their priests would not give them this baptism.[26]

The Maya before the conquest also apparently attempted to control the sexual conduct of their people. According to Pedro de Santanilla, the encomendero of the Maya town of Muxuppipp, "In their paganism, they had fasting as a good custom, and they ate only a little; and they punished the vices of the flesh very cruelly, not consenting that there should exist any man or women who committed adultery, and if there were, they both died for it; and they did not eat human flesh before, nor did they commit the nefarious sin [*pecado nefando*]."[27] Fray Diego de Landa echoed the encomendero's claim that sodomy had not existed before the conquest. He observed that sodomy, or the nefarious act against nature, appeared oddly absent, writing that "I have not learned of their doing this in this country, nor do I believe they did so."[28]

Apparently, the Maya did have defined categories and sanctions for adultery, incest, and rape. Gaspar Antonio Xiu, a descendant of a ruling Maya dynasty at Mani, wrote in his own historical recollections that the Indians here punished vices and sins with rigor. . . . the man or women who committed adultery were killed, shot with arrows. . . . they abhorred all types of sins of the flesh and they punished them severely, even among very important and prominent people. . . . He who raped or violated a young girl received the death penalty. . . . and he who had relations with a married women was also put to death. . . . and he who impregnated a slave woman or married her would be made a slave himself.[29]

Other early observers and later Franciscan historians such as Fray Diego López de Cogolludo also noted the precontact Maya's rigorous punishments for sexual crimes such as adultery and rape.[30] Maya concepts of sexual conduct and sexual perversion can be understood by examining the surviving colonial dictionaries (only a few examples of Maya terms for sexual conduct are found in table 1). However, due to their high number of terms that deal with explicitly lustful and promiscuous sexual practices, the earliest Franciscan dictionaries themselves appear to contradict any effective pre-Columbian systemic control over Maya sexual conduct. Although Maya culture and custom dictated against sexual perversions, the Maya appear to have been quite promiscuous if we accept Maya vocabulary recorded in these dictionaries. Though mainly monogamous in their marriages, the Maya colonial dictionaries contained many words in Maya to describe promiscuous extramarital liaisons between men and women. Thus, the earliest Spanish observers noted that preconquest Maya society had distinct concepts of sexual propriety that helped to control what the Spanish clergy viewed as the sexually destructive behavior of adultery and sexual promiscuity. Nevertheless, most Mayas, especially women, apparently followed a strict code of sexual behavior that was rigorously enforced by their Maya priests and rulers.

Maya Sexual Encounters and Collisions: A Sexual Conquest?

Putería ni hurto nunca se encubren mucho.
(Neither sexual promiscuity nor theft is long covered up.)
—Sixteenth-century Castilian proverb

Any image of a chaste and sexually pure Maya world that might have existed before the conquest quickly came under assault. Many clergymen believed that Maya sexual conduct changed when the Maya came into contact with the Europeans. According to most early colonial observers, pre-

Table 1. Maya terms for various sexual acts and relations

Maya Sexuality: Adultery		
Maya Term/Word	Spanish Definition	Source
Ah calpach	*adultero*	*Calepino de Motul*, 11
Ah pay bey	*alcahueta, o alcahuete*	*Calepino de Motul*, 38
Ah tzubancil	*amancebado*	*Calepino de Motul*, 48
Caapatcunah	*poner los cuernos la mujer al marido o el marido a la muger*	*Calepino de Motul*, 111

Maya Sexuality: Prostitution		
Maya Term/Word	Spanish Definition	Source
Ah concooil/Ix cooil	*rufián que vende mujeres, para que pequen con ellas*	*Calepino de Motul*, 15
Ah con tzubul	*puta, que ella se convida y vende*	*Calepino de Motul*, 16
Ah ppen	*pecador carnal, lujurioso, putañero*	*Calepino de Motul*, 42
Ix kakat na pel	*puta que anda de casa en casa dando su cuerpo*	*Vocabulario de Maya Than*, 547
Ah kakat na cep	*putañero que anda todo, vagabundo con su miembro*	*Vocabulario de Maya Than*, 547

Maya Sexuality: Lust and Fornication		
Maya Term/Word	Spanish Definition	Source
Ah coo tzicbal	*parlero deshonesto y carnal*	*Calepino de Motul*, 16
Ah nocchan keban	*gran pecador, que tiene grandes pecados*	*Calepino de Motul*, 36
Ah oppchek box coo	*malo y perverso, que no entiende su mala vida hasta que lo cogen en el delito*	*Calepino de Motul*, 38
Ah oppchek box cooech	*eres malo y perverso*	*Calepino de Motul*, 38
Ah tzucach than	*deshonesto en hablar*	*Calepino de Motul*, 48
Ah tzucyah	*deshonesto, lujurioso*	*Calepino de Motul*, 48
Dziboolach	*deseoso de mujeres, con deseo carnal*	*Calepino de Motul*, 216
Dziboolachil	*aquel deseo*	*Calepino de Motul*, 216

Table 1. Continued

Dzib olal	*deseo carnal y tenerle y el que le tiene*	*Calepino de Motul*, 216
Dzib oolil	*el deseo carnal*	*Calepino de Motul*, 216
Pak keban	*pecar, generalmente por fornicación*	*Vocabulario de Maya Than*, 509
Ah Pak keban	*fornicador*	*Vocabulario de Maya Than*, 355

Maya Sexuality: Masturbation

Maya Term/Word	Spanish Definition	Source
Baxalaan tan ba	*tocarse unos a otros impúdicamente*	*Calepino de Motul*, 80
Baxal ba	*tocarse impúdicamente, y los tales tocamientos*	*Calepino de Motul*, 80
Baxta ba	*tocarse con tactos impúdicos a si mismo*	*Calepino de Motul*, 80
Baxtah cucutil	*cometer pecado de molicie consigo mismo o con otro*	*Calepino de Motul*, 80
Colach	*contratarse o sobajarse uno sus vergüenzas o las de otro*	*Calepino de Motul*, 133
Colbakel	*idem, polución voluntaria*	*Calepino de Motul*, 133

Maya Sexuality: Purity and Sexual Abstinence

Maya Term/Word	Spanish Definition	Source
Chabtan	*hacer penitencia darse a ayunos y abstenerse de delitos de la carne*	*Calepino de Motul*, 253
Chabtan uinic	*hombre abstinente continente y observante de la ley de Dios*	*Calepino de Motul*, 253
Cuxtal ool	*perder la virginidad*	*Calepino de Motul*, 150

Maya Sexuality: Oral Sex

Maya Term/Word	Spanish Definition	Source
Chii keban	*pecado que se comete con la boca, chupando las vergüenzas*	*Calepino de Motul*, 242

Table 1. Continued

Chijl Keban	pecado vergonzoso y sucio que se lo mete el miembro del varón con la boca mamando o chupando las vergüenzas	Vocabulario de Maya Than, 509
cuchpach keban	pecado de carne cometido versa facie al revés	Calepino de Motul, 143

Maya Sexuality: Homosexuality		
Maya Term/Word	Spanish Definition	Source
Ah topchun	sodomita, garzón	Calepino de Motul, 46
Ah toplom Chun	idem	
Ah toplom it	sodomitas	Calepino de Motul, 46
Ix ppenil keban	pecar un hombre con otro, sodomia y cometerla	Vocabulario de Maya Than, 510, 595

conquest Yucatec Maya women lived chaste and virtuous lives.[31] Although they wore little clothing, their modesty was such that they avoided looking men in the eye for fear of provoking their desire. If a girl did look at a man, her mother punished her indiscretion. This idyllic view of Maya chastity and sexual purity, whether exaggerated or not, quickly changed after the initial contact with the Europeans. Landa stated that Maya women were so chaste before the arrival of the Spaniards that it was a marvel to behold.[32] To explain the virtue of Maya women, Landa gave an example of the violence of the sexual conquest: "The captain Alonso López de Avila, father-in-law of the *adelantado* Francisco Montejo, captured a handsome and graceful Indian girl during the war at Bacalar. She, in fear of death for her husband, had promised him never to yield herself to another, and for this nothing could persuade her, even fear of death, to consent to violation; so that they threw her to the dogs."[33] Maya women were not always the victims, sometimes they fought back. Another story tells of an Indian maiden who, being raped by a Spanish soldier, took his dagger from his holster and plunged it into his heart, only to be run through by the sword of one of his friends. Not all of these forced unions ended in the suicide or murder of Maya women. A large number of illegitimate mestizo children are mentioned after the conquest and many were recognized by their Spanish fathers, who left them inheritances. Even the Spanish conqueror of

Yucatán, Francisco de Montejo, had a mestizo son, Diego, by an unknown Indian woman, and favored him with *encomiendas* and other benefits.[34]

Nevertheless, violent sexual encounters of conquerors and conquered were quite common during the early days of the conquest. The Spanish soldiers, who had no women in their parties, took native women as their concubines and lovers. Some Spaniards were given women as gifts, and others took them by force. In fact, the first conflicts during the military conquest resulted from the Maya's anger when the Spaniards raided their villages for the prettiest girls. The earliest conquerors attempted to curb the sexual appetites of their soldiers, but to no avail. Francisco de Montejo, the conqueror of Yucatán, prohibited his soldiers from taking young Indian girls from their villages and allowed no soldier to engage in sexual intercourse with an Indian maiden unless he married her.[35] However, like most sexual prohibitions, Montejo's orders fell on deaf ears. Gaspar Pacheco, according to colonial reports one of the most unscrupulous of the early conquerors, began to prostitute the young women his troops had gained as tribute from their allied caciques. One soldier in his company reportedly wrote that "the Spaniards are allowed to choose among one hundred and fifty Indian maidens, the ones they liked best, paying for each one an arroba of wine or oil, or vinegar, or a pig."[36]

So great was the impact of the sexual conquest that the Maya wrote in their books of Chilam Balam that the Spaniards were "whoremongers":

> When the Spaniards arrived, they brought shameful things. . . . The black sickness. . . . The coveting of the beauty of girls. . . . Whore-mongering came with them. . . . The prostitution of the village girls came with them. . . . Before they came, Oh brothers, there was not lust, there was not envy. . . . Before the Strangers came there was no suffering, nor was their robbing of men's wives. . . . With them came shameful things. . . . With them came the selling of the women and the unclean things. . . . With them came the end of the flower people.[37]

Even the more scrupulous of the Spanish conquistadors of Yucatán had many *naborías*, or indigenous slaves, including Maya women, some of them as young as fourteen. The sexual abuse of Maya slaves and servants became widespread. Many Maya naborías of Spanish conquistadors of Yucatán were forced to offer sexual favors to their masters and other soldiers.[38] Several of Montejo's captains became infamous for their sexual abuse of their naborías. Others apparently amassed "collections of the prettiest women that they could find, and rented them out to their fellow soldiers," making for themselves a decent fortune.[39] Native Maya accounts after the conquest lamented this sexual slavery: "Many village girls were forced to become prostitutes. . . . and they forcibly took them. . . . These young girls did not understand the expectations of the foreigners: neither their Christianity, nor their demands. . . . these Spaniards brought shame when they came. . . . They lusted after the younger and the prettiest girls."[40]

The organized plundering of the most beautiful Maya women from the provinces of Tabasco and Yucatán began shortly after the Montejos gained control of the region.[41] Young Indian women, especially those held in encomienda by the Montejos or their supporters, found themselves the victims of what can only be called an organized prostitution ring. According to witnesses, one of Francisco Montejo's captains, Juan de Aguilar, trafficked in the most beautiful Indian women from all over Mesoamerica, forcing them to serve as prostitutes and concubines of Spanish conquerors of Yucatán.[42] On one occasion, Aguilar purchased a pretty girl for a sack of cacao beans.[43] Diego Martín later testified that Alonso López admitted that he gave these pretty girls to others to use as they pleased and in his various trips to Campeche "gave these girls to whomever he wanted."[44]

Landa was right later to blame much of the conquest's sexual brutality on Alonso López. It was common knowledge during the conquest that López rounded up hundreds of girls and sent them to Francisco Montejo. Others claimed that the Indians of their encomiendas complained incessantly about López's confiscation of the most beautiful Indian women. According to other testimonies, the cacique and Indians of Tamulte (an encomienda belonging to the adelantado) attempted to hide the town's most beautiful girl. Apparently, López often sent his servant Diego Romero to towns to collect girls. More than fifty other young women faced a similar fate as Romero rounded them up and sent them to López in early 1541. López's depredations did not affect only Indians. On other occasions he took pretty young women from Spaniards who held them legally as naborías. For example, Alonso de Eliva testified that he had lost an Indian couple stolen by López; the young Indian woman was beautiful and she and her husband were taken from his encomienda. López apparently sold the Indian man as a slave to a soldier in Campeche and gave the young woman to Diego de Aranda, a conquistador.[45] Another Spaniard from Tabasco, Juan de Ayllón, reported that he had seen firsthand the abuse of several of his own young Maya naborías. López had taken two very pretty young naborías from him and sent them to his friends in Campeche. On a voyage to Campeche, Ayllón ran into the two girls, who looked badly abused, one apparently pregnant. The two Indian women grabbed at him and "cried profusely, begging to return to their own land."[46]

Regardless of pre-Hispanic Maya conceptions of sexual morality, things changed with the violent confrontations and forced sexual encounters of the conquest. Maya women were forcibly taken from their husbands and families, raped, and often kept as concubines or sold and traded like sexual slaves to other conquerors.[47] Their Maya husbands, if not killed, would often flee or take another wife, never to see their previous spouse again. Maya girls as young as twelve were given to Spanish conquistadors as prizes and plunder throughout the conquest.[48] Apparently, the dislocations and forced relocations of large numbers of Maya forced a change in Maya sexual mores, with many Mayas after the conquest marrying and having sexual relations at a younger age than before the arrival of the Europeans.[49] This breakdown in the family structure of Maya families was paralleled by a breakdown in indigenous government and administration, which only partially recovered during the early colonial period. Once powerful regional Maya lords, or Halach Uinic, such as the Xiu lords of Mani, could not exercise the same power or control over the daily lives and sexual attitudes and activities of their Maya commoners. No longer, as Spanish observers later cited, could these Halach Uinic punish the Maya for unacceptable carnal sins. Instead of punishing Maya sodomites by burning them alive, as many Halach Uinic such as the Xiu lords at Mayapan had done to enforce codes of sexual conduct, Maya lords and their subordinate *batabob* found themselves removed from office and replaced by commoners or other Maya collaborators with the Spanish (see fig. 4).[50]

Many Spaniards saw the subsequent lack of punishment and vigilance by native lords as the main reason for an increase in sexual promiscuity and crimes of the flesh. The encomendero Diego Brizeño put it most succinctly in 1579: "Since this land has been conquered, they [the Maya] have begun to lose these good customs due to the lack of punishment that they receive for so many carnal sins evident today."[51] Other Spaniards echoed Brizeño's assertion that the Maya's sexual morality changed for the worse with the conquest. Iñigo Nieto went further: "Since there have been Spaniards in this land, [the Maya] have been losing the custom of punishing [these sins of the flesh], and there are more of these vices today than there have been for the last fifty years."[52] Whether or not Maya sexual promiscuity increased, the sexual encounters and collisions that resulted from the Spanish conquest changed many things for the Maya.

Sexual Encounters: Colonial Maya Sexuality

With the advent of forced sexual relations between the Europeans and Maya women, Maya conceptions of sex and sexuality began to change. The "sexual conquest" violently assaulted traditional Maya views of

Figure 4. Maya image of the "seizing" of the chiefs because they are "lacking understanding," from the Colonial Maya book of Chilam Balam of Chumayel. Image drawn after figure 21 in Ralph Roys, *The Maya Book of Chilam Balam of Chumayel* (Washington, DC, 1933). Drawing by Argelia Segovia Liga

morality and sexuality. Tellingly, the Maya books of Chilam Balam also connected the arrival of the Europeans with the advent of their suffering: "When misery came, when Christianity came from these many Christians who arrived with the true divinity, the True God. For this indeed was the beginning of misery for us, the beginning of tribute, the beginning of tithes, the beginning of strife over purse snatching, the beginning of strife with blowguns, the beginning of strife over promotions, the beginning of the creation of many factions."[53] The Chilam Balam of Chumayel also noted that the arrival of the Spaniards coincided with the advent of shameful lust and a loss of virtue: "The foreigners who have come here, have brought shame when they came. . . . Lust and sex are their priests that are coming to administer things here because of the foreigners."[54]

Landa's and other observers' earlier images of the virtue of Maya women before the conquest conflict with the seventeenth-century view of general Maya sexual promiscuity found in the writings of Fray Diego López de Cogolludo. López de Cogolludo lamented the loss of this chastity and decency and the increase in adultery and rape: "Today when they should be better Christians, it is a sad thing to observe the lasciviousness that exists among them, and this is no doubt caused because they do not punish these sins with the rigor that they did before."[55] The Spanish encomendero of the town of Muxuppipp near Motul complained about the Maya's sexual promiscuity and even outright perversion: "Among them there now exists an innumerable amount of sins of the flesh, incest, and above all many other evil customs."[56] The royal *visitador* of the Real Audiencia of Guatemala, don Diego García de Palacio, who had previously studied Maya customs in Yucatán, concluded in 1576 that "the most notorious things [observed] among them are their incest, sodomies, rapes, adulteries, and other crimes that occur commonly among these natives due to the fact that they live in large families together and do not make houses for their own families, but rather choose to remain with their parents and in-laws."[57]

The violence and rape that were part of the Spanish conquest and the introduction of a new system of morality and government no doubt changed the Maya's concepts of sexuality and sexual morality. No longer could their caciques and *batabob* sentence commoners to death for adultery, rape, or sexual promiscuity. Instead they had to rely on the secular Spanish officials and judges, who were notoriously lax in their persecution of sexual offenses. Even the Holy Office of the Inquisition had no power to enforce sexual morality among the Maya.[58] This was left to the bishops, their ecclesiastical courts of the Provisorato de Indios, and their officials, called *vicarios*, in Maya towns. The earliest bishops gave explicit instructions to the local ecclesiastical judges or vicarios concerning Maya sexual crimes and sexual morality. Fray Francisco de Toral, the first bishop, ordered that the local vicarios be especially vigilant in teaching the Maya about the sacraments of confession and matrimony and with the aid of interpreters have them confess their sins and lusts of the flesh.[59] Many Spanish observers believed that this was to no avail, for Maya women had become more promiscuous. According to Giraldo Díaz de Alpuche, Maya women "are shameless and every day become greater whores."[60] Other Spaniards claimed that more than sixty years after the conquest, promiscuity among young Maya had grown such that many of the prettiest Maya women went to towns looking for Spaniards to fornicate with.[61] Subsequent bishops continued to order their vicarios to be vigilant and control the sexual morality of their Maya parishioners. As late as 1765, church authorities in the province revealed their continued preoccupation with the Maya's sexual offenses when they ordered their parish priests to be especially careful about these vices and preach against them.[62]

Many Maya women apparently became sexually fascinated with the Spaniards and their African slaves.[63] Colonial observers remarked that "the most beautiful of the young women quickly became 'friends' of the Spaniards, seeking them out in whatever town they might be." Other Spaniards commented with disdain that these beautiful young women prostituted themselves out of a desire for sexual novelty. To have sex with a Spaniard, according to other colonial sources, was irresistible for young Maya women.[64]

Initially, the early colonial Maya became fascinated not only with the Spaniards and their strange bodies, but also with their European livestock. The contact with unusual people and animals caused the Maya to experiment with new aspects of sexuality, much to the horror of the clergy. During the early contact period, many Mayas were caught experimenting sexually with the strange animals that the Spaniards had brought with them. By the 1560s, the Spanish system had attempted to conquer Maya sexuality, and several Maya were punished for bestiality. In one instance, Pedro Na, a fifteen-year-old Maya boy from the town of Mani, was caught committing bestiality with a Castilian chicken.[65] On Monday, 11 January 1563, Juan Camal and his wife, Francisca Tun, while walking along the road, discovered Pedro Na seated on the ground with his pants open and his virile member in his hands. According to their later testimony, the hen was bleeding from its rear, and it was obvious that Pedro had just finished having carnal relations with the animal.[66] During the trial, it became apparent that the boy had had carnal access with animals on many other occasions. He stated that he had no idea that his actions were wrong, pleading innocence and begging for mercy. The horrified Spanish prosecutor called his perversion "a sin so atrocious and abominable against God and nature" that it deserved the harshest penalty.[67] On 30 January 1563, the judge issued his sentence, which was executed four days later: the boy was marched through the streets of Mérida with the dead hen tied around his neck. He was taken to the public square, where he was castrated, his genitals thrown into a bonfire with the dead hen.[68]

As this example illustrates, Spanish conceptions of sex and sexuality differed greatly from Maya conceptions. Although the Maya might have had a natural sexual curiosity to engage in sexual relations with animals, they soon came to realize that such conduct would be severely punished. The violent Spanish reaction against an "abominable sin" would be repeated many times in response to other aspects of Yucatec Maya sexuality and sexual conduct. From the earliest contact with the Franciscan friars in the 1540s, to the frequent sermons and preaching of the secular parish clergy, the Maya's different cultural concepts of sexual morality collided with the church's message on the dangers of sex and sexuality.

Sexual Collisions: The Church's Message on Sex and Sexuality

Lust is the most debilitating of vices. . . . No evil attacks us earlier, pricks us more sharply, covers more territory, or drags more people to ruin.
—Erasmus of Rotterdam, *Enchiridion Militis Christiani* (1503)

One of the first actions of the early friars was to stop all pre-Hispanic practices they considered "deviant or sexually promiscuous," such as Maya concubinage and promiscuous sexual relations, especially those of the Maya nobility. The early friars viewed this effort as "civilizing" the Maya. Fray Bernardo de Lizana wrote in 1633 that the early Franciscans had the job of "domesticating [the Maya] and placing them in good order and civility, procuring clothes, because before they went around naked, and making them form orderly republics and towns." [69]

The later missionary friars' views differed greatly from the initial positive observations of precontact Maya sexual morality. The later friars viewed the Maya and their religion and culture as savage and inhuman. They remarked that their religion and culture broke all "divine and natural laws." [70] Especially in their observations of Maya sexual practices and marital relations, the Franciscans and Spanish authorities found practices that they wished to change.

As early as 1553 Spanish officials in the province issued *ordenanzas* that attempted to regulate Yucatec Maya sexual morality and marital relations. The royal *visitador* from the Audiencia of Guatemala issued a series of ordenanzas at the request of the Franciscans in an effort to reform and restrict Maya sexual practices. From that point onward, the Catholic Church and the Spanish authorities regulated and controlled Yucatec Maya sexuality, desire, and sexual relations. The ordenanzas of Tomás López Medel included several decrees concerning fornication and Maya marital relations. The royal official noted that, "even though the sacrament of matrimony was used among the natives of this province, they commit grave errors and abuses." [71] The decree ordered that "all of those who, after having been baptized, have lived with many women are to manifest all of the women that they have to the bishop or the friars, who will examine them to determine which should be the legitimate wife so that they leave behind all the others."[72]

Anyone who continued to fornicate with many women or who refused to leave his other wives would be punished with "one hundred lashes." The decrees also mandated a similar penalty for Mayas who committed adultery. According to the decree, those caught committing adultery would receive "one hundred lashes and have their hair shorn off."[73] Similarly, those who continued to practice polygamy or adultery faced harsher penalties. The ordenanzas also prohibited Maya caciques and principals from keeping Maya women as slaves because the Spaniards believed that these female slaves were kept as "lovers and concubines in great offense of their legitimate wives and the sacrament of matrimony." Fray Diego de Landa mentioned that the caciques often engaged in sexual relations with their female slaves, because they believed that it was "a man's right to do with his own property as his wished."[74]

Regardless of these prohibitions and the harsh penalties attached to them, more than twenty years after the conquest the Spaniards and the clergy began to observe an increase in sexual promiscuity among the Yucatec Maya. For example, the Spaniard Juan Hernández, during the trial of several Maya for sexual promiscuity, testified: "I have seen that the natives here in this province commonly get married while they are still young boys. . . . many marry at the age of ten or twelve, and they live a married life with their wives; and it is common among them that they have carnal access with women at a very early age, unlike the Spaniards."[75] Other friars and parish clergy continued to decry what they viewed as increasing Maya sexual depravity. Concerning the sexual misconduct of Mayas in his own district, Fray Juan de Benavides wrote that many fled his region "with their women, their own daughters, or the wives of other Indians, secretly hiding them and living with them in sin. . . . They even commit incest with their own daughters and close relatives. . . . Both I and Fray Beleña have tried to put an end to these customs, remedying them with severe punishments. . . . but my efforts have not been sufficient to uproot from them this evil and those of their incests."[76]

By the 1560s, the clergy had learned the Maya language, congregated the Maya into orderly towns, forced them to wear clothing, and begun instructing them in Spanish Christian concepts. One of the most important goals of evangelization now became teaching Catholic sexual morality, a task that fell to both the Franciscan order and the secular clergy of the newly established bishopric.

Sexual Collisions: Inculcating a "healthy abhorrence of sexual relations"

To sin with a single woman is simple fornication; with a married woman, adultery; with a young virgin, estupro [rape]; with a relative, incest; and with a religious person or one dedicated to God, sacrilege or spiritual adultery.
—Fray Luis de Granada (1504–88), *Memorial de la vida cristiana* (1565)

The above definitions by the Spanish Dominican Fray Luis de Granada are perhaps the best summary of Spanish Catholic concepts of the dangers of sexuality, lust, and other sins related to sexual relations. Christian morality, as Louise Burkhart also has noted for the Franciscans' work among the Nahua, was defined according to the Ten Commandments and the Seven Mortal Sins, "which were part of the basic doctrine that everyone was expected to memorize."[77] The official view of the Catholic clergy enforced by the Council of Trent in 1563 was that "virginity or celibacy is better and more conducive to happiness than marriage."[78]

Within this concept of sexuality, vaginal intercourse by a married couple remained the only sexual expression permitted. However, even this was viewed as shameful and only served the purpose of procreation. The clergy, in essence, hoped to inculcate in the Maya what they viewed as a "healthy abhorrence of sexual relations." The clergy taught that the "less pleasure sustained during sex the better, and if it was possible one ought to experience no pleasure at all."[79] The friars also preached often on the virtue of virginity and the sinfulness of sexual activity outside of marriage.[80]

Thus the most important message taught to the Maya was that celibacy was the most desirable state and that sex was sinful and dirty. The early friars also taught the Maya that the Catholic clergy were celibate and had to remain celibate, not only when conducting religious services, but throughout their lives. This concept of clerical celibacy conflicted with traditional Maya concepts of ritual celibacy, which, though required in certain religious ceremonies and feasts, was not a permanent characteristic of the Maya priesthood.[81] At the same time, the early Franciscans arriving from Spain began in the late sixteenth and early seventeenth century to stress in their sermons the newly invigorated doctrine of the Immaculate Conception of the Virgin Mary. It was Fray Diego de Landa himself who brought the first major image of the Virgin of the Immaculate Conception from Guatemala in 1558. Placed in the Franciscan monastery at Izamal, the carved wooden image of the Virgin immediately acquired a devoted following among the Maya from throughout Yucatán.[82] The cult of the

Virgin of Izamal was used by the friars to evangelize and instruct the Maya in the glories of virginity and the sins and dangers of sexual relations (see fig. 5).

On occasions throughout the year, the Franciscans would bring out and parade the image of the Virgin of Izamal. This beautiful, perpetual girl served as an example of the perfect state for all women and girls. Young Maya converts were taught to emulate the Virgin of Izamal's chastity and modesty. The friars hoped that holding up this image as a role model would make young Maya women less likely to engage in promiscuous sexual relations with boys and men. For married Maya women, the Virgin also symbolized chastity and submission to husband and church. The Virgin also represented a nonsexual image of perfect motherhood. Maya women, then, were to see in the Virgin of Izamal the epitome of their socially mandated roles: chastity and obedience. The friars hoped by this means to make Maya women chaste and modest again, restricting sexual relations to marriage and never endangering the social order of their missions with sexual promiscuity or fornication. The Maya themselves record with wonder the arrival of the Virgin. They wrote that "it was at Izamal where the daughter of the true God, Lord of Heaven, descended, the Queen, the Virgin, the miraculous One. . . . It was she, the miraculous one, the merciful one, who was so declared here."[83] The message of the dangers of the sins of sexuality that the fathers taught them made their way even into many of the Maya's clandestine books of Chilam Balam.[84] These sins quickly permeated colonial Maya understanding of all things sexual.

The Colonial Clergy and Sexuality: Attempts at Sexual Control

> La mayor parte de los hombres, aunque alaban la virtud, siguen el vicio.
> *(The majority of men, though they praise virtue, follow vice.)*
> —Fray Luis de Granada (1565)

The clerical preoccupation with sexual morality and sexual practices is evident in the earliest doctrines and Christian confession manuals published in the Maya language.[85] For instance, a surviving seventeenth-century confession manual translated into Yucatec Maya, *Confesionario breve para confesar a los indios*, placed a great deal of emphasis on discovering and making the Maya confess their sexual sins and other perversions.[86] One of the longest sections of this confession manual deals with fornication.

Figure 5. Engraving of Nuestra Señora de Izamal (Franciscan Virgin of the Immaculate Conception brought from Guatemala on orders of Fray Diego de Landa, 1558). Drawing of plate in Fr. Bernardo de Lizana, *Devocionario de Nuestra Señora de Izamal y conquista espiritual de Yucatán*, ed. Rene Acuña (Mexico City, 1995 [1633]). Drawing by Argelia Segovia Liga

The priest or confessor is instructed to ask questions that followed a sup-posedly normal exchange between confessor and Maya confessant. For example:

> *Yanxin açipil ti hunpay chuplal* [Have you fornicated with some woman?]
>
> *Haytulx tubaob* [With how many?]
>
> *Hay tenhi ti hun tulicunx tihuntuli* [How many times with one and with the other?]
>
> *Yan uxiblil cuchi* [Did she have a husband?]
>
> *A uenelob xin* [Are they your relatives?]
>
> *Bicx auonelil ti* [How are they related to you?]
>
> *Yonelob xin a chuplil* [Are they relatives of your wife?]
>
> *Yanxin a dziboltic huupay chuplal* [Have you desired any woman?]
>
> *Haytulx tubaob* [How many?]
>
> *Haytenhi a dzibolticob* [How many times have you desired them?]
>
> *Yanhi ua auoltiçipil tiob cuchi* [Did you have the will to fornicate with them?]
>
> *Yanxin abaxtic aba* [Have you touched yourself dishonestly?][87]

The Spanish clergy's preoccupation with sexual deviance and sexual morality is evident not only in this confession manual but also in many of the words that they elicited from their Maya informants for their earliest dictionaries. For instance, in many of the Franciscan dictionary entries that dealt with sex and sexuality, the clergy attached the Maya *keban* to words for sexual practices and sexual positions (fig. 6).

The clergy used the word *keban*, which meant "a sad or miserable thing,"[88] to roughly translate the Spanish *pecado* (sin). The Catholic Christian relationship between sex and sin was thereby perpetuated by the later friars' teachings. Just as Burkhart noted for the Franciscans' missionary efforts among the Nahuatl-speaking natives of central New Spain, the Yucatán missionary's "aim was translation, not linguistic investigation."[89]

As table 2 and many other examples of Maya terms for sexual posi-tions and sexual acts illustrate, the Franciscan friars associated Maya sexu-ality and sexual practices with sinfulness and dirtiness. The friars began to record common Maya sayings, which also show the Spaniards' view of the increase in Maya sexual promiscuity. One such common phrase was *Baxalech choo u baxalech kuch*, which meant "You are the plaything of mice and buzzards." The friars glossed this phrase as "You are an evil woman who gives herself to everyone and everyone comes to you like rodents go

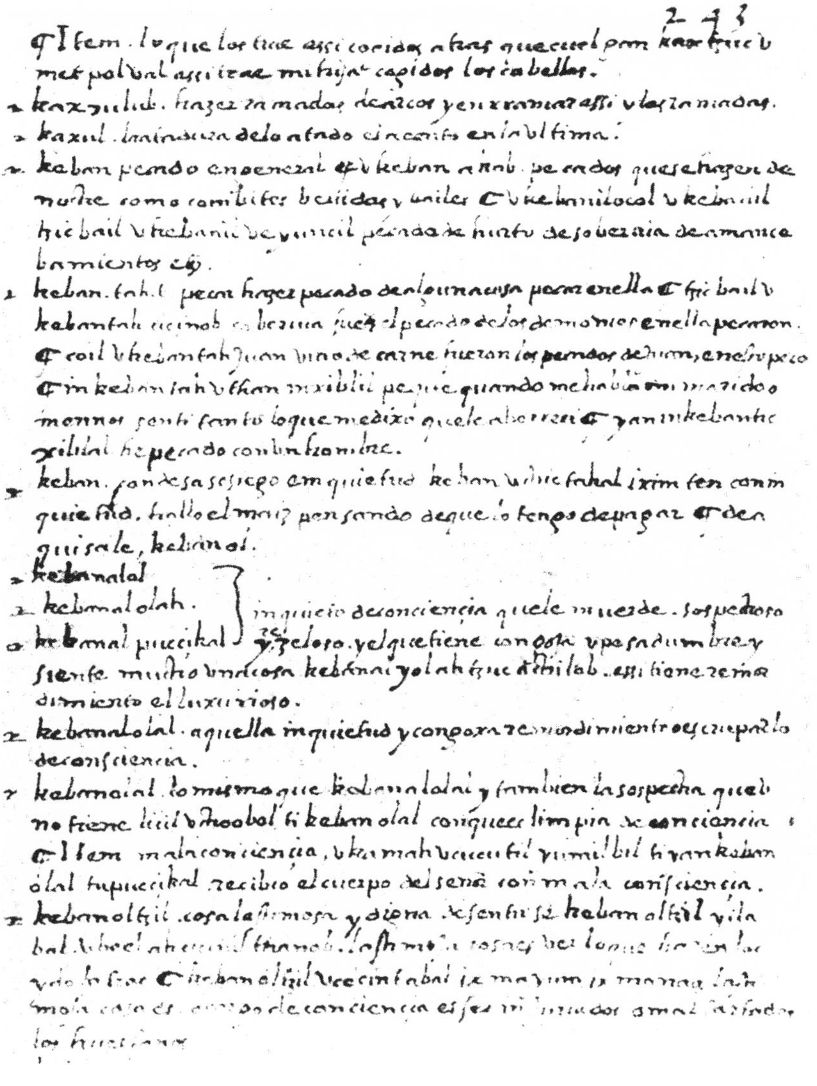

¶ Item . lo que los tiene assi cogidos a tras que cuel pan kaxthie ¿
met polbal assi teae mi hijas cogidos los cabellos .

↳ kaxghib . hazer ramadas deares y enramar assi v la ramadas .

↳ kaxul . laminaria delo atado cincoss en la ultima .

↳ keban pecado en general ⊕ v keban a tab pecados que se hazen de
noche como combites beuidas y uiles ⊂ v kebanil ocal v keban al
hie bail v kebanii de ymail pecado de hurto de sobervia de amone
bramientos ⊕ .

↳ keban . tah l pecar hazer pecado de alguna cosa pecar en ella ⊂ hie bail v
kebantah ycinob es berina fues el pecado delos demonios en ella pecaron .
⊂ coil v kebantah Juan vino de carne fueron los pensos de tum, e nestropeo
⊂ in keban tah v than misiblii pe quie quando me habia un marido
mennos senti canto lo que me dixo que le aborrese ⊂ yan in kebantse
xiblal he pecado con un hombre .

↳ keban . confesa se se cego em que fue keban v hie cabal ixim ten comin
quie fue . hallo el maiz pensando de que lo tengo de mgar ⊂ den
guisale, keban os .

↳ kebanalal

↳ kebmal olah . } in quieto de conciencia que le muerde . sospechoso

◦ kebmal puccikal y zeloso. y el que tiene un ooh v pesadumbre y
siense mucho vn cosa kebmai yol ah que athilab . essi tiene rema
dimiento el luxurioso .

↳ kebmalolal . aquella inquietud y congoxa re mordimiento o escrupulo
de consciencia .

↳ kebmaial . lo mismo que kebanalalai y tambien la sospecha que b
no tiene liuil v theobol ti keban olal conques cerlimpia de consciencia
⊂ Item mala consciencia, v ka mah veue ti vmilbil ti yan keban
olal tupuccikal recibio el cuerpo del señor con mala consciencia .

↳ kebanolkii cosa la firmeza y digna de sentirse keban olkil y la
bal v hee l ah emil thanob . lafh mi la conge bel lo que he en las
v de lo fae ⊂ keban olkiil vee en kabal ia me um u manca lah
mola cosa es enojos de consciencia es ser in imador a mal arindos
los huessos .

Figure 6. Maya Calepino de Motul of Fray Antonio de Ciudad Real, entry dealing with the Maya term *keban*, meaning roughly "sin." Author's photograph of fol. 243 from *Calepino de Motul: Diccionario maya-español*, vol. 1 (Mexico City, 1995), 417

to bread and buzzards to putrid flesh."[90] In this way, they attempted to inculcate a horror of sexual promiscuity and lasciviousness. Their conceptions came from the Christian Catholic view of sexuality dictated by the Council of Trent in 1563.

The Maya, however, had a preconquest sexual morality that did not view sex as inherently evil. Maya conceptions defined and placed sexual pleasure and sexual relations within certain constructs and relationships that depended on one's social class and one's status in society. Whereas Maya commoners were only allowed to enjoy sexual relations within the confines of a monogamous marriage, the Maya nobility and caciques were allowed during the precontact period to engage in and enjoy sexual relations with many wives and with many of their female slaves and servants. Even during the colonial period, the Maya nobility continued to claim sexual prerogatives over many women, even including wives of their commoners. For instance, in 1569 the Maya nobleman and governor from the region of the town of Tabi tried to force a commoner's wife to have sex with him. According to the commoner: "The worst thing that he did was that he came into my house four times, trying to take my wife by force in order to sow sin [fornicate] with her. He desired this, but he did not fulfill his desire. This is what don Jorge Xiu did."[91] As this case illustrates, with the full force of Spanish colonial society and the church on their side, Maya commoners could thwart the continued prerogatives and sexual advances of the Maya nobility. During the later colonial period, Maya women too were able to use the Spanish system to protect themselves from lascivious Maya noblemen and even unwanted sexual advances from Spaniards.[92]

Colonial Realities: Sexual Immorality among the Clergy

Attempts to correct abuses and reform the clergy were the main preoccupations of the final session of the Council of Trent (1562–63). Efforts to control the morality and inhibit and punish the sexual immorality of parish clergy were made in several major Mexican provincial councils and three separate diocesan synods in the bishopric of Yucatán. Apparently, as successive bishops proclaimed, there was a problem with enforcing celibacy and continence among the clergy (especially the secular parish clergy).

All of the church's efforts at reform appear to have been in vain. Especially in later colonial Yucatán, sexual immorality among the higher clergy appears to have been commonplace. For example, as late as 1700 a priest of the cathedral, Gaspar Joseph Rodríguez, complained that the

Table 2: Maya sexual terms associated with the word *sin* by the colonial Franciscan friars

Maya Word	Spanish Definition	Dictionary or Source
Chii keban	*pecado que se comete con la boca, chupando las vergüenzas*	*Calepino de Motul*, 242
Chijl keban	*pecado vergonzoso y sucio que se lo mete o chupando las vergüenzas el miembro del varón en boca mamando*	*Vocabulario de Maya Than*, 509
Cuchpach keban	*pecado de carne cometido versa facie al revés*	*Calepino de Motul*, 143
Pak keban	*pecar, generalmente por fornicación*	*Vocabulario de Maya Than*, 509
Ah Pak keban	*fornicador*	*Vocabulario de Maya Than*, 355
Ix ppenil keban	*pecar un hombre con otro, sodomía y cometerla*	*Vocabulario de Maya Than*, 510, 595

entire ecclesiastical membership of the cathedral chapter engaged in sexually immoral behavior. He wrote to the Crown:

> Many of the priests and even the *prebendados* have illicit relationships with women, and they even have children by them. . . . The Dean of the Chapter does not go to the meetings, instead he screws around with four girls and gives them his pensions as "dowries." . . . the Archdean also has a lover with whom he fornicates. . . . The *Maestroescuela* also has a lover with whom he fornicates, a *mestizo* woman named Josefa Montalvo, whom he offered as a whore informally to a member of the secular *cabildo*. They all fornicate with mestizas and indias. . . . but I should tell no more so as not to offend Your Majesty's chaste ears.[93]

If this is an accurate image of the higher, more educated clergy in Mérida, what could one expect from the undereducated and often illiterate clergy who served in the Maya parishes and *guardianías*?

Renewed Sexual Encounters and Collisions:
The Priests/Confessors and the Maya

> *While he was confessing me in his room[,] . . . he reached out under my garment and groped my breasts and said to me, "You are very pretty. . . . I think I should like to see your breasts. . . . They are quite fine indeed. . . ."* Then, being the first time that I had been to confession, I fled his room in horror and have never confessed since that day.
> —María May, nineteen-year-old Maya woman from the village of Peto (1589)

Since the Fourth Lateran Council of 1215, the Catholic Church has emphasized the obligation of every Christian of both sexes to confess before the local priest at least once a year. Moreover, from the decrees of the Council of Trent (1553–63) onward, confession became mandatory on certain feast days of precept. The council decreed that "for those who after baptism have fallen into sin, the Sacrament of Penance is as necessary unto salvation as is baptism itself for those who have not yet been regenerated."[94] In 1585, the Catholic Church in Mexico went a step forward when the Third Mexican Provincial Council required parish priests to keep a book for this purpose, and every year during Lent they had to enter into it the names of those who had come to confession as well as report those who did not confess. This procedure was required by most synods.[95] The provincial council also decreed which holy days of precept were to be observed by the indigenous people in their parishes.[96] In colonial Yucatán, Maya parishioners had to appear and confess before their priest on four separate occasions each canonical year according to the bishopric's first synod in 1563.[97] These four mandatory confessions were to occur during the Feast at Easter, Corpus Christi, the Feast of the Patron Saint of the village, and one other feast day.[98] In other words, the Maya were required by law to be interrogated regularly about their sexual conduct by their parish priests and Franciscan friars in the intimacy of the confessional.[99] This quickly enabled the Maya to understand the clergy's obsession with the intimate details of their sexual lives. Many Mayas soon realized that the act of confession could be a powerful tool in their dealings with each other and with their parish clergy.

Moreover, for the Spanish Catholic Church during the colonial period, the single most abhorrent crime that a clergyman could commit was *solicitación*, or solicitation *ad turbia intra confessionem*.[100] According to medieval Spanish law, the clerical crime of soliciting sex in the confessional was tantamount to heresy and a grievous sin, considered one of the worst committed against the majesty of God. The old Castilian law of the *Siete*

(a)   (b)

Figure 7. Confessions made before confessors in "open" confessionals in New Spain prohibited by decrees of the Council of Trent (1563). (a) Image detail from a Nahuatl confessional manual (1611) showing a priest confessing a Nahua penitent in an open confessional. Drawing adapted from Fray Martín de León, *Camino del Cielo en Lengua Mexicana* (México City, 1611). (b) Recreated drawing of a Franciscan friar "improperly" administering a confession to a female Maya penitent in a similar open confessional. Drawings by Argelia Segovia Liga

Partidas, on which many of the laws of the Indies were based, declared that "ecclesiastics are always bound to live in a chaste manner, especially after they have taken holy orders."[101] Any clergyman who solicited sex in the confessional or who engaged in open fornication would be removed from his parish.[102] The Holy Office of the Inquisition also issued several edicts specifically denouncing the sin of solicitation and requiring all Christians to denounce any cases of solicitation to their local commissary of the Inquisition.[103] The Inquisition and church authorities also attempted to regulate the act of confession by mandating the use of a formal enclosed "confessional," which would physically separate the confessor from the person confessing.[104] Mindful of the dangers and temptations that existed for the solicitation of sex during confessions, the Council of Trent and numerous church councils in New Spain and its bishoprics attempted to require the use of enclosed confessionals. However, as late as the seventeenth century, even the illustrations in colonial Mexican *confesionarios* showed priests confessing penitents who openly knelt before them (see fig. 7a). This type of "open" confessional often led to both temptations and abuses of penitents (see fig. 7b). In many cases in colonial Yucatán, this type of confessional, without any enclosures separating the penitent from the confessor, remained common late into the eighteenth century (see fig. 8).

Figure 8. Eighteenth-century open-front confessional from the Maya convent church at Mani. Photograph by the author

Technically in canon law, solicitation was the use of the sacrament of penance, either directly or indirectly, to draw others into sins of lust.[105] In the province of Yucatán and in New Spain in general, the term *solicitación* took on a wider meaning and a broader definition. It came to be associated with any attempt to initiate sexual contact between a priest or confessor and anyone else before, during, or after a confession. The actual solicitation of sex in the confessional was not absolutely necessary to try a priest for solicitation. The actual act of soliciting sex or engaging in sexual relations could take place before or after a confession either in the church, the priest's private dwelling, or any other place close to or attached to the church or convent.[106] The mere fact that the soliciting priest was also a licensed confessor made any sexual overture or act of the priest a sin against the sacrament of penance and an abuse of office.[107]

The seriousness of an accusation of solicitation of sex in the confessional made such charges a powerful weapon for the Maya in battles against their parish priests.[108] In many instances, the Maya used their knowledge of their priests' and friars' illicit sexual relations.[109] They had learned well the lessons that the priests and friars had taught them about sexuality and sexual perversion, and they used these lessons to attack their clergymen when they had no other means of resistance. For example, in one instance in 1774 an anonymous Maya wrote a long petition denouncing the hypocrisy of the local parish priests.[110] The Maya denounced them for sexual depravity, stating:

> I, the informer of the truth, tell you what you should know about Father Torres, Father Díaz, squad corporal, Father Granado, sergeant, and Father Maldonado. They say false baptism, false confession, false last rites, and false mass. Nor does the True God descend in the host when they say mass, because they have stiff penises. Every day all they think of is intercourse with their mistresses. In the morning their hands smell bad from playing with their mistresses. Father Torres only plays with the vagina of that ugly black devil Rita. He whose hand is disabled does not have a disabled penis. It is said that he has up to four children by this black devil. Likewise, Father Díaz, squad corporal, has a woman from Bolonchen called Antonia Alvarado, whose vagina he repeatedly penetrates before the whole community, and Father Granado bruises Manuela Pacheco's vagina all night. Father Maldonado has just finished fornicating with everyone in his jurisdiction and has now come here to carry out his fornication. The whole community knows this. When Father Maldonado makes his weekly visit, a woman from Pencuyut named Fabiana Gómez pro-

vides him with her vagina. Only the Priests are allowed to fornicate without so much as a word about it. If a good commoner does that, the priest always punishes him immediately. But look at the priests' excessive fornication, putting their hands on these whores' vaginas, even saying mass like this. God willing, when the English come may they not be fornicators equal to these priests, who only lack carnal acts with man's arses. God willing that smallpox be rubbed into their penis heads. Amen. I, the Informer of the truth.[111]

This petition is illustrative of the Maya's abilities to turn the Catholic teachings on the immorality of sexual behavior against their own priests and friars. In this petition, the author, no doubt a Maya nobleman, subtly challenges the clergy's teachings against fornication and polygamy. His use of the phrase "If a good commoner does that" shows that he is trying to relate and identify himself as a common Maya, but his education and erudition betray him as a member of the noble class that was most affected by Franciscan and clerical prohibitions of polygamy and fornication. As Sigal has noted, this petitioner reveals quite a bit about Spanish colonialism and the impact of the sexual conquest.[112] This petition is also a brilliant act of Maya resistance against the clergy. The author achieved his desired effect of shocking the ecclesiastical authorities. The official of the Inquisition who translated the document was so offended that he added his own opinion to the translation saying that the accusations were "scathing, audacious, and grossly excessive," since he argued that it was well known that the clergy treated the Maya with "respect and veneration."[113] The anonymous Maya petitioner successfully used his knowledge of Spanish sexual morality to attack his parish priests: during the pastoral visitation of the region several of the friars and priests mentioned in this petition were removed and tried for solicitation.[114]

In one of the earliest cases against a clergyman for soliciting sex in the confessional, a similar Maya petition complained that the parish priest and vicario Andrés Mexía solicited sex in the confessional. According to the Maya officials of the town of Ekpedz, "While [Mexía] gives confession to women, he says, 'If you do not give yourself to me, I will not give you confession.' This is how he abuses the women. He will not give them confession unless the women go to him. Unless the women fornicate with him. This is the whole truth about why the women are so upset."[115]

Initially, Mexía was removed, but after a long trial he was eventually reinstated in the Peto region from 1582 to 1589.[116] Mexía claimed that the Maya were quick to lie under oath and often committed perjury. He stated before the inquisitors that the Maya "very easily commit perjury and . . . ordinarily get drunk and are easy to convince and persuade to give testimony against someone contrary to the truth. . . . They are out to see whom they can take advantage of and for any small occasion or interest they contradict themselves [make false declarations]."[117] Apparently, the Inquisition officials believed Mexía's arguments. The Maya officials from the local town of Tetzal quickly realized that the reinstated Mexía might harbor a grudge against them. Showing the Maya's cunning and understanding of the reality of colonialism, the town government of Tetzal wrote a letter of apology to the Inquisition asking for Mexía's forgiveness and blaming the scandal on the gossip of Maya women. Using Spanish ideas of Christian virtue, they wrote: "Because of Christianity we gave up our anger with the padre and that which we previously said about him. Nor do we ask anything of him. Nor do we have anything else to say about it, because it is all over. We tell the truth. We will remember none of it a second time, because we know nothing about it except for tale-telling and women's gossip."[118]

It was not long, however, before the Maya used another accusation of solicitation of sex in the confessional against Padre Mexía. In late March 1589, a group of Maya women from the Peto region denounced Mexía again for sexually abusing them in the confessional.[119] Once more, Mexía argued that they held animosity against him, but he was not as successful this second time.[120] Eventually condemned, Mexía was sentenced to the perpetual privation of confessing women as well as to banishment from the province for two years and a fine of one hundred pesos.[121]

In another case, from 1599, the Maya again denounced sexual impropriety in the confessional to defend themselves against an abusive Franciscan friar. A group of Maya women from the towns of Motul and Cacalchen denounced their friar for soliciting sex in the confessional and for molesting them while they confessed. Through the interpretation of Fray Julián de Quartas, four young Maya women denounced their friar to the Franciscan provincial Fray Alonso de Río Frío.[122] They accused Fray Pedro de Vergara of soliciting sexual relations from them and ultimately raping them during their confessions. According to Ana Kuk, a Maya woman from Motul, Vergara had said "lascivious words to her and shown her his penis after which she grew saddened and left without confessing."[123] Beatriz Dzib, also from the town of Motul, accused Vergara of soliciting her during confession. She claimed that Vergara "placed his hands on her breasts and tried to make her touch his penis."[124] In the town of Cacalchen, however, María Cocom made the most damning allegations, alleging that Vergara made her sit between his legs before him while he "touched her breasts and forced her to touch his penis."[125] When the girl began to cry, the friar reportedly forced her to her knees and raped her, telling her when he finished that "she should not tell anyone about what had happened there."[126]

According to other information gathered later, Vergara had also raped Maya women in other towns.[127] More petitions from Maya women and men arrived. The scandalized provincial of the Franciscan order wrote that after having been warned the friar still "had not changed his ways, but rather continued these vile actions and did other things worthy of punishment."[128] Based on the Mayas' petitions and testimony, the provincial removed the friar. However, by October 1600 Fray Miguel López, a Franciscan official who visited the province, heard of the case and reviewed it. He discovered that many of the husbands of the same Maya women who denounced Vergara previously had been punished by him for the crime of idolatry.[129] Fray Miguel wrote that the Inquisition should reconsider the case:

> These Maya [who testified against Vergara] are less than firmly planted in the faith, and they have proceeded to denounce Fray Pedro de Vergara out of desire for revenge, since they had ample cause to hold hatred for him, because as the *guardián* of their convent and as a translator of their language he had persecuted them for their idolatries with all of the care and diligence necessary of his office, and in punishing them he used harsh measures and cruelty and because of his extirpation of idolatry there has not been a single convent in which the Indians have not raised severe complaints against him for his excessive cruelty, and even now during the present Chapter meeting of our order I have received verbal petitions from the Indians of several villages where he has never yet served as *guardián* not because he has done anything, but rather because out of their fear and knowing the fame of his cruelty they hoped that he would not be assigned to their *guardianía*. . . . For these reasons I am sure that the Indians referred to in this case have the same hatred for him since he was the translator in various cases against idolatry in their town. . . . Thus I am of the opinion that we delay any punishment for some time until we can be sure that if any of the witnesses in this case wish for revenge they will not be able to gain it in this manner.[130]

The 1609 case against the parish priest Cristóbal de Valencia discussed at the beginning of this essay is another typical case in which the Maya used denunciations of sexual impropriety against a clergyman who had punished them for their own excesses. Clemente Ek was not the only one who denounced Padre Valencia. More than one hundred other Maya gave depositions against the priest. One of these witnesses was Pablo Chan, a resident of the town of Hoctun. According to Chan, Valencia, "with a diabolical soul and unworthy of the ministry and office of a priest, called the said Indian one day and ordered him to put his virile member into his mouth and that the said Indian placed his virile member into the mouth of the accused and he took his own member into his hands and he played with it until he spilled his own natural seed."[131]

Valencia, in his own defense, argued similarly that Pablo Chan, Clemente Ek, and many of the other Maya witnesses used their denunciations to take revenge against him. He stated "that the natives give this false testimony against him because he had punished them for their own crimes against the faith and their idolatries and drunkenness that they engage in frequently, and for this reason they declare these falsehoods against him."[132] As in the case against Fray Pedro de Vergara, the Maya apparently used accusations of sexual impropriety to rid themselves of a repressive clergyman. During the same period, the bishop of Yucatán stated that the Maya often lied and testified falsely against their clergymen. In a letter to the Crown, he wrote: "I, inquiring about the matter, discover that the Indians come with lies because they are obligated to go and hear mass or the doctrine, or that proceedings for some crime or sin against the faith are brought against them."[133] More important than whether the Mayas told lies or the truth is that their accusations proved effective in removing their clergymen, at least for the duration of the trial. As these and many other cases show (see table 3 in the appendix), many Mayas may have used denunciations of solicitation to remove priests and friars who punished or abused them for what they viewed as the Mayas' own sins. Accusations of solicitation empowered Maya men to take revenge against the repressive measures of clergy seeking to extirpate idolatry. Maya women also empowered themselves by taking the initiative and denouncing their parish priests or friars for sexual advances in the confessional or in the church.

These accusations also allowed Maya women to protect themselves from the abuse of a jealous husband. For example, two Maya women from the Peto region denounced their interim parish priest, Bachiller Antonio Ramón de La Cueva, in 1730 for the crime of solicitation *ad turpia intra confessionem*. Fearful that their husbands might discover that they were not virgins when they married, they blamed their lost virginity on a parish priest well known for exploiting his parishioners.[134] Whether or not they were actually raped in the confessional, the Maya women used the accusation as a shield against their jealous husbands. In order to minimize their own public shame, the two women intelligently asked a second Spanish confessor to denounce the priest for them.[135] Another Maya woman, María

Uxul, brought a similar case against the assistant parish priest of the town of Mama, Bachiller Félix de Malavar, in the same year.[136] Apparently, her husband also had abused her for suspected infidelity.

In many other cases, Maya men used similar claims about priests and Maya women to take revenge for abuses committed against them. For example, in 1780 Félix Cocom, the Maya *maestro de capilla* of the town of Uman, denounced his own parish priest Bachiller Luis Antonio de Echazarreta for sexual misconduct and solicitation.[137] According to later testimony, the priest not only solicited sex during confession, he also mistreated young pregnant Maya women. Apparently, he frequently attacked unwed mothers or pregnant Maya women by yelling at them: "Come here you whores, you little pigs, mules of the devil that is what you are, slaves of the devil's fornication, come and tell me who are the fathers of the bastard children that you have in your womb."[138] Padre Echazarreta's offenses did not stop with insults. Many of the younger Maya women who attempted to marry, such as Francisca Cauiche, testified that the priest had raped them during their marriage talks and confessions while they resided in the church.[139] Apparently, while they stayed in the church at night the priest called them to his room. Francisca Cauiche later testified that after dinner one night she was summoned to his quarters by the priest's sister doña Ignacia, who dragged her by her arms and locked her in the priest's room.[140] Father Echazarreta then pulled her forcibly to the bed and threatened her, "If you do not have carnal relations with me I will not marry you." Francisca kicked and resisted and told him, "My Lord, I cannot have relations with you because you are Christ on earth!" The priest replied: "My daughter, I have permission and a license to have relations with anyone, even a young virgin like you. . . . I should be the first to taste of the fruits that will soon belong to those *cabrones*. Besides if you have any trouble in the future with your husband because of this just come to me and tell me so I can punish him."[141] According to other witnesses, the parish priest apparently molested all of the girls who came to him for marriage instruction and confession.[142] In his initial denunciation, Félix Cocom argued that Father Echazarreta's sexual scandals were so horrendous that they set a bad example for the entire town. Cocom appealed to Catholic fears of public scandal when he wrote sarcastically in his petition: "All of this, My Lord, appears upon seeing it to cause me many sins, because if a Spiritual Padre can do and consent to these things in his Holy Convent, what will I not do with this bad example?"[143]

Cocom's denunciation was motivated less by altruistic interest in protecting the Maya women of his town than by personal revenge. Padre Echazarreta had had him whipped and ordered the Maya *fiscales* to smear human excrement in his mouth.[144] Apparently, this punishment was for appearing drunk in public and swearing at the priest.[145] The Maya women involved in this case were at first reluctant to press the issue, but Cocom's denunciation forced them to testify. Although the priest's sexual abuse of the women was a fact, it was not the motivating factor in his denunciation. In fact, two of the women who were molested by the priest received much grief from their husbands for participating in the case.[146] The Maya women and one Spanish woman, whom the priest also molested, would have preferred to keep their molestation a secret. However, the denunciation of sexual impropriety proved an irresistible weapon for Félix Cocom and for his fellow members of the Uman town council, angered at Echazarreta's failure to pay them or feed the town employees for work conducted on the church.[147] In the end, the authorities removed the priest from his parish, not for his host of abuses and extortions, but rather for his few sexual indiscretions.

A large corpus of similar trials for clerical solicitation exists. The few examples given here illustrate how the Maya used denunciations of sexual abuse to rid themselves of clergymen who abused and punished them for their own supposed crimes against the Catholic faith.[148] Although sexual abuse almost certainly did occur in most of these cases, it was not until the Maya found themselves abused in other ways that they used the accusations of sexual impropriety against their clergymen. In most cases, the Maya accepted and even covered up the sexual indiscretions of their clergymen.[149] As long as the clergy did not engage in open violation of traditional Maya concepts of celibacy during the conducting of religious rituals (such as the mass, confession, baptism), the Maya would ignore their sexual impropriety. But if a clergyman attempted to punish the Maya of his parish too rigorously for their traditional religious practices or for what he viewed as their sexual immorality, the Maya would complain about the priest's hypocrisy. When local priests enforced the Spanish Catholic code of sexual morality, the Maya complained about the "priests' excessive fornication," as they did in the anonymous 1774 petition reproduced above. In many instances, the accusation of sexual immorality was the last of many attempts to remove abusive clerics. In the cases against Andrés Mexía and Luis Antonio de Echazarreta, a long series of complaints of economic and labor abuse preceded denunciations for solicitation. However, the Spanish authorities, themselves complicit in Mexía's and Echazarreta's corruption and extortion of the Maya, turned deaf ears to their complaints. Only after the Holy Office of the Inquisition got involved in solicitation cases did the Maya manage to remove abusive priests.

The Colonial Maya and the Sexual Conquest:
Who Conquered Whom?

The Maya response to the "sexual conquest" illustrates the ability of a militarily conquered people to exploit every weakness in the colonial system to preserve the traditional culture. The Maya who denounced their priests skillfully used the Spaniards' contradictory worlds of sexual morality against them. If we believe the testimonies of the Mayas who denounced their parish priests as pedophiles or sexual abusers, the picture we gain is one of rampant sexual promiscuity among the clergy. Although many of the testimonies may have been exaggerated, there is evidence of the clergy's lax morality in the frontier province of Yucatán. To argue that the Maya used accusations of sexual abuse in political and cultural self-defense is not to deny that abuse took place with alarming frequency throughout the colonial era. Maya testimony suggests a pattern of widespread sexual abuse, which appears to continue past independence in the nineteenth century.[150] This leads to the question of whether the Maya accusations are evidence of sexual deviance or brilliant use of Catholic sexual preoccupations and conceptions against the clergy. This question, however, ignores the most important arena of sexual conflict, where traditional Mayan sexuality collided with the contradictory Spanish worlds of morality and lasciviousness. In these encounters, sexually abused Mayas found themselves used as political weapons against the colonial system by Maya lords who resented their loss of sexual prerogatives.

In the end, one is left with the lingering and unanswerable question of who actually won the "sexual conquest." Perhaps the best way to explore this question is with Guido Ruggiero's metaphor of European sexual worlds. The first world of Spanish Catholic morality, with its virtues of chastity and virginity, clearly failed to conquer the Spanish, much less the Maya. The second world of Spanish lasciviousness found itself checked by the first world and also failed to "conquer" the Maya. At the same time, the Maya world of pre-Columbian sexuality found itself under assault by both worlds of Spanish sexual mores. In this culturally complex universe of sexual worlds there were neither winners nor losers, only an intermingling, colliding, and chaotic brew of clashing cultures that was the colonial Yucatán. The wreckage of worlds colliding, reforming, and colliding again is the best metaphor for the creation of a unique postconquest Maya culture that successfully protected itself from both the Spaniards' sexual aggression and their alien concepts of Catholic sexual morality, even as the conflict itself transformed Maya traditions.

Appendix

Table 3. Sample cases of clerical solicitation in the diocese of Yucatán, 1578–1808

Date	Accused Clergyman	Crime	Accuser	Incident	Outcome
1578	Andres Mexía, cleric [Yalcon, Ekpedz, Tetzal, others]	solicitation *ad turpia intra confessionem*	Maya cabildo and numerous Maya women from towns of Ekpedz and Tetzal	solicitation of sex and sexual relations in confessional	temporary removal
1580	Various clergymen	solicitation *ad turpia intra confessionem*	Maya women and men	solicitation of sex in confessional	permanent removal
1580	Fray Juan de Santanella, Franciscan	solicitation *ad turpia intra confessionem*	Maya women, town government	solicitation of sex in confessional, sexual molestation	permanent removal
1582	Fray Pedro Núñez, Franciscan	solicitation *ad turpia intra confessionem*	Various Maya women	solicitation of sex in confessional, molestation	permanent removal
1589	Andrés Mexía, cleric [Calotmul, Peto]	solicitation *ad turpia intra confessionem*	Maya women and cabildos of towns of Peto and Calotmul	solicitation of sex and rape in the confessional	permanent removal
1599	Fray Pedro de Vergara, Franciscan [Motul]	solicitation *ad turpia intra confessionem*	Maya women from the towns of Motul and Cacalchen	solicitation of sex in the confessional, rape, molestation	temporary removal, reinstatement

Table 3. Continued

Date	Accused Clergyman	Crime	Accuser	Incident	Outcome
1600	Bachiller Andrés Fernández de Castro, cleric	solicitation *ad turpia intra confessionem*	several Spanish and Maya women	solicitation of sex during confession	temporary removal
1605	Diego de La Camara, cleric	solicitation *ad turpia intra confessionem*	Maya women	solicitation of sex during confession	temporary removal
1610	Cristóbal de Valencia, cleric	solicitation *ad turpia intra confessionem, pecados contra natura, actos nefandos*	Maya men and boys from Hocaba, Sanlahcat, Hoctun	solicitation of sex during confession, homosexual acts, forced oral sex	permanent removal
1613	Fray Cristóbal de Moreno, Franciscan [Campeche]	solicitation *ad turpia intra confessionem*	Maya women	solicitation of sex in confessional	permanent removal
1621	Fray Francisco Gutiérrez, Franciscan	solicitation *ad turpia intra confessionem*	Maya women	solicitation of sex in the confessional	permanent removal
1624	Fray Julian Orbita, Franciscan	solicitation *ad turpia intra confessionem*	Maya and Spanish women	solicitation of sex in the confessional	permanent removal
1730	Bachiller Antonio Ramón de La Cueva, cleric	solicitation *ad turpia intra confessionem*	Bernardina Chan, Thomasa Huchim	solicitation of sex in the confessional	permanent removal

Table 3. Continued

Date	Accused Clergyman	Crime	Accuser	Incident	Outcome
1730	Bachiller don Félix de Malaver, cleric	solicitation *ad turpia intra confessionem*	Cecilia Uxul (Mama)	solicitation of sex in the confessional	permanent removal
1750	Bachiller Alfonso Pérez, cleric	solicitation *ad turpia intra confessionem*	Maya women	solicitation of sex in the confessional	permanent removal
1751	Fray Francisco Guzmán, Franciscan	solicitation *ad turpia intra confessionem*	Maya women	solicitation of sex in the confessional	permanent removal
1757	Bachiller Mateo González, cleric	solicitation *ad turpia intra confessionem*	Maya, mulatta, and Spanish women	solicitation of sex in the confessional	permanent removal
1777	Fray Francisco Guzmán, Franciscan [repeat offender]	solicitation *ad turpia intra confessionem*	Marcela de Campos, other women	solicitation of sex in the confessional, assault	died during trial
1780	Luis Antonio de Achazarreta, cleric	solicitation *ad turpia intra confessionem, fornicación,* other crimes	Francisca Cauiche, Manuela Pacheco, Félix Cocom	solicitation of sex in confessional, sexual misconduct	permanent removal
1780	Fray Pedro Ortega, Franciscan	solicitation *ad turpia intra confessionem*	Spanish, mestiza women	solicitation of sex in the confessional	permanent removal
1781	José Manzanilla, cleric	solicitation *ad turpia intra confessionem*	Maya, mulatta, and Spanish women	solicitation of sex in the confessional	died during trial

Table 3. Continued

Date	Accused Clergyman	Crime	Accuser	Incident	Outcome
1785	Pablo Ray-mondi, Italian cleric	solicita-tion *ad turpia intra confessionem*	Various Maya and mestiza women	solicitation of sex in the confessional	permanent removal
1794	Bachiller Julián Qui-jano, cleric [Bacalar]	solicitation *ad turpia intra con-fessionem, sodomía, acto nefando*	Francisco Uicab	solicitation of sex in the confessional, sodomy, homosexual acts	permanent removal
1795	Antonio Pacheco, cleric	solicita-tion *ad turpia intra confessionem*	Micaela Dzib	solicitation of sex in the confessional	died during trial
1797	Juan Dio-nisio Frasqui, cleric	solicita-tion *ad turpia intra confessionem*	Maya women	solicitation of sex in the confessional	permanent removal
1798	Bachiller José Rafael Jiménez, cleric [Tixkokob]	solicita-tion *ad turpia intra confessionem*	María Isabel Torralbo, mestiza	solicitation of sex in the confessional	permanent removal
1808	Fray Lorenzo de Avila, Franciscan	solicita-tion *ad turpia intra confessionem*	María Encarnación	solicitation of sex in the confessional	false accusation

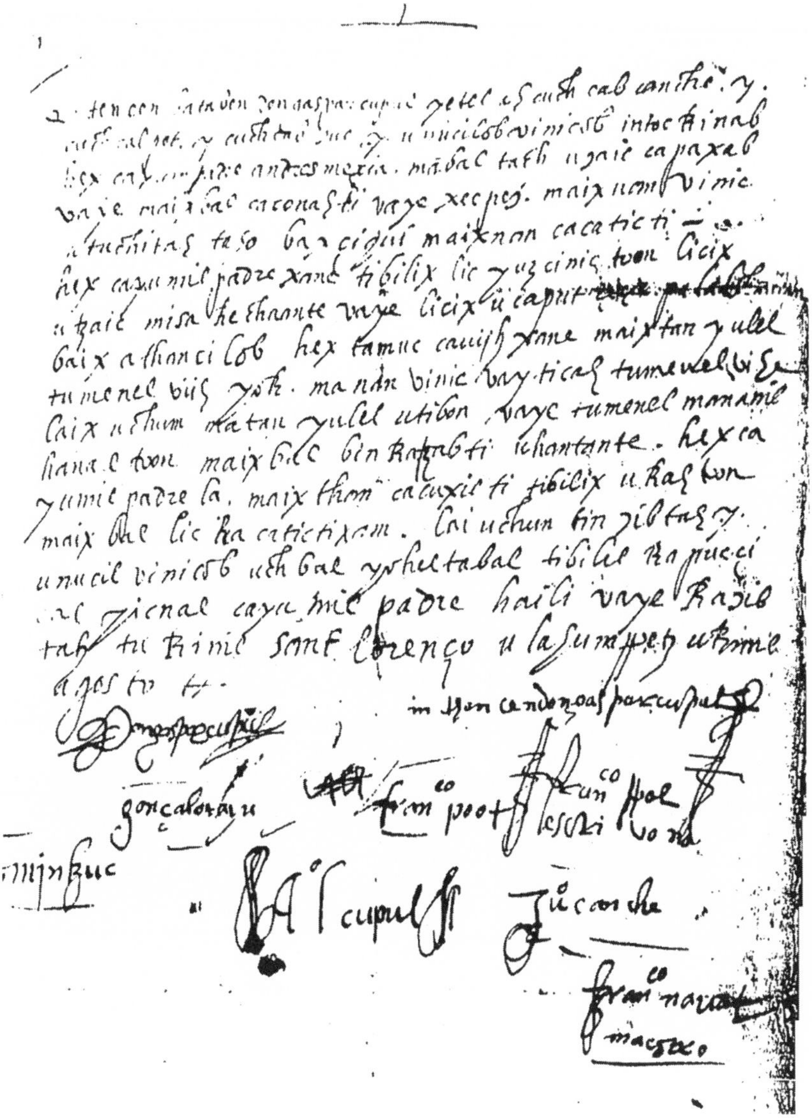

Figure 9. Petition from Maya batab and cabildo officials from the town of Ekpedz in protest against their priest and vicar, Padre Andrés Mexía (1589)

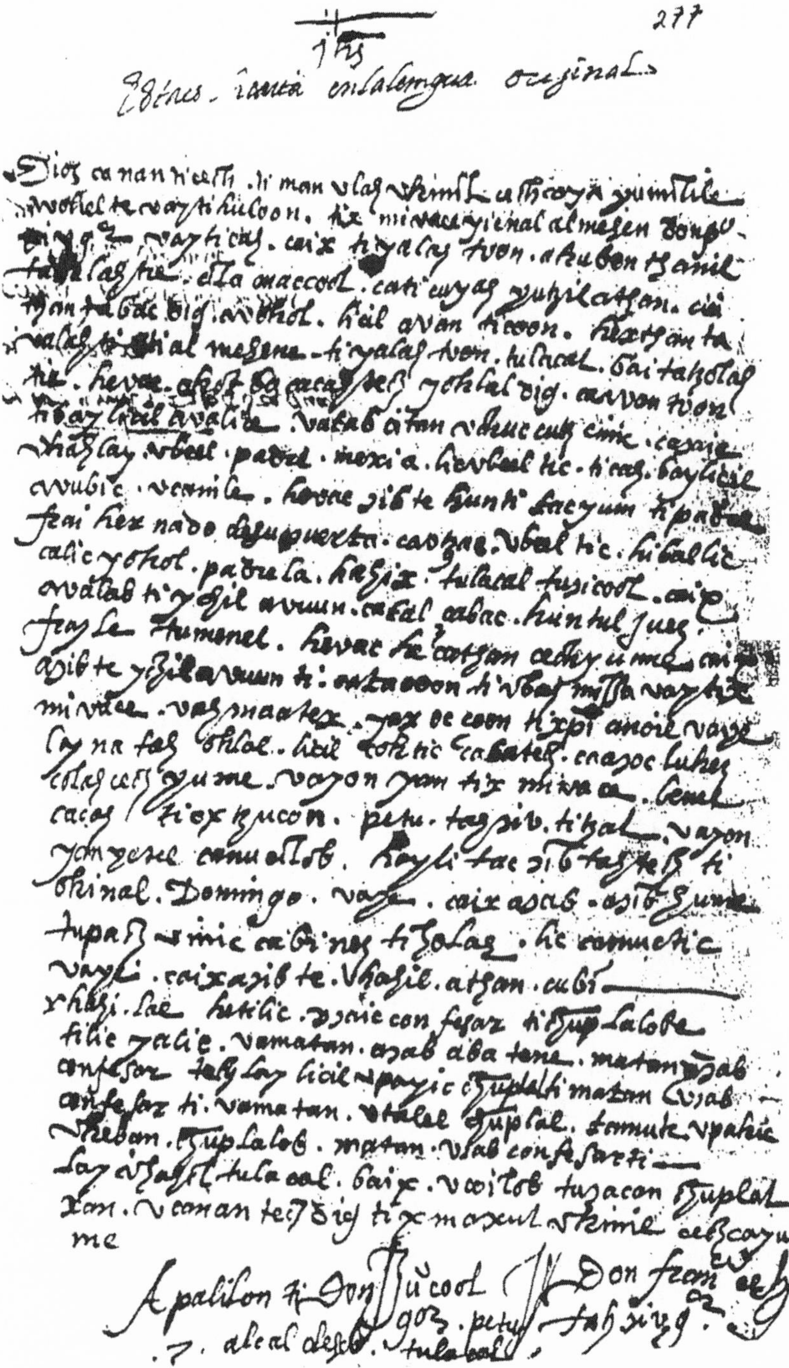

Figure 10. Petition from Maya batab and cabildo officials from the Maya town of Tixhualatun, complaining about sexual abuse from their parish priest, Andrés Mexía (1589)

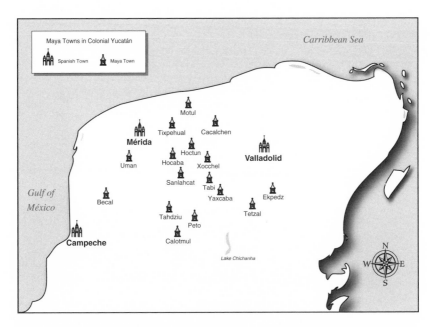

Figure 11. Maya towns discussed in this article. Map concept by the author. Copyright 2006 by Robin Gold/Forbes Mill Press

Notes

Spanish spellings have been modernized throughout, and, unless otherwise noted, all translations are mine.

1 "Petición en lengua maya de Clemente Ek y Francisco Ek su padre contra el cura beneficiado del pueblo de Hocaba, Cristóbal de Valencia por varias cosas indecentes" (6 July 1609), Archivo General de la Nación (hereafter AGN), Ramo de Inquisición, legajo 472, expediente 5, fols. 1v–3r.

2 AGN, Ramo de Inquisición, legajo 472, expediente 5, fol. 2v.

3 "Testimonio y declaración de Clemente Ek en contra de su cura Cristóbal de Valencia" (6 July 1609), AGN, Ramo de Inquisición, legajo 472, expediente 5, fol. 10r.

4 Ibid., fols. 10r–10v.

5 "Mandamiento de prisión contra Padre Cristóbal de Valencia hecha por su paternidad Fr. Fernando de Nava, comisario del Santo Oficio" (6 July 1609), AGN, Ramo de Inquisición, legajo 472, expediente 5, fols. 4r–4v. As the commissary's reaction illustrates, the ecclesiastical authorities were especially adamant about rooting out "sodomy," the "nefarious act," or any type of homosexual relations between clergymen and parishioners. For a complete study of Christian intolerance of and historical views on homosexuality, see David F. Greenberg and Marcia H. Bystryn, "Christian Intolerance of Homo-

sexuality," *American Journal of Sociology* 88 (1982): 515–48. Also, for the case of colonial Latin America, see Federico Garza Carvajal, "An Emasculation of the 'Perfect Sodomy' or Perceptions of Manliness in the Harbours of Andalucia and Colonial Mexico City, 1560–1699" (paper presented at the 1998 Latin American Studies Association Meeting, Chicago, 24–26 September 1998). For an earlier discussion of the connection between the Christian concept of "crimes against nature" and homosexual behavior, see F. E. Frenkel, "Sex-Crime and Its Socio-historical Background," *Journal of the History of Ideas* 25.3 (1964): 333–52.

6 Especially damning evidence from several of Padre Valencia's younger male parish assistants (such as his sacristans and other acolytes) pointed to his abuse of small children. For several examples, see "Testimonio de Pablo Chan, indio vecino del pueblo de Hoctun, en contra de los abusos de Padre Cristóbal de Valencia" (July 1609), AGN, Ramo de Inquisición, legajo 472, expediente 5, 5 fols. See also "Denuncia de Pedro Couoh de Sahcaba, sacristán del dicho pueblo, en contra de los abusos de Padre Cristóbal de Valencia" (July 1609), AGN, Ramo de Inquisición, legajo 472, expediente 5, 6 fols.

7 For a few of the more than one hundred denunciations, see "Testimonio y declaración de Juan May, vecino de Tixpehual, contra Padre Cristóbal de Valencia" (July 1609), AGN, Ramo de Inquisición, legajo 472, expediente 5, fols. 11v–13r; see also "Presentación de capítulos y cargas en contra del padre Cristóbal de Valencia hecha por los indios del pueblo de Hocaba" (August 1609), legajo 472, expediente 5, fols. 13v–17r; and "Petición del cacique y oficiales del pueblo de Xocchel en contra de su cura Padre Cristóbal de Valencia" (July 1609), legajo 472, expediente 5, fols. 17r–32r.

8 According to canon law and tradition, parish priests who had concubines or engaged in illicit sex had to be warned three times by the local bishop before he could remove them from office. For specific examples of Spanish custom and law concerning the sexual immorality of clergymen, see the statutes of the *Siete Partidas* in *The Medieval Church: The World of Clerics and Laymen*, vol. 1 of *Las Siete Partidas*, trans. Samuel Parsons Scott, ed. Robert I. Burns, S.J. (Philadelphia, 2001), 100–103. See also the decrees concerning sexual offenses, clerical celibacy, and misconduct in the Council of Trent's proceedings; Ignacio López de Ayala, *El sacrosanto y ecuménico concilio de Trento* (Mexico City, 1855). For the case of New Spain (Mexico), see Mariano Galván Rivera, *Concilio III provincial mexicano celebrado en México el año de 1585* (Mexico City, 1859). For specific Yucatec examples of these ecclesiastical regulations, see "Sínodo diocesano celebrado por Su Señoría Ilustrísima el Dr. Juan Gómez de Parada" (1721), Archivo General de Indias, Seville, Spain (hereafter AGI), Audiencia de México, legajo 1030. See also "Sínodo diocesano celebrado en el año de 1737 en el obispado de Yucatán" (1737), AGI, Audiencia de México, legajo 3168. This laxity in dealing with the clergy's sexual offenses was not a New World phenomenon: even in Europe before the reforms of the Council of Trent, the church turned a blind eye to all but the most open and scandalous violations of the vows of celibacy. For the best and most complete study of the concepts of sex and sexuality and the dilemma between sexual practices and church doctrine, see Asunción Lavrin, "Sexuality in Colonial Mexico: A Church Dilemma," in *Sexuality and Marriage in Colonial Latin America*, ed. Asunción Lavrin (Lincoln, NE, 1989),

47–95. For a good description of the European reality, see Merry E. Weisner-Hanks, *Christianity and Sexuality in the Early Modern World: Regulating Desire, Reforming Practice* (London, 2000), 118–21. For other discussions of the historical trajectory of Christian intolerance and laxity, see Christie Davies, "Sexual Taboos and Social Boundaries," *American Journal of Sociology* 87 (1982): 1032–63.

9 To date the most complete discussion of solicitation in the confessional is Stephen Haliczer, *Sexuality in the Confessional: A Sacrament Profaned* (New York, 1996). See also Jorge René González M., "Clérigos solicitantes, perversos de la confesión," in *De la santidad a la perversión, o de porqué no se cumplía la ley de Dios en la sociedad novohispana*, ed. Sergio Ortega (Mexico City, 1986), 239–52. For a study of the types of punishments and censures given to *solicitantes*, see Solange Alberro, "El discurso inquisitorial sobre los delitos de bigamia, poligamia y de solicitación," in Alberro et al., *Seis ensayos sobre el discurso colonial relativo a la comunidad doméstica: Matrimonio, familia y sexualidad a través de los cronistas del siglo XVI, el Nuevo Testamento y el Santo Oficio de la Inquisición* (Mexico City, 1980), 215–26.

10 "Repuesta y confesión del padre Cristóbal de Valencia a las cargas hechas contra el por los Mayas del pueblo de Hocaba y su partido" (1 October 1609), AGN, Ramo de Inquisición, legajo 472, expediente 5, fols. 117r–34r.

11 For an excellent analysis of Renaissance sex and sexuality, see Guido Ruggerio, *The Boundaries of Eros: Sex Crime and Sexuality in Renaissance Venice* (Oxford, 1985). See also Ruggerio, *Binding Passions: Tales of Magic, Marriage, and Power at the End of the Renaissance* (Oxford, 1993).

12 As Weisner-Hanks posits in *Christianity and Sexuality*, the term *sexuality* itself is "a more problematic word, because no one in the centuries I am discussing used it" (3). She also notes aptly that the term *sexuality* did not enter the English language until 1800. In this article as well, I use the term *sexuality* as a construct to mean, as Weisner-Hanks describes it generally, "the possession or exercise of sexual functions, desires, etc." It is also interesting to note that the word or concept of *sexual* did not enter Spanish dictionaries until 1843; see *Diccionario de la lengua castellana por la Real Academia Española*, 9th ed. (Madrid, 1843), 666. The earliest use of the term *sexo* appears in the 1739 version of the dictionary, but here it merely conveys the meaning of "male and female gender"; see Real Academia Española, *Diccionario de la lengua castellana, en que se explica el verdadero sentido de las voces, su naturaleza y calidad, con las frases o modos de hablar, los proverbios o refranes, y otras cosas convenientes al uso de la lengua*, vol. 6 (Madrid, 1739), 106. It was not until the 1984 Spanish dictionary that the term *sexo* became associated with the sexual organs and the study of human sexuality (*sexología*).

13 "There is always a licit sexual culture side by side with an illicit one liable to persecution and punishment, and in between the two a grey area, often a very large one, in which the two come together." Lawrence Stone, *The Past and the Present Revisited* (London, 1987), 350; cited in Brett Kahr, "The History of Sexuality: From Ancient Polymorphous Perversity to Modern Genital Love," in *Journal of Psychohistory* 26 (1999): 764–78.

14 The documents in the inquisitorial record are invaluable, regardless of any possible bias or clerical lens through which testimony was collected. Things so private and concealed as sexual acts leave scant evidence in the historical

record, and even less in the archaeological remains of ancient cultures. We know that most sexual relations considered "normal" took place behind closed doors, or in private places, with no witnesses other than the participants themselves, almost none of whom left any record of their encounters. Even modern science is incapable of revealing any real details of sexual practices and sexuality in the skeletal record of past societies. Similarly, most historical sources are also silent concerning sex. Most colonial documents in New Spain (even letters and diaries) contain no references to sex or sexuality. When sexual relations are hinted at in the documentary record, the documents were most often written by men. The testimony of young Maya women in these inquisitorial trials, for instance, is thus an incredibly valuable source that may give us some notion of colonial Maya women's experiences, attitudes, and understandings of sexual relations and sexuality.

15 For a more in-depth examination of the history of sexual misconduct in the confessional in colonial Yucatán, see John F. Chuchiak, "Secrets behind the Screen: *Solicitantes* in the Colonial Diocese of Yucatán, 1570–1785," in *Religion in New Spain: Varieties of Colonial Religious Experience*, ed. Susan Schroeder and Stafford Poole (Albuquerque, NM, forthcoming).

16 The modern word *perversion* describes those types of human behavior that established authorities consider to deviate from what is orthodox or normal. It was originally defined as a "deviation from the original meaning or doctrine," literally a "turning aside" from the norm. Thus sexual perversity would mean in the colonial context the deviation from the norms of sexual relations. The Spanish term *perversidad*, for instance, was glossed as meaning "a great evil or corruption of customs and manners, or of the proper conduct or quality." Someone who was *perverso* was believed to be "totally evil, defective in his actions, depraved in his customs and obligations to his proper state"; *Diccionario de la lengua castellana* (1739), vol. 5, 238.

17 See LeBaron, "Sexual Relations," 1.

18 See Pete Sigal, introduction to *From Moon Goddesses to Virgins: The Colonization of Yucatecan Maya Sexual Desire* (Austin, TX, 2000), xiii–xv.

19 See ibid., 8–10. Much has been written recently concerning sexuality and gender in the context of the archaeological record of Classic Maya society. Especially in surviving portrayals and iconography in several recently uncovered murals and other ceramic pottery, themes of Classic and pre-Classic Maya sexuality and sexual intercourse are prevalent.

20 According to Sigal, "There is no evidence that the Maya would have considered these sexual, and for yet others (e.g., ritualized intercourse between humans and gods), there is no place in modern Western discourse" (ibid., 10).

21 In many of the *relaciones* of Maya towns along the coasts, the respondents remarked that the Indian women went about bare breasted, while those of the interior described them as wearing a triangular garment (*huipil*) that covered their breasts. For a more detailed description and comparison, see Martín Sánchez, "Relación de Dzindzantun" (1581), in Mercedes De la Garza, *Relaciones histórico-geográficas de Yucatán*, 2 vols. (Mexico City, 1983): "Los hombres y mujeres se labraban por bien parecer, como las más veces andaban desnudos, y se embijaban cada día con tierra colorada" (1:413).

22 See "Relación de Tabi y Chunhuhub" (1581), in De la Garza, *Relaciones histórico-geográficas de Yucatán*. Here the encomendero wrote that "the Maya

married when they were older and they did not have more than one wife . . . and they were enemies of the vices of the flesh which they took to be great sins . . . and they punished adulterers both male and female with the death penalty" (1:164).

23 Alonso Julián, "Relación de Tetzal y Textual" (1581), in De la Garza, *Relaciones histórico-geograficas de Yucatán*, 1:238.

24 Martín de Palomar, "Relación de Motul" (1579), in De la Garza, *Relaciones histórico-geograficas de Yucatán*, 1:270.

25 Juan Gutiérrez Picón, "Relación de Ekbalam" (1579), in De la Garza, *Relaciones histórico-geograficas de Yucatán*, 2:139.

26 See Palomar, "Relación de Motul," 1:270.

27 "Relación de Muxuppipp" (1579), in De la Garza, *Relaciones histórico-geograficas de Yucatán*, 1:378–79.

28 See Matthew Restall and John F. Chuchiak, "The Friar and the Mayas: Fr. Diego de Landa's *Relación de las cosas de Yucatán*," unpublished ms., 35. Or see Fr. Diego de Landa, *Yucatan before and after the Conquest*, ed. and trans. William Gates (New York, 1978 [1566]), 52.

29 See Gaspar Antonio Xiu, "Relación de los costumbres de los indios" (20 March 1582), AGI, Audiencia de México, legajo 110.

30 López de Cogolludo echoes Gaspar Antonio Xiu in his observations of Maya policing of sexuality: "They punish vices with rigor. . . . The man or woman who commits adultery received the death penalty by shooting them with arrows. . . . thus they abhorred this sin and they punished even noble and principal persons"; Fray Diego López de Cogolludo, *Los tres siglos de la dominación española en Yucatán, o Historia de esta provincia*, 2 vols. (Graz, Austria, 1971), 1:331.

31 Landa, *Yucatan before and after the Conquest*, 54–55.

32 Ibid., 54.

33 Ibid., 54.

34 See "Petición de don Diego Montejo, hijo natural de Francisco de Montejo, a don Carlos de Arellano para poder casar con Ana de Campos, viuda mujer que fue de Julián Doncel," 22 November 1571, private collection, Mérida.

35 "Instrucciones y ordenanzas para Francisco de Montejo el mozo sobre la conquista de Yucatán, hecha por el Adelantado en el Ciudad Real de Chiapas" (1540), AGI, Audiencia de México, legajo 299.

36 "Testimonio de Juan Bote en la residencia del Adelantado de Yucatán" (1549), AGI, Justicia, legajo 300, 5 folios.

37 Chilam Balam of Chumayel. See Munro Edmonson, *Heaven Born Merida and Its Destiny: The Book of Chilam Balam of Chumayel* (Austin, TX, 1986).

38 See the large number of testimonies and declarations in the residencia trials of Francisco de Montejo in "Residencia de Francisco de Montejo, gobernador de Chiapas, Yucatán y Cozumel por el Licenciado Juan Rogel, oidor de la Audiencia de los Confines" (1546–47), AGI, Justicia, legajo 300, 789 folios; see also "Residencia de los alcaldes mayors, regidores y escribanos de la villa de Valladolid de Yucatán, hecho por el Dr. Diego Quijada, gobernador de Yucatán" (1563), AGI, Justicia, legajo 244, 678 folios.

39 See various declarations of the conquistadors who participated in the logistics of conquest in Yucatán in "Pleito del Fiscal de su majestad contra Alonso López, Alcalde de Tabasco" (1541–45), AGI, Justicia, legajo 195.

40 Chilam Balam of Chumayel. See Edmonson, *Heaven Born Merida and Its Destiny*.

41 For more information concerning the roles of indigenous men and women in the conquest of Yucatán, see John F. Chuchiak, "Forgotten Allies: The Role of Native Mesoamerican Auxiliaries and *Indios Conquistadores* in the Conquest and Colonization of Yucatán, 1526–1697," in *Indian Conquistadors: Native Militaries in the Conquest of Mesoamerica*, ed. Michel Oudjik and Laura Matthew (Norman, OK, forthcoming).

42 There is evidence and testimony that Aguilar trafficked and sold or exchanged as prostitutes or concubines more than one hundred Indian women from several provinces to his fellow conquistadors of Yucatán. Alonso López, a supporter of Aguilar and the Montejos, is also said to have sold or sent more than two hundred pretty young Indian women to Yucatán and Campeche for similar purposes. "Testimonio de Francisco de Cuesta sobre los abusos hechos por Alonso López y otros españoles contra las indias naborías" (1545), AGI, Justicia, legajo 195, 5 folios.

43 "Testimonio de Francisco de Cuesta sobre los abusos hechos por Alonso López y otros españoles contra las indias naborías" (1542), AGI, Justicia, legajo 195, 5 folios.

44 "Testimonio de Diego Martin sobre los abusos hechos por Alonso López" (1541), AGI, Justicia, legajo 195, 4 folios.

45 "Testimonio de Alonso de Elvira sobre los abusos hechos por Alonso López y su robo de algunos indias naborías que tenia" (1541), AGI, Justicia, legajo 195, 5 folios.

46 "Testimonio de Juan de Ayllón en el proceso del fiscal de Su Majestad en contra de Alonso López" (1541), AGI, Justicia, legajo 195, 7 folios.

47 See various documents in "Residencia de Francisco de Montejo, gobernador de Chiapas, Yucatán y Cozumel por el Licenciado Juan Rogel, oidor de la Audiencia de los Confines" (1546–47), AGI, Justicia, legajo 300, 789 folios.

48 For Maya testimony concerning female Maya slaves as young as twelve and fourteen years old who were handed over to the conquistador Gaspar Pacheco by the Maya of the town of Calkini, see Tsubasa Okoshi Harada, "Los Canules: Un Análisis etnohistórico del códice de Calkini," PhD diss., Universidad Nacional Autónoma de México, 1992, 82–83.

49 Large numbers of illegitimate children (*hijos de la iglesia*) appear in the baptismal parish and convent registries, indicating a larger number of Maya children born out of wedlock in the later sixteenth century. See Michel Antiochiw, "Los Registros de Bautizo de Yucatán: Los Libros de Bautizo de Ticul, 1594–1635" in *Los Mayas de Ayer y Hoy, Memorias del Primer congreso Internacional de Cultura Maya*, ed. Alfredo Barrera Rubio and Ruth Gubler (Mérida, Mexico, 2005), 848–62.

50 See Sergio Quezada, *Pueblos y Caciques Yucatecos, 1550–1580* (Mexico City, 1992), 127–43.

51 See Diego Brizeño, "Relación de Tekal" (1579), in De la Garza, *Relaciones Histórico-Geográficas de Yucatán*, 1:440.

52 "Relación de Citilcum y Cabiche" (1579), in De la Garza, *Relaciones Histórico-Geográficas de Yucatán*, 1:182–83.

53 See Edmonson, *Heaven Born Merida and Its Destiny*, 109–10.

54 Ibid., 148.

55 Fray Diego López de Cogolludo, *Historia de Yucatán*, 3 vols. (Campeche, 1996 [1688]), 1:331.

56 See "Relación de Muxuppipp" (1581), in De la Garza, *Relaciones Histórico-Geograficas de Yucatán*, 1:377. Other Spaniards blamed the Maya's consumption of the alcoholic beverage *balché* for their sexual excesses and incest. For instance, Diego de Contreras commented that "it was because of their drunkenness that they had carnal access with their sisters, their daughters, and other relatives, and in order to avoid this great sin [the friars] took from and prohibited this wine to them"; see "Relación de Nabalam, Tahcabo, Cozumel" (1579), in De la Garza *Relaciones Histórico-Geograficas de Yucatán*, 2:187.

57 See "Relación y forma que el Lic. don Diego García de Palacio, oidor de la audiencia real de Guatemala, hizo para los que hubieren de visitar, contar, tasar y repartir en las provincias de este distrito" (1576), AGI, Audiencia de Guatemala, legajo 128. It is interesting to note that as late as 1813 parish priests in Yucatán continued to complain about incest and sexual encounters between relatives. See "Informe del cura de Yaxcaba sobre los indios de su beneficio" (1813), AGI, Audiencia de México, legajo 3068. Bachiller Baeza complained that "once they are married it is indispensable to observe their domestic lives. . . . and the priest should oblige them to set up a house apart from their parents, in order to avoid so many abuses and sins that would occur between fathers-in-law and their daughters-in-law, and even between fathers and daughters."

58 The Crown and church early on excluded the Indians from the jurisdiction of the Holy Office of the Inquisition and placed them under the jurisdiction of the episcopal courts of the Provisorato de Indios. See Richard E. Greenleaf, "The Inquisition and the Indians of New Spain: A Study in Jurisdictional Confusion," *Americas* 22 (1965): 138–66. For a complete study of the Provisorato de Indios in the diocese of Yucatán, see John F. Chuchiak, "The Indian Inquisition and the Extirpation of Idolatry: The Process of Punishment in the Provisorato de Indios of the Diocese of Yucatán, 1563–1821," PhD diss., Tulane University, 2000.

59 See "Avisos del muy ilustre y reverendísimo señor don Fray Francisco de Toral, obispo de Yucatán, para los padres curas y vicarios de este obispado" (n.d.), AGI, Audiencia de México, legajo 369, 12 fols.

60 "Las mujeres también son tan desvergonzadas y cada día se hacen mayores putas." "Relación de Dzonot" (1579), in De la Garza, *Relaciones Histórico-Geograficas de Yucatán*, 2:87.

61 "Las mujeres por el propio tenor son tan desvergonzadas, tanto que ellas propias se van en busca de los españoles, en sabiendo que en algún pueblo de indios los hay, especialmente las que han sido amigas de ellos." Juan Farfan el Viejo, "Relación de Kancopolche y Chochola" (1579), in De la Garza, *Relaciones Histórico-Geograficas de Yucatán*, 2:327.

62 "Instrucción que dio el juez provisor y vicario general de la provincia de Yucatán para los curas de almas y sus tenientes" (19 July 1765), Archivo Histórico del Arzobispado de Yucatán, Mérida (hereafter AHAY), Asuntos terminados, 5 fols. Earlier episcopal synods also focused on specific clerical preoccupations with the Maya's fornication, bestiality, and other "crimes against nature," such as sodomy (*pecado nefando*). See the documents of the synod of 1722, especially "Formula del edicto de pecados públicos que todos

los domingos primeros de Cuaresma se ha de publicar por los curas y vicarios de este obispado" (1722), AGI, Audiencia de México, legajo 1040, fols. 230r–32v.

63 See Matthew Restall, "The Runaway Slave and the Maya Postman: African-Maya Relations in Colonial Yucatan," (paper presented at the American Society for Ethnohistory conference, Portland, Oregon, November 1996).

64 See "Testimonio de Gaspar Pacheco en el juicio de residencia del Adelantado Francisco de Montejo" (1549), AGI, Justicia, legajo 300, 5 folios.

65 "Proceso contra Pedro Na, indio, por cometer actos contra natura teniendo acceso carnal con una gallina" (1563), AGI, Justicia, legajo 248, 30 fols.

66 "Testimonio de Juan Camal en contra de Pedro Na en el proceso contra acceso carnal con una gallina" (12 January 1563), AGI, Justicia, legajo 248; see also "Testimonio de Francisca Tun en el proceso contra Pedro Na" (12 January 1563), AGI, Justicia, legajo 248, 2 fols.

67 "Declaración del fiscal Gabriel Hernández en contra de Pedro Na por el crimen contra natura y el pecado nefando con una gallina" (14 January 1563), AGI, Justicia, legajo 248, 2 fols.

68 "Testimonio de la ejecución de la sentencia en contra de Pedro Na por el crimen del acto nefando con una gallina" (3 February 1563), AGI, Justicia, legajo 248, 2 fols.

69 Fr. Bernardo de Lizana, *Devocionario de Nuestra Señora de Izamal y conquista espiritual de Yucatán*, ed. René Acuña (Mexico City, 1995 [1633]), 67.

70 Ibid., 68.

71 López de Cogolludo, *Historia de Yucatán*, 1:93, gives the complete set of ordenanzas of Tomás López Medel.

72 Ibid.

73 Ibid.

74 Landa, *Yucatan before and after the Conquest*, 46.

75 "Testimonio de Juan Hernández, vecino de Mérida en el proceso contra pecados nefandos" (15 January 1563), AGI, Justicia, legajo 248, 3 fols.

76 See "Parecer y testimonio del padre Fr. Juan de Benavides, guardián del convento de San Antonio de Ichbalche en las Montañas" (1 February 1615), AGI, Audiencia de México, legajo 138, 8 fols.

77 Louise M. Burkhart, *The Slippery Earth: Nahua-Christian Moral Dialogue in Sixteenth-Century Mexico* (Tucson, AZ, 1989), 25.

78 Ibid., 152.

79 Ibid., 153.

80 See Sigal, *Moon Goddesses to Virgins*, 94–128. See also Burkhart, *Slippery Earth*, 154.

81 For a complete discussion of the Maya priesthood and the colonial survival of traditional Maya religious practices, see John F. Chuchiak, "Pre-conquest *Ah Kinob* in a Colonial World: The Extirpation of Idolatry and the Survival of the Maya Priesthood in Colonial Yucatán, 1563–1697," in *Maya Survivalism: Acta Mesoamericana*, vol. 12, ed. Ueli Hostettler and Matthew Restall (Markt Schwaben, Germany, 2001), 135–60. For specific information on the ritual celibacy of the Maya priesthood, see Sigal, *Moon Goddesses to Virgins*, 18–21.

82 See Lizana, *Devocionario*. The original sixteenth-century image of the Virgin

of Izamal was a focus of Maya cult worship until it was destroyed by fire in 1829.

83 Chilam Balam of Chumayel. See Edmonson, *Heaven Born Merida and Its Destiny*.

84 The Chilam Balam of Tusik contains more than fifteen parables and examples concerning clerical conceptions of the sins of lust and fornication. The Chilam Balam of Ixil and of Chan Cah have similar Maya passages discussing, commenting, and warning about "the sins of the flesh." See Héctor M. Calderón, *Manuscritos de Chilam Balam de Tekax y Nah* (Mexico City, 1981); and the *Chilam Balam of Tusik* (Mexico City, 1984). See also Ralph L. Roys, "The Book of Chilam Balam of Ixil," *Notes on Middle American Archaeology and Ethnology* 3, no. 75 (1946): 90–103.

85 Catholic attempts to control and reshape Maya sexual practices have recently been discussed in Sigal, *Moon Goddesses to Virgins* (2000). Catholic confession manuals were useful tools to police the sexuality of Mesoamerica's indigenous people. In these manuals, the clergy attempted to "conquer," "reform," and reshape indigenous conceptions of sex, sexuality, eroticism, and acceptable moral behavior. Several recent studies have analyzed these confession manuals in order to understand more about both colonial Catholic and indigenous sexual practices and sexual morality. For a few examples, see Luis Arias González and Agustín Vivas Moreno, "Los manuales de confesión para indígenas del siglo XVI: Hacia un nuevo modelo de formación de la conciencia," *Estudios de historia moderna* 10–11 (1992–93): 245–59. These confession manuals, they argue, reveal much about the interaction of priests and indigenous peoples and the mind-sets of both groups. For another example of the use of confession and confession manuals to dominate and change indigenous conceptions of eroticism and sexuality, see Sylvia Marcos, "Missionary Activity in Latin America: Confession Manuals and Indigenous Eroticism," in *Religious Transformations and Socio-political Change: Eastern Europe and Latin America*, ed. Luther Martin (New York, 1993), 237–53. Similarly, for the now classic study of the use of the sacrament of confession and as a form of domination and social control, see Serge Gruzinski, "Individualization and Acculturation: Confession among the Nahuas of Mexico from the Sixteenth to the Eighteenth Century," in *Sexuality and Marriage in Colonial Latin America*, ed. Asunción Lavrin (Lincoln, NE, 1989), 96–117. Gruzinski described the sacrament of Christian confession of sin as a form of ideological control and subjugation. A similar interpretation of the confessional as a tool of colonial domination is found in Jorge Klor de Alva, "Sin and Confession among the Colonial Nahuas: The Confessional as a Tool for Domination," in *Memorias de la Reunión de Historiadores mexicanos y norteamericanos*, Oaxaca, October 1985 (Mexico City, 1992), vol. 1, 91–101. Klor de Alva also portrays Christian confession as a means of social control. He was one of the first to suggest that questions posed in Nahuatl-language confessionals hold vital information about indigenous sexuality and worldviews.

86 The entire title of the *Confesionario* is illustrative of the early clergy's goals in controlling and dominating Yucatec Maya sexual practices: *Confesionario breve, para confesar a los indios, ponense las preguntas ordinarias en la lengua y la de Castilla, según las culpas que acostumbran cometer y en que ordinariamente pecan y se les pregunta*, private collection, Mérida, Yucatán.

87 These questions and others related to confessing sexual sins are found in ibid.,
234v–35v.
88 For various colonial definitions of the word *keban*, see *Calepino de Motul:
Diccionario maya-español*, vol. 1 (Mexico City: UNAM, 1995), 417–18.
89 See Burkhart, *Slippery Earth*, 23.
90 *Calepino de Motul*, 80.
91 Quoted from Sigal, *Moon Goddesses to Virgins*, 90. The same document and
incident is also discussed in Matthew Restall, *The Maya World: Yucatec Culture and Society, 1550–1850* (Stanford, CA, 1997), 144. Restall also discusses
this document in "He Wished It in Vain: Subordination and Resistance among
Maya Women in Post-conquest Yucatán," *Ethnohistory* 42 (1995): 577–94.
The original can be found in the *Documentos de Tabi*, held in Tulane University's Latin American Library.
92 Several instances of Maya women using the Spanish system to protect themselves from Maya noblemen and Spaniards are found in various documents
submitted by the bishop of Yucatán against the sexual misconduct of parish
priests and Franciscan friars. See especially "Informaciones del obispo de
Yucatán contra los abusos de algunos frailes y clérigos del obispado" (1702),
AGI, Audiencia de México, legajo 1035.
93 "Carta del Dr. don Gaspar Joseph Rodríguez Vizario, clérigo presbítero del
obispado de Yucatán sobre los beneficios de la provincia y su mala conducta"
(1700), AGI, Audiencia de México, legajo 312, 7 fols.
94 See Council of Trent, session 14, canon 2, cited in D. Ignacio López de Ayala,
*El Sacrosanto y Ecuménico Concilio de Trento Traducida al idioma Castellano,
Librería de Garnier Hermanos.*
95 Mariano Galvan Rivera, *Concilio III Provincial Mexicano celebrado en Mexico
el año de 1585* (Mexico City, 1859).
96 Ibid., 139.
97 See "Avisos del muy ilustre y reverendísimo señor don Fr. Francisco de Toral,
primer obispo de Yucatán, Cozumel y Tabasco, del consejo de Su Majestad,
para los padres curas y vicarios de este obispado y para los que en su ausencia
quedan en las iglesias" (1563), AGI, Audiencia de México, legajo 369.
98 Galván Rivera, *Concilio III provincial mexicano*.
99 See "Instrucción que dio el juez provisor y vicario general para los curas de
almas y sus tenientes" (1785), AHAY, Asuntos terminados, 5 fols.: "Item . . .
Desde la septuagésima deberán concurrir todos juntos con el cura para des-
pachar la feligresía en el cumplimiento del precepto anual orando así todos
juntos por todo el partido para el desahogo de las conciencias de los feligreses,
sin permitirse de ninguna manera que el Teniente que reside en el pueblo sea el
que despache las confesiones de el por sí solo, pues cuando por alguna causa
no puedan concurrir todos el cura propio los deberá mudar enviando al uno,
al otro pueblo y así con los demás en lo que se le encarga al citado cura la
conciencia por ser la materia de tanta gravedad. . . . durante la semana saliese
cada uno torna a su residencia esta misma concurrencia deberán tener el día
de Corpus para la mayor solemnidad de tan venerable sacramento y el día del
Patrón la misma y no otro día de los que llaman de Provincia."
100 Haliczer's *Sexuality in the Confessional* remains one of the best treatments of
the crime of solicitation.
101 Scott and Burns, *Medieval Church*, 102.

102 Ibid., 102.

103 For several of the more important edicts of the Holy Office in Mexico against the crime of solicitation, see "Edicto de fe de los Inquisidores de México contra el crimen de la solicitación" (30 April 1620), AGN, Edictos, legajo 1, fols. 2–3; "Edicto de fe de los Inquisidores de México contra los solicitantes" (13 May 1624), AGN, Edictos, legajo 3, fols. 45–46; "Edicto de fe de los Inquisidores de México contra los solicitantes" (13 May 1651), AGN, Indiferente General, 3 fols. For a study of these edicts and the crime of solicitation, see Jorge René González Marmolejo, "El delito de solicitación en los edictos del tribunal del Santo Oficio, 1576–1819," in Solange Alberro et al., *Seis ensayos sobre el discurso colonial relativo a la comunidad doméstica: Matrimonio, familia y sexualidad a través de los cronistas del siglo XVI, el Nuevo Testamento y el Santo Oficio de la Inquisición* (Mexico City, 1980), 169–211.

104 See the various decrees concerning the sacrament of penance and the modes and requirements for confessors and confessionals in D. Ignacio López de Ayala, *El Sacrosanto y ecuménico Concilio de Trento traducida al idioma castellano* (Mexico City, 1855).

105 Definition of *solicitation* in *The Catholic Encyclopedia*, (New York, 1911). However, the definition and scope of the crime of solicitation was often confused by the bishops and inquisitors who investigated these crimes. For several instances in which commissaries of the Inquisition and bishops inquired and sought information concerning the definition and methods to define the actual crime of solicitation, see "Carta de Fr. Diego de Landa, obispo de Yucatán, consultando sobre casos de solicitación y averiguando sobre su jurisdicción" (1578), AGN, Ramo de Inquisición, legajo 90, expediente 8, 3 fols. See also "Carta con dudas del Maestro Alonso Martín Bermejo, comisario del Santo Oficio en Yucatán sobre confesores solicitantes" (1580), AGN, Ramo de Inquisición, legajo 85, expediente 8, 2 fols.

106 In terms of the surviving documents concerning the crime of solicitation committed by Yucatec clergy, it appears that the term *solicitación* was used most often to describe soliciting sex from a parishioner in the priest's private chamber or the sacristy. Many of the cases involved the solicitation of sex while confessing women and men in these places. See table 3 in the appendix for descriptions of specific cases under study. Many of the major cases against priests and friars who solicited sex in the confessional can be found in the following archives: AGN, Ramo de Inquisición, legajos 35, 69, 85, 90, 122, 123, 249, 281, 288, 295, 303, 337, 926, 935, 954, 988, 1046, 1250, 1284, 1369, 1373, 1380, 1468; also many documents relating to *solicitantes* in Yucatán are found in AGI, Audiencia de México, legajos 1030–36, 3063, 3068; similar documents relating to Inquisition trials and proceedings are found in Archivo Histórico Nacional, Madrid (hereafter AHN), Inquisición (1735); AHN, Competencias.

107 All parish priests and confessors needed an explicit license from their bishop in order to conduct and take confessions. In the diocese of Yucatán, a special license was required to confess both women and men. Each cleric or priest was examined and periodically inspected during pastoral visitations to ensure that he did not abuse the sacrament of penance and solicit sex in the confessional. During the pastoral visitations of the province, the Yucatec bishops issued a series of questions to the Maya town officials and principal

residents of each town. The most important questions focused on the lifestyle and abuses of the clergy. The bishops wanted to know if "the Indians know of or have heard that the priests and their assistants have women or have engaged in illicit relations with them publicly or secretly." See "Interrogatorio por el cual deben ser examinados los sujetos mas dignos de cada pueblo sobre las conductas y operaciones de sus curas de alma," in "Visita pastoral al pueblo de Oxkutzcab" (1782), AHAY, Visitas pastorales, legajo 1, expediente 4, fols. 13r–15v. The answers to all thirty questions are then recorded. Most often the Maya hid the sexual crimes of their clergy, but in a few instances they revealed their priests' sexual indiscretions.

108 For other excellent studies that examine the relationship between indigenous people and their parish priests and the conflicts that arose between them, see William B. Taylor, *Magistrates of the Sacred: Priests and Parishioners in Eighteenth-Century Mexico* (Stanford, CA, 1996). See also Robert Haskett, "Not a Pastor, but a Wolf: Indigenous-Clergy Relations in Early Cuernavaca and Taxco," *Americas* 50 (1994): 293–336.

109 "Expediente de las quejas de los indios del pueblo de Becal contra su cura Br. Bernardo Echiverria" (1768), AGI, Audiencia de México, legajo 3053, 63 fols.

110 Restall (*Maya World*, 161) was one of the first to note that this petition served as a form of revenge against what the Maya perceived as the hypercritically punitive reaction of Spanish priests to Maya sexual activity. Restall argues that the issue was control, for the "Maya view priests as outsiders without the authority or status to pass judgement and demand punishment over this aspect of Maya life." However, I believe that the Mayas at heart in this petition were not challenging the priests' authority but getting back at the entire Spanish system of sexual morality that had attempted to "conquer" Maya sexuality and encompass it within the more restrictive sexual morality of Spanish Catholicism. Restall does note that the allegation of "public sexual behavior" was a potent weapon. Thus, Spanish Catholic fears of "public scandal" meant that these types of charges could lead to the removal of a priest. For more detailed discussions of the removal of priests for solicitation, see González M., "Clérigos solicitantes."

111 The original document can be found in AGN, Ramo de Inquisición, legajo 1046. This fascinating Maya petition has been examined and analyzed previously by Restall (*Maya World*) and Sigal (*Moon Goddesses to Virgins*). Although exceptionally vivid in its detail and the quality of its sarcastic prose, this document is not unique. Other similar petitions also remain in the archives; see AGI, Escribanía de Camara, legajos 313B (1630, 1660, 1667, 1670, and 1671), 317 (1660–79); and AGN, Ramo de Inquisición (1578–89), legajo 69, expediente 472.

112 Sigal, *Moon Goddesses to Virgins*, 65.

113 Restall (*Maya World*, 141–42) notes the Inquisition official's horror and his notations in reaction to the petition. The original is found in AGN, Ramo de Inquisición, legajo 1187, expediente. 2, fols. 59–61.

114 See AHAY, Visitas pastorales (1781), legajo 1.

115 See Sigal, *Moon Goddesses to Virgins*, 75–76. The original Maya petition is found in AGN, Ramo de Inquisición (1589), legajo 69.

116 Andrés Mexía was partially exonerated when he proved to the Inquisitors

that many of the Maya who declared against him were ones he had punished for idolatry and other "faltas de doctrina." Also, he stated that the Maya denounced him under the inducement and sinister plot of their local Spanish encomendero, whom Mexía had punished for his own sexual indiscretions with two local Maya women. Mexía declared in his own defense, "All that they said against me was done out of the sinister inducement of their Encomendero, who wishes me ill because I conducted a trial against him for living in concubinage in the said town with two married Indian women, and for this reason he has had animosity, and he has openly stated that he would do anything in his power to harm me." See response to charge no. 46 in "Respuestas del clérigo Andrés Mexía contra los cargos que le hicieron los indios de su partido" (1578), AGN, Ramo de Inquisición, legajo 69, expediente 5, fol. 191v.

117 "Respuestas del clérigo Andrés Mexía" (1578), AGN, Ramo de Inquisición, legajo 69, expediente 5, fol. 192r.

118 Taken from Restall, *Maya World*, 164. The original Maya document can be found in the Inquisition trial against Andrés Mexía. See AGN, Inquisición (1589), legajo 69, expediente 5.

119 See "Testimonio y declaración de María Tun, india del pueblo de Peto, contra su cura Andrés Mexía" (1589), AGN, Ramo de Inquisición, legajo 69, expediente 5, fols. 318r–19r; see also "Testimonio y declaración de María Col, india del pueblo de Peto, contra su cura Andrés Mexía" (1589), legajo 69, expediente 5, fols. 319r–20r; and "Testimonio y declaración de Mencia Puc, india del pueblo de Peto, contra su cura Andrés Mexía" (1589), legajo 69, expediente 5, fols. 320r–21r. Other testimonies and denunciations are found in the same volume, AGN, Inquisición (1578–89), legajo 69, expediente 5, fols. 268–78.

120 See "Petición de Andrés Mexía beneficiado de Calamud y Peto en que se opone de enemistad contra los indios que le han informado contra el delito de solicitud y presenta recaudos como ya son amigos" (1589), AGN, Ramo de Inquisición, legajo 69, expediente 5, fols. 273r–74v.

121 "Sentencia y votos hecho por los inquisidores de México contra el clérigo presbítero Andrés Mexía por el crimen de solicitación a sus hijas de confesión" (13 July 1590), AGN, Ramo de Inquisición, legajo 69, expediente 5, fol. 325r.

122 "Carta del provincial del orden de San Francisco, Fr. Alonso de Río Frío dando cuenta de unas peticiones de algunas indios en contra de Fr. Pedro de Vergara por el delito de solicitación" (1599), AGN, Ramo de Inquisición, legajo 249, expediente 1, 3 fols.

123 "Declaración de Ana Kuk, en contra de Fr. Pedro Vergara por el crimen de solicitación" (16 November 1598), AGN, Ramo de Inquisición, legajo 249, expediente 1, fol. 12.

124 "Declaración de Beatriz Dzib, en contra de Fr. Pedro Vergara por el crimen de solicitación" (16 November 1598), AGN, Ramo de Inquisición, legajo 249, expediente 1.

125 "Declaración de María Cocom, en contra de Fr. Pedro Vergara por el crimen de solicitación" (16 November 1598), AGN, Ramo de Inquisición, legajo 249, expediente 1.

126 "Carta del provincial del orden de San Francisco en Yucatán sobre el caso de

solicitación en contra de Fr. Pedro de Vergara" (1598), AGN, Ramo de Inquisición, legajo 249, expediente 1.

127   "Carta de Fr. Juan de Santa María, guardián del convento de Campeche en contra Fr. Pedro de Vergara y sus abusos de los indios" (14 March 1599), AGN, Ramo de Inquisición, legajo 249, expediente 1.

128   "Carta de Fr. Alonso de Río Frío contra Fr. Pedro de Vergara escrita a los Señores Inquisidores de México" (16 November 1599), AGN, Ramo de Inquisición, legajo 249, expediente 1, fol. 26.

129   "Carta del visitador Fr. Miguel López acerca del caso de Fr. Pedro de Vergara con información sobre el odio que le tienen los indios que han declarado contra el en el caso de solicitación" (20 October 1600), AGN, Ramo de Inquisición, legajo 249, expediente 1.

130   "Carta de Fr. Miguel López" (20 October 1600), AGN, Ramo de Inquisición, legajo 249, expediente 1. Interestingly, this is the last document in the Inquisition trial against him. There is no record of any punishment administered. No doubt the Inquisitors believed that the Mayas had testified falsely to remove their priest. Vergara would go on to serve in the Franciscan missions of the Sierra, where he appeared around 1603.

131   "Declaración y testimonio hecho por Pablo Chan, indio natural del pueblo de Hoctun, en contra de su cura Cristóbal de Valencia" (July 1609), AGN, Ramo de Inquisición, legajo 472, expediente 5, 4 fols.

132   "Confesión del clérigo Cristóbal de Valencia con sus respuestas a los cargos impuestos contra el por los indios de su partido" (1609), AGN, Ramo de Inquisición, legajo 472, expediente 5, 14 fols.

133   "Carta del obispo de Yucatán sobre sus relaciones con el gobernador" (10 October 1606), AGI, Audiencia de México, legajo 369, 4 fols.

134   See "Proceso del Santo Oficio contra el Br. don Antonio Ramón de La Cueva, cura interino que fue del partido de Peto, por solicitante" (1730), AGN, Ramo de Inquisición, legajo 1046, expediente 4, fols. 107–26.

135   "Carta del comisario del Santo Oficio, Br. Nicolas Leyton, con información sobre la solicitación ad turpia de unas indias en la confesión por Padre don Antonio Ramón de La Cueva, cura interino de Peto" (21 March 1730), AGN, Ramo de Inquisición, legajo 1046, expediente 4, fols. 108r–9r.

136   "Carta del comisario del Santo Oficio, Br. Nicolas Leyton, con información sobre otra delito de solicitación" (29 March 1730), AGN, Ramo de Inquisición, legajo 1046, expediente 4, fols. 112r–13r.

137   "Petición en lengua yucateca contra el cura don Antonio hecho por el Maestro de Capilla del pueblo de San Francisco de Uman" (1781), AGI, Audiencia de México, legajo 3064, 10 fols.

138   "Petición en lengua yucateca contra el cura don Luis Antonio de Echazarreta" (1781), AGI, Audiencia de México, legajo 3064, 10 fols.

139   See various denunciations of Padre Echazarreta in AGI, Audiencia de México, vol. 3064 (1781).

140   "Declaración y testimonio de Francisca Cauiche en contra el cura de Uman" (26 April 1781), AGI, Audiencia de México, legajo 3064, 4 fols.

141   "Petición y denuncia hecha por Félix Cocom, maestro de capilla del pueblo de Uman contra su cura por abuses que le había hecho" (1781), AGI, Audiencia de México, legajo 3064, 4 fols.

142   "Declaración de don Andrés Tinal, cacique del pueblo de Tahuman contra su

cura" (1781), AGI, Audiencia de México, legajo 3064, 4 fols.; see also "Carta y petición del cacique y oficiales indios del pueblo de Uman con unas quejas contra su cura" (1781), AGI, Audiencia de México, legajo 3064, 6 fols.

143 "Petición en lengua yucateca contra el cura don Antonio hecho por el maestro de capilla del pueblo de San Francisco de Uman, Félix Cocom" (1781), AGI, Audiencia de México, legajo 3064, 10 fols.

144 "Petición y denuncia hecha por Félix Cocom, maestro de capilla del pueblo de Uman contra su cura por abuses que le había hecho" (1781), AGI, Audiencia de México, legajo 3064, 4 fols.

145 "Declaración de don Ignacio Quintal, español, sobre los abusos del cura de Uman" (1781), AGI, Audiencia de México, legajo 3064, 4 fols.

146 Both Francisca Cauiche and Manuela Pacheco, a Spanish woman, complained that their troubles with their husbands resulted from their having been raped by the priest. See "Carta y petición del cacique y oficiales indios del pueblo de Uman con unas quejas contra su cura" (1781), AGI, Audiencia de México, legajo 3064, 6 fols.

147 See the official complaints of the cacique don Andrés Tinal and the other town officials of Uman: "Petición en lengua yucateca con traducción de las quejas del cacique y cabildo del pueblo de Uman contra los abusos de su cura interino" (1780), AGI, Audiencia de México, legajo 3064, 4 fols. Specific instructions and official ecclesiastical quotas were set to regulate the clergy's use of Maya labor. A table of fees, called the *arancel*, existed to regulate these economic interchanges. For an example of these regulations and other laws prohibiting clerical exactions in the province of Yucatán, see "Arancel de lo que cada indio debe contribuir para el sustento de su cura en el discurso del año" (1737), AGI, Audiencia de México, legajo 3168; see also "Arancel para los derechos que se deben llevar en este curato y vicaria de Campeche" (1763), AHAY, Asuntos terminados, legajo 1, expediente 14. For a detailed examination of the abuses and exploitation of the Maya by both legal and illegal means, see John F. Chuchiak, "*Ca numiae, lay u cal caxtlan patan lae*: El tributo colonial y la nutrición de los Mayas, 1542–1812 — Un estudio sobre los efectos de la conquista y el colonialismo en los Mayas de Yucatán," in *Iglesia y sociedad en América Latina colonial* (Mexico City, 1995), 117–225.

148 It is interesting to note that a large number of priests and friars denounced for solicitation had previously punished their accusers for serious infractions of Catholic law such as witchcraft, idolatry, and public drunkenness. See Chuchiak, "Indian Inquisition," 512n119.

149 The complicity of many Maya parishioners in the sexual misconduct of the clergy is evident in transcripts of many Inquisition and episcopal court trials for sexual misconduct. For one example, see "Información del obispo de Yucatán sobre los excesos de religiosos saliéndose de noche vestidos de seglares y los escándalos públicos y concubinatos que tienen" (1703), AGI, Audiencia de México, legajo 1035, 42 fols.

150 Accusations of sexual abuse by the clergy continued long into the early national period. The section of the National Archives of Mexico containing material confiscated from the church archives (*Bienes nacionales, Bienes nacionalizadas*) shows that as late as the mid-nineteenth century parish priests were accused of abuse and sexual misconduct by the Maya.

From Sodomy to Superstition: The Active Pathic and Bodily Transgressions in New Spain

Laura A. Lewis, *James Madison University*

Abstract. Engaging primary documents and scholarly debates, this article examines an array of practices in colonial Mexico as it undertakes a discursive account of how gender ideologies informed the politics of discipline and a range of behaviors from atypical sexuality to cross-dressing and witchcraft. It speaks to a lived world set ambiguously between violations of social norms and the uncertainties of official culture as it examines these heterodox practices, especially as they relate to Indians.

In 1658, authorities of Mexico City's criminal court called before them a woman named Juana de Herrera, who was a mestizo laundress from Mexico City. Herrera told them that she had been out washing clothes one September day when several young boys ran up to her and, with voices raised, told her that two men were "playing like dogs" near the ditch where she was doing laundry. She walked over to a point some distance from where she had been washing in order to get a better view and was able to observe the two men committing a *pecado nefando*, a phrase that translates literally as an unspeakable sin and figuratively referred to male same-sex relations, particularly to sodomy (*sodomía*), understood as anal penetration.[1] Both of the men had their pants pulled down, Herrera testified, and the man on top had covered the one below with his cloak (*capa*).

Herrera did not dare get any closer for fear that the two men would kill her, which suggests that both she and the men were aware of church and state repression of sexual relations between men. She was, however, able to recognize the individual on top, whom she knew as a free mulatto named Juan de La Vega.

Ethnohistory 54:1 (Winter 2007) DOI 10.1215/00141801-2006-041

The authorities subsequently sought La Vega at the home of Doña Melchora de Estrada, where he was thought to be renting a room. La Vega had already moved, but other boarders described him to the investigators as a "feminized" mulatto (*mulato afeminado*), whose nickname was Cotita.[2] They described how La Vega would cinch his waist and wear the kind of kerchief over his brow that women used. He adorned the sleeves of his white bodice with ribbons, and he sat like a woman on a small platform placed on the ground as he made tortillas, washed, and cooked. Young men would visit him, the investigators were told, and La Vega would refer to them affectionately as "my soul, my life, my heart" (*mi alma mi vida mi corazón*), taking offense if they did not call him Cotita. These companions would also sleep with La Vega in his room.[3]

La Vega's story ended tragically when he was caught and burned at the stake in Mexico City along with thirteen other men alleged to have committed the pecado nefando.[4] The Iberian laws that condemned him had been in place since the thirteenth century. Based on the medieval Spanish legal code known as the *Siete Partidas*, those laws sentenced individuals convicted of same-sex acts to death by stoning. The vast majority of those so sentenced were men, and the high rate of execution for people identified as sodomites in Spain attests to extraordinary state and church concern with male-male sexual relations.[5] That rate intensified during the late fifteenth century, when the Spanish Inquisition was established to prosecute Jews and other heterodox subjects. In 1497, burning at the stake—the fate La Vega and the others suffered—took the place of stoning as the punishment for convicted sodomites.[6]

Spanish law—especially under the Inquisition—has been characterized as "quite repressive" when compared with other early modern legal regimes.[7] Yet legal records from Spain suggest that executions of sodomites, at least by the Inquisition, which was granted jurisdiction over this sexual crime only in the eastern province of Aragon,[8] had all but ceased by the mid-seventeenth century. In contrast, executions of sodomites by secular tribunals in both Spain and Protestant Europe continued through the mid-eighteenth century.[9] Studies also show that although passive sodomites—referred to as *putos* in Spain and in the New World—were socially disdained,[10] they were in fact less likely to be severely castigated than active ones, especially when the passives were minors or were otherwise deemed to have been coerced.[11] Concerned with the youth of many defendants, the late-sixteenth-century Spanish Inquisition raised the minimum age for sodomy persecution from twenty-one to twenty-five.[12]

The proceedings against Juan de La Vega suggest that at least some of the legal practices held in Mexico. For while we do not have a great deal of information about the sexual acts in which he and his cohorts were said to engage, we do know from the documentation that La Vega, at least, had acted as the "active" penetrator, and that he and other men were having sexual relations with boys. While some of the condemned men in this case were indeed designated *pacientes* (passives), the life of at least one of the boys was spared, that of a fifteen-year-old who was given a whipping and condemned to six years of forced labor.[13]

In his essay on Juan de La Vega and a seventeenth-century Mexican "wave of repressions" against "homosexual" men,[14] the historian Serge Gruzinski notes that in contrast to New Spain's Indians, Jews, blacks, and women, such men "continue molesting," for the archives hold few traces of their lives.[15] My intention here is not so much to focus precisely on those lives, about which indeed we have scant information,[16] as it is to use the idea of pecados nefandos to begin a discursive account of how gender ideologies informed both the politics of discipline and the enactment of heterodox practices—ranging from atypical sexual behaviors to cross-dressing and superstition—in sixteenth- and seventeenth-century Mexico. Gruzinski remarks on the "terminological coincidences" that held between sodomy and idolatry during that period.[17] With this observation in mind, in this essay I counterpose sexual with other kinds of social practices to explore how Indianness in particular came to be articulated as both a feminized passivity and as the source of dangerous contagions. I suggest that in the colonial imagination Indians embodied the paradox of the womanly "pathic" or passive, who was simultaneously condemned and pardoned but who also returned "from below" to contaminate the body politic. Such a perspective may help resolve a recent conflict between Richard Trexler and Michael Horswell over whether the "feminine" in the New World only degraded subjects or was in fact a construct that empowered them.[18] Could it not have done both?

In addition to prosecuting sodomites, colonial authorities sought out and persecuted heterodoxy in various realms. I refer to these practices and their symbolic expressions, in shorthand, as the "grotesque," following Peter Stallybrass and Allon White's analysis of the carnivalesque in Modern Europe. That analysis develops Mikhail Bakhtin's distinction between the "low" realm of human experience, which is mapped onto the social and the corporeal, first, as "heterogeneity, masking, protuberant distension, disproportion, exorbitancy, clamour, decentred or eccentric arrangements[, and] . . . physical needs and pleasures of the 'lower bodily stratum,'" and, second, as a more complex hybridization that forever questions and destabilizes the system itself.[19] Though contrasted by elites (and, subsequently, by scholars themselves) with the bourgeois legitimacy of the

"high," "classical" realm constituted by symmetry, centeredness, homo-
geneity, and increasing rationalism, the grotesque was not an independent cultural domain. Instead, it derived from the "higher discourses . . .
associated with the most powerful socio-economic groups,"[20] even as it
helped to constitute and define those discourses. As the high designated
the low, moreover, it also symbolically included it "as a primary eroticized
constituent of its own fantasy life."[21]

I draw material from colonial legal codes and from proceedings and
inquiries by various branches of the judiciary. Although the records derive
from church and state sources and thus filter accounts through the minds
and pens of elites, they are nevertheless the closest we will ever come to
understanding the realities of ordinary people, who often crossed paths
with inquisitors, criminal prosecutors, ecclesiastics, and myriad other
enforcers.[22] In fact, I conclude by suggesting that the crossing of such paths
actually helps to illuminate those realities by deepening our understandings of the origins of certain expressions of the grotesque. This is because,
in the final analysis, the "low" realm of human experience in colonial
society likely drew on ambiguities encoded in official culture—especially
religious culture—itself. I thus draw attention in the final parts of this essay
to Christian ritual, including the symbolism of blood, priestly dress, and
the alleged sexual practices of clergy. Religious culture not only provides
clues to what was condemned; it also provides insights into how Indians
turned into problematic subjects as they became the "active pathics" at the
heart of the colonial Mexican imaginary.

The Feminization of the Indian and
the Conundrum of Contamination

Recent scholarship on the Iberian conquest of the Americas has examined
the ways gender ideals mapped onto the politics and social dynamics of
conquest. Such scholarship pays particular attention to the construction
and subordination of the feminine and how it came to be represented most
consistently by the Indian.[23] As I have argued elsewhere, and can only
briefly summarize here, conquest itself had a gendered dimension, and
during the following centuries, juridical, social, and religious practices
in Mexico worked to produce an Indian whose alleged incapacities and
vulnerabilities mirrored the qualities dominant gender ideologies assigned
to women.[24] Thus the Spanish theologian Juan Ginés de Sepúlveda promoted women/Indian analogies to defend the legitimacy of conquest; the
language of colonial judicial documents rendered women and Indians
"weak," "sinful," and "ignorant"; colonial ideologies denied both Indians

and women the full capacity to reason;[25] colonial practices confined women to domestic spaces and Indians to the villages of their republic; colonial elites insisted on the moral guidance of women by men and Indians by Spaniards; and colonial labor became the domain of subordinated women and Indian producers in both the private and public spheres. As legal "minors" and dependents, women and Indians were in many respects rendered as children, and they were also the colony's quintessential witches, infected with the pathogen of superstition through inveterate contact with the devil.

Trexler's ambitious and controversial work on the implications of Iberian and Native American sexual culture for the discourse and practice of conquest brings the entwined issues of gender and violence to bear on the question of male same-sex practices. Arguing that male-male sexual subcultures existed in both contexts, and that Iberians and Native Americans equally disdained "passive" receptors more than active inserters, Trexler maintains that indigenous homosexuality, especially as represented in his interpretation by the transgendered and transvested figure of the berdache, fed Iberian understandings and discourses of conquest that feminized New World natives.[26] While my intention is not to endorse Trexler's position on berdaches as debased males who performed the sexual and social roles of women, and while Trexler has been criticized for what some scholars consider to be an anachronistic separation between "actives" and "passives," who might not have been so distinguished in Iberian or perhaps in indigenous American culture,[27] I believe that the distinction between the active and the passive in the realm of sexuality provides compelling clues to the broader implications of acting and being acted upon.

We can take as a starting point Trexler's attention to the paradoxical situation that resulted in individuals depicted as actives in the sources, who were "generally admired or at least tolerated" for their manly roles as penetrators, being more harshly punished than their disdained pathic partners, especially in Iberian culture.[28] Trexler suggests that this difference can be attributed to the fact that while the penetrated were linked to defeat and being "infected," the penetrators were held to be the source of contagions.[29] I argue that in the colonial imagination the devil took on an "active" role as infector, while feminized Indians—the most susceptible of his many prey—came to taint the populace with the devil's malady. Thus feminized Indians were, paradoxically, also empowered.

Spanish and Spanish colonial discourses were replete with references to the dangers posed by the social contagions allegedly borne by the myriad actors whose actions and essences placed them outside of what was construed as a healthy and functioning social body. Thus, as Gruzinski tells us, the head of the Criminal Court in the matter of Juan de La Vega and his cohorts described pecados nefandos in a letter to the king as a "contamination . . . [a] cancer . . . so widespread, so rampant."[30] In sixteenth-century Spain, as Mary Elizabeth Perry has written, "male homosexuality appeared so dangerous that men accused of homosexual behavior were isolated from others in the Royal Prison of Seville, their deviance regarded as a contagion that could easily infect others."[31] Moors, foreigners, and sailors came to be particularly associated with sodomy in the Old World,[32] where Moriscos were also condemned as "weeds."[33] One viceroy described New World mulattoes and blacks as weeds,[34] and New World authorities also asserted that the mostly non-Spanish vagabonds, as well as the northern nomadic Chichimec Indians, "infested" the roads surrounding Spanish towns, and that Spanish territory was to be kept "clean" of "loose people" (*gente suelta*),[35] while Indians "infected" the populace with witchcraft they had received from the devil.[36]

Women were also seen as potential contaminators. The Spanish ethos stressed self-control,[37] lineage "purity," and family honor. Honor referred both to social status (distinguished by wealth and "blood") and to the preservation of virtue in the form of virginity, which signified a morally pure life and respect for the church while guaranteeing the character of future lineages. In theory, the sexuality of both men and women was subject to control.[38] But women were judged to be more emotional, passionate, and carnal than men and therefore in need of supervision by male superiors such as fathers, husbands, and priests. Such supervision was thought to protect women from their own proclivities and make them good. More generally, it conserved male salvation and honor, which could be corrupted by out-of-control women who might pollute men with lust, weakness, and venereal diseases.[39] Women therefore might have been devalued, but they also bore perils that could unsettle the social hierarchy.

To explore the gender issue further, and to link it more specifically to witchcraft, we can turn briefly to *The Malleus Maleficarum*, the fifteenth-century witchcraft manifesto that had been issued in thirty editions in German, French, and Italian by 1669. In this text, the Dominican Inquisitors Heinrich Kramer and James Sprenger wrote extensively of the defects they believed constitutive of female nature.[40] As much a condemnation of women as it is of the superstition in which women were thought to ordinarily engage, the work is a diatribe linking "loose" women to perverse sexualities and to the sins of witches, both of which originated with a seductive devil who took advantage of women's inherent weaknesses to impose his will on theirs. The Dominicans' argument was taken up by colonial authorities, who believed that women who pulled free of church authority and male kin fell naturally into a kind of fecklessness that made them vulnerable to the devil's corruption. For those authorities and, it seems, for much of the populace, the devil turned such women into witches, and it was the devil to whom such women often turned for what Inquisition documents describe as passionate bouts of sexual intercourse. The dangers to men were made clear by the Spaniard Francisco, who accused a mulatto woman of having had intercourse with the devil and then using her powers to make Francisco "not a man."[41]

Like the women described by Kramer and Sprenger as without "moderation in goodness or vice,"[42] Indians might embrace the Spanish God if guided properly by Spanish clergy. But without such guidance, Indians were as likely as women to be enticed by the devil, a vector not only of loose sexual mores and the contagion that was witchcraft, but also of the sin of sodomy. Indeed, Bartolomé de Las Casas wrote that demons infected Guatemalan Indians with homosexuality, while Cieza de León identified the devil as the source of homosexuality in coastal Peru.[43] As Indians gained the reputation as the most notorious of the colony's witches and became the suppliers of the supernatural remedies that other subjects sought out,[44] they were also depicted by religious authorities as sexual degenerates.[45] The anchoring of religious and sexual decadence in the same evil sheds light on why the terms "whore" (*puta*) and "witch" (*hechicera*) are often found paired in colonial Mexican stories about wayward women, and why, more generally, there existed Gruzinski's "terminological coincidences"[46] linking sexual and religious aberrations.

The records suggest that *puta*—denoting a woman who was excessively sexual—and *puto*—signifying a man who performed sexual acts with other men but in the vernacular more precisely a man who was acted upon[47]—were used as insults in everyday speech. These insults were often directed at Indians,[48] whose alleged moral and physical debilities were also conflated, and whose bodies were made the objects of often sexual violence.[49] In Juan de La Vega's case, we have the interesting conflation of the terms *puto* and *puta*, for the documentation indicates that the putos—as some of the men referred to themselves in the text—took on the names of notable Mexico City putas.[50] The records are interesting, then, for the ways they join excess to perversions of the proper sexual order, thus conveying the sense that these men were doubly "out of control."

Spanish legal attitudes toward sodomy, which seemed to have deemed penetrators in sodomy cases as more responsible than the penetrated, were echoed in the codes and practices bearing on witchcraft offenses, which were surprisingly lenient. First, colonial authorities held that both women and Indians were "blinded" and "tricked" by a devil who took advan-

tage of their ignorance. Second, while again the Inquisition has a reputation for brutality, both women and Indians were treated with relative
leniency by this judicial body. In Spain, for instance, witches were never
burned at the stake after the early sixteenth century. Mostly women, they
were instead often "rehabilitated" by forced removal to villages where
their "unsavory reputation was not known."[51] In New Spain a high pro-
portion of witchcraft accusations were never brought to trial, especially
when defendants were women and especially in later periods when witchcraft came to be more consistently seen as "superstition" born of ignorance and a lack of "good sense."[52] Women often voluntarily confessed to
witchcraft, and their punishments included the occasional whipping but,
especially in later periods, mostly fines, public confessions and humilia-
tions, temporary exile, and confinement to the feminine spaces of home
and church.[53] Moreover, although indigenous supernaturalism, variously
coded as idolatry and witchcraft, was condemned in Mexico, and several
Indians were put to death for such offenses around the middle of the sixteenth century, by the last quarter of that century the Inquisition had lost
complete authority over Indians, in part because they were seen as "weak,
and of little substance," as one priest wrote, and in part because the institution's methods were considered to be too harsh for these New Christians.[54]
Unlike blacks, Indians had been freed from slavery some decades before,
and, as *miserables* or dependents, they were also made special wards of
the Crown, which mandated judicial institutions and processes meant to
facilitate equity between them and non-Indian groups. In the final analysis,
then, degraded and feminized Indians, who were routinely associated with
the devil, were also in theory protected from the harshest reaches of colonial officialdom.

In a Mérida Church

At this juncture I turn to another Juan. Juan Ramírez, like Juan de La Vega,
was a free mulatto in seventeenth-century Mexico. Caught with another
man near a Mérida church, he was also accused of a pecado nefando.[55]
While the records concerning La Vega do not clarify who his consort was,
those concerning Ramírez describe his partner as an Indian. As I shall
argue, the textual narrative contains elements of sexual aggression, feminizing the Indian in relation to the macho mulatto, even in the context of
an act that was itself deemed to be a violation of gender norms.

The matter of La Vega comes to us through reports by officials of the
criminal court and the viceroy himself. In contrast, the proceedings against
Ramírez were heard by the Inquisition. The consequent wealth of detail

does not make what occurred transparent, for the layers of meaning and interpretation hide some matters and reveal others, and the documentation does not indicate culpability or sentencing. Indeed, the matter might have been turned over to secular authorities, since the Inquisition did not have the authority to prosecute sodomy or Indians.[56] But the extant documentation does provide further insight into the discourses around, and the social contexts of, what were construed as homosexual acts.

The incident came to the attention of the Inquisition after an Indian sacristan named Pascual Couoh encountered another Indian, whom he did not know but who was later named as Andres Chan,[57] in the company of Ramírez. Couoh told the authorities that he had found the two committing the "pecado nefando" next to the church one evening as he was on his way to see his own live-in *compañero*, another Indian named Miguel Tun. On his way to finding Tun, Couoh passed by the priest's house, which was located to one side of the church. In the breezeway that presumably joined the two buildings, he had seen two indistinct forms (*bultos*), one on top of the other. Couoh went back to his own house to find a candle, and then returned to have another look. At this point he recognized one of the men as Ramírez; the other was Chan, whom Couoh recognized as an Indian even though he did not know his name.

As Couoh approached Ramírez and Chan, the mulatto got off of the Indian. According to Couoh, Ramírez then tied up his trousers and sat on the parapet of the breezeway. Couoh subsequently addressed him, saying, "Juan, what are you doing here? You must be a woman, since you're with a man." Ramírez replied that he was just "playing around" (*jugando*),[58] at which point Chan stood up and attempted to leave. As Tun approached the corridor, Couoh yelled out to him, "Friend, grab that Indian for me." Tun seized the Indian's poncho, which ripped as the Indian and Ramírez both ran. Couoh then turned to Tun and asked, "Friend, what do you think about these scoundrels, who come to do their shameful acts next to the church?"

When Ramírez was brought before the inquisitors, he testified that he had met with the Indian, whom he did not know, on the church patio, where he had gone to rest following a visit with a friend of his, a mulatto woman named Gracia. The Indian asked Ramírez where he was from. When Ramírez replied that he was from Campeche, the Indian told him how much he himself wanted to go there. Ramírez then told the Indian that he would take him, and asked him where he was from. The Indian responded that he was from Valladolid, and that in Mérida he had worked for a man who gave him decent clothes on holidays, but only to go to mass, after which the man would take the clothes away. The Indian then pulled a pair of white trousers out of his shirt and gave them for safekeeping to the mulatto.

Ramírez told the inquisitors that he had been with the Indian until four o'clock in the afternoon, at which point he himself went to church for mass. When Ramírez returned, he found the Indian in the same place and sat down next to him. They then proceeded to chat about Campeche. After a while, the Indian sacristan Couoh came by and asked Ramírez what he was doing. Ramírez answered that he was doing "nothing." As Couoh left, Ramírez lay down next to the Indian. By his own admission, he touched the Indian's penis, but only with the intention of agitating or annoying him (*alterarse*).

The Indian Andres Chan had obviously been caught, because he came before the inquisitors on the same day as his accuser. When they showed him the piece of poncho that had remained in Tun's hands, Chan told them that he remembered having bumped into Tun the previous night. Tun was drunk, Chan contended, and he let him have the poncho so that Tun would not attack him. According to Chan's version of events, he had been sleeping in the corridor when the mulatto—whom he also said he did not know—came by and grabbed a hat that Chan had set between his legs. This woke Chan up, and he went off for water. When he returned, Ramírez started chatting with him, telling him that he was waiting for some muleteers he was going to accompany to Campeche. Chan wanted to go there as well, and, hoping to get a lift, he moved closer to the mulatto. Suddenly, he claimed, the mulatto began to pinch him (*pelliscar*), to poke him (*triscar*), and to touch his penis (*tocarle el miembro*). Chan tried to flee ("as a man," he told the inquisitors), but somehow two hours later the mulatto was still touching him. Finally, the mulatto went off to buy tobacco. When he returned, he suggested to Chan that they move off of the patio, where there was "too much air," and go sit in the breezeway instead. Chan followed him there and lay down with his poncho over him.

At this point, the mulatto again began to pinch him and to touch his penis. Chan asked him how he could do these "shameful acts." "You are not a man," the mulatto apparently told him, to which the Indian replied, "Yes I am, and I have a penis just like you." The mulatto then accused Chan of not being his friend, because all of his friends "let all of their parts be touched and inspected" (*se dejan manosear y registrar todas sus partes*). Chan then moved away from the mulatto, who came after him and at the same time began to untie his pants. This was the point at which Couoh arrived, and as Tan grabbed at his poncho Chan hid behind a wall with a cross in bas-relief.

The symbolism of the church setting, Chan's cross-infused subter-

fuge, and perhaps the presence of male church officials should not go unremarked. Taken together, these components of the narrative might reference
a church culture that protected Indians, especially from inquisitorial punishment, but which may have maintained a kind of homoerotic subculture
even as it punished sodomy. For now I leave that issue aside and note that
while we do not know the outcome of this particular case, we can be fairly
certain that the Indian was released. This result would be in keeping with
church and state attitudes toward Indians, who, as I have already noted,
were dependants and not under the Inquisition's jurisdiction. It might also
follow from attitudes toward passives in homosexual encounters, if they
were indeed chastised more moderately than actives because they were
frequently youth and/or were understood to have been coerced. Furthermore, mulattoes were subject to the Inquisition and were thought of more
generally as "aggressive" and likely to tyrannize Indians.

Whether or not Chan was, in fact, willfully mounted by the mulatto
and was therefore the "paciente," the passive participant, as the Indian
sacristan Couoh told the inquisitors, or whether Chan was simply annoyed
that the mulatto touched his genitals, the textual narrative clearly ren-
ders Chan the "victim" while portraying the mulatto Juan Ramírez as
the aggressor. Yet Ramírez's friend Gracia also told the inquisitors that
Ramírez had gone shopping for a woman he helped around the house; he
also cooked, ground corn, washed and starched clothes, and made chocolate—all women's tasks.

There is undoubtedly a caste dimension to this encounter.[59] For as I
have shown elsewhere,[60] and as I have intimated above, Indians were often
depicted as victims of mulatto aggression even as they were recognized as
the most powerful practitioners of witchcraft. In the case just reviewed,
the details of the mulatto's social affiliations and practices spoke—like
Juan de La Vega's—to the accused's feminine qualities. But with respect
to the actual sexual act described—which is variously referred to in an
elaborate cross-pollination of terms and concepts as an *acto diabólico* (diabolical act), a *pecado nefando* (unspeakable sin), a *crimen somético* (crime of
submission), and a *pecado contra natura* (a sin against nature)—the Indian
Chan emerges as the more feminized of the two, for he was the one on the
bottom.

Given what can be discerned about official attitudes toward Indians
it would not be difficult to read Chan's tale of his encounter with the
mulatto in Mérida as a strategizing discourse that consciously appealed to
colonial ideas about Indians, and about the relationships between Indians
and members of other castes. We really have no way of knowing what the
truth was. Nevertheless, the narrative of the text feminizes the Indian and

turns him into the victim of the mulatto's aggression, as it again points to the issue of seduction, which, in its sexual and more general senses, was central to understanding the chain of "contamination" and therefore the latent dangers of feminized Indianness. It was in fact precisely their weakness or passivity that bound Indians and women to sacrilege.[61] Like the qualities assigned to some actors in male same-sex encounters—who might have been youthful and who gave themselves over to an "aggressor"—passivity underscores the lack of conviction that can lead to being coerced. This helps to explain why passives in male same-sex acts might have been more disdained than actives but also not as severely punished: although they engaged in forbidden behaviors, they were—like Indians, women, and children—not to be held entirely accountable for the acts that polluted them. Thus the Indian Chan contended that Ramírez had "come on" to him even as he admitted to remaining in the mulatto's company voluntarily for hours on end.

Cloaked in Secrecy

Although Juan Ramírez was not transvested, like Juan de La Vega he reportedly engaged in feminine domestic tasks. Trexler associates transvestism and female practices (*oficios*) with passives.[62] But clearly this association did not hold for La Vega, a mulatto who dressed and acted like a "passive" but was also seen mounting another man. Neither did it hold for the mulatto Ramírez, whose case, like La Vega's, is of interest in this respect because the narrative again exposes an anomalous combination—if Trexler's claims are accurate—of an otherwise effeminate man also tagged as the penetrator, a combination that might be connected to the aggression colonial authorities imputed to mulattos. It also again exposes the limits of what we know about "homosexuality," and gender and caste identities in New Spain.

Yet it is clear that because relationships were inferred between "men dressing and acting like women," male same-sex sex acts and general "lasciviousness,"[63] public attention was drawn to men like La Vega and Ramírez. Whatever their actual behaviors, because of the dissonance between clothing, social behavior, and sex, people like them were marked as exposing what Marjorie Garber describes as the "ungroundedness of identities on which social structures and hierarchies developed."[64] "Acting like a woman" and transvestism were not in and of themselves punishable by death, however. As Trexler writes of cross-dressing, "laws against transvestism were often not taken seriously . . . [and] traditional Europeans in general were much readier to think of transvestism as a normal product of social interchange."[65] Yet without suggesting, for instance, that the lives of La Vega and his transvested cohorts would have been spared had they "looked like" men, it certainly appears that the question of dress was central to the concerns of the authorities who chased La Vega down and killed him. Indeed, much of the narrative of his case focuses not so much on the details of his and the others' sexual practices as it does on exactly what kinds of clothes they typically wore, for that clothing signified deeper forms of deviance.

In this respect, cross-dressing women also drew attention, and accounts of such women can be found in both Spanish and colonial Mexican records.[66] However, while they were clearly and explicitly violating gender norms, these women were not associated with female same-sex sex acts in the ways that cross-dressing men were deemed to be sodomites of one sort or another.[67] In fact, until the eighteenth century, when the role of the *sapphist*—a woman who preferred female sexual partners—emerged in European discourse, same-sex sex practices were rarely associated with women.[68] When they were, these practices were not defined as sodomy, which generally meant anal penetration with a penis.[69] The cross-dressing women that we know of from sixteenth- and seventeenth-century Spain and the New World either had sexual relations with men or claimed to be chaste. Thus, their sexual comportment did not deny at least those moral codes that cultivated heterosexuality. Moreover, transvested women might have drawn less condemnation than transvested men because "maleness" was the more highly valued Spanish ideal. Women who dressed as men might therefore have been more comprehensible and tolerable to the authorities than men who expressed their femininity through dress and therefore freely chose to limit their social power.[70]

A good example of a woman who cross-dressed and was tolerated by the authorities, and one of the few examples that in fact exists, is the Spanish nun Catalina de Erauso. Said to be a "virtuous" woman and a proven virgin, she was granted a royal license to don men's clothing by the Spanish Crown in the sixteenth century. Dressed like a soldier, she traveled throughout the New World, including to Mexico.[71]

And then we have Ursula de Las Vírgenes, a Spanish widow and resident of Mexico City, who also dressed in men's clothing in order to escape the confines of domesticity. She was called before the ecclesiastical authorities in the late seventeenth century for what they described as her "disorderly way of life." First, her disconcerting habit of wearing men's clothing, especially during Lent,[72] subjected her to censure. Second—and this would explain ecclesiastical interest in her case—Las Vírgenes donned not just male attire, but male religious attire, which is described in the text as the hooded garment of a penitent (*una tunica de penitencia con su capirote*). Dressed as a monk, she allegedly had the custom of going about the city and entering people's homes. As the married Spaniard Augustina Rodríguez reported to the authorities, Las Vírgenes would move "with confidence" while dressed in men's clothing, a rather subtle indication, one imagines, of the insolence with which Las Vírgenes carried out her indecent subterfuge, at least in public. Further allegations came from Las Vírgenes's own servant, a mestiza named Cathalina who apparently told Augustina Rodríguez that Las Vírgenes often dressed as a man in order to go out on the street at night. And another Spanish witness claimed that even when Las Vírgenes's husband was dying she would don men's clothing to go where she wanted when darkness fell.[73] Las Vírgenes thus ventured into public spaces coded as male—the streets of the nighttime city—while, as we have seen, both Juans stayed home to make tortillas.

Las Vírgenes was portrayed as a noisy and rumor-mongering trouble-maker. She was certainly not chaste, for she went around "illicitly" with men. This speaks to the kind of lasciviousness ascribed to men like La Vega, "putos" who engaged in homosexual acts. Furthermore, women like Erauso and Las Vírgenes who wore men's clothing did so in tandem with masculinized behaviors designed to give them mobility and freedom from the domestic confines of home and church. Thus, like their male counter-parts, such women drew suspicion because they violated the spatial and temporal coordinates in which "legitimate" bodies moved. Yet they did not violate the basic hetero norms of sexual conduct itself.

The sartorial rules widespread in the early modern world, including Mexico, were designed to facilitate what Garber calls "cultural legi-bility,"[74] but not just with respect to gender codes. In Mexico, legal stipu-lations regarding dress also applied to caste, and much legal activity took place around the implementation and contestation of caste dress codes. Presumably, dress norms did not have to be dictated when it came to gender, for such norms were encoded in the Bible itself. Violations, then, were much more egregious than the ones caste statutes provoked.

The category of clothing that included capes, cloaks, and shawls is of particular interest because it spoke to the uncertainties of gender and caste, while also blurring the secular and sacred divide. Thus Span-iards were allowed to wear one kind of cape and Indians another; men donned cloaks (*mantos*), women used shawls (*mantas*); men did not wear skirts but women did, and monks wore a particular kind of long garment called a habit (*abito*). These kinds of garments seem to have played central roles in gender and caste subterfuge. For instance, drawing on an indige-nous planting ritual depicted by the colonial Andean chronicler Guaman

Poma, as well as on contemporary ethnographic accounts, Horswell links women's shawls worn by male ritual practitioners to "third-gender subjectivity" and to mediation of "absolute gender opposites."[75] In his work on gender and the sartorial adornment of religious statues in Spain, Italy, and the New World, Trexler also refers to cloaks and tunics—particularly the garb of priests and the Virgin Mary—as "sex-neutral" or "unisexual."[76] Garber makes the more general observation that "bodies concealed under robes are objects of suspicion,"[77] and the colonial documentation on cross-dressing often includes references to long garments that support magical and otherwise carnivalesque acts, often with a sexual twist. Juan de La Vega, for instance, used his cape to cover his partner, thus "hiding" both the sexual act and his own body, which was otherwise described as sartorially feminine. Another of the men condemned with him, a seventy-year-old mestizo, would dance with other men with his cape tied around his waist while complaining that he felt ill and was pregnant.[78] The Indian Chan's poncho also played a role in his alleged transgressions.

Certainly Las Vírgenes's wandering the streets as a man dressed in a monk's tunic speaks to the useful indefiniteness and symbolic fluidity of robes that conceal. So do the actions of a seventeenth-century Mexico City baker, who turned to similar clothing to invent a new persona for his slave, in the process violating a number of categorical boundaries. The baker used a long tunic "like those of monks" to punish the slave, whom he accused of rebelling. Dressing the man up in the tunic, the baker paraded him around in the public plaza in front of Mexico City's cathedral. To enhance his message he transformed the slave's other bodily signs by shaping his hair into a monk's tonsure and whitening his face with flour. The authorities thought he was showing contempt for the clergy, but the baker explained that he was rather punishing and "shaming" the slave.[79]

Clearly both religious and caste meanings—for whiteface aside, monks were by definition Spanish—informed the baker's attempt to disgrace his slave. And once again those meanings seem to be encoded in a long garment. Moreover, one could also read a latent feminization in the baker's actions because he not only dressed up his slave as a presumably asexual—and hence not-male—monk, he had also, as he told the authorities, fashioned the garment out of some of his wife's old clothes. He thus directly transposed a woman's skirts onto a man's cassock.

The Devil and the Indian: Dressing for Success

I have thus far suggested that Indians were feminized, that they were "infected" with pollutants that came from the devil, and that clothing was a symbolic focal point for a variety of heterodoxies. It remains now to bring these various issues together. I begin to do this with an account of a devil, whose name was Mantelillos and who became the helpmate of a mestizo cowhand named Juan Luis. When he first appeared to Juan Luis, Mantelillos was wearing a waterproof cloak (*capa aguadera*). He also happened to have two faces, which Juan Luis asked him not to display in future encounters because they disturbed him. Juan Luis told the inquisitors that he adored this demon "like God," and he would kneel before him as he asked him for help.

The name Mantelillos, which is also attached to the devil in another instance,[80] is something of a puzzle. I have never encountered a translation in the texts, although the inquisitors often asked defendants and witnesses to explain unfamiliar terms. This suggests that what "Mantelillos" meant was understood, at least to sixteenth- and seventeenth-century colonial Mexicans. I can only speculate here, but I believe that the moniker might have derived from a *manto* (a man's cloak) or a *manta* (a woman's shawl) or—perhaps more likely—from a *mantel*, an altar cloth. The devil's name, then, might have meant something like "little altar cloth," and he was wearing a cape when Juan Luis first encountered him.[81] We therefore again see long and coded garments (both the one that Mantelillos wore and the one that probably informed his name) playing what seem to be significant roles in the enactment of heterodoxy. This time, such garments are linked to a devil whose face itself was unsettled.

The document also features a connection between the caped figure of the devil and an Indian, for in the course of what was a rather long Inquisition trial, Juan Luis admitted that an Indian had introduced him to Mantelillos.[82] The inquisitors considered the Indian's role to be so central that they interrogated Juan Luis about who the man was, where Juan Luis had met him, and whether Juan Luis had "dared" at any point to call on the devil himself, without the Indian's intervention. When the Indian was questioned by the inquisitors he admitted that he and his Indian forefathers had learned everything that they knew from the devil.[83]

Yet another Indian on intimate terms with the devil came to the aid of the mulatto slave woman Antonia, who lived in the northern reaches of Spanish territory at the end of the seventeenth century. As I have discussed at length elsewhere,[84] Antonia, using "herbs and powders" supplied by the Indian, escaped her master's house and dressed as a man. Although the clothes are not described in detail, in her magical disguise she maintained her male identity with the help of the Indian's remedies, which she would rub all over her body while "calling and invoking the devil to help her." The devil would do everything she commanded, and with his help she was able to engage in activities coded as male, including fighting bulls and taming horses as she "served different masters as a cowboy."[85]

Antonia was careful to explain to the authorities—to whom she eventually turned herself in—that none of the men with whom she had contact had discovered that she was a woman. In fact, she had never had "illicit friendships" with her male companions. The implication, of course, was that Antonia had remained chaste in her interactions with men despite her sartorial and gender transmutations, and that her clothing in and of itself not only transformed her gender; it also allowed her to maintain the fiction.

Antonia went on to tell the inquisitors that one night she awoke to find herself flying through the air toward a mountain. As it became light she saw a male figure dressed in a dark habit (*abito*) with a palm frond in his hand and a haircut "like a priest's." She followed him down the mountain and as he disappeared she went to confess. It was San Antonio, she said, and she knew it was him because the previous day she had asked for his help.

That Antonia turned herself in after seeing an apparition of San Antonio bathed in light speaks to the indeterminacies of bodily forms in this colonial setting. For the saint's body could also be read as a mirror image of the devil who, in Antonia's account, was a white man and who disappeared as soon as San Antonio materialized. Following Stallybrass and White's analysis of the carnivalesque, we might see Antonia's journey as a "fantasy *bricolage*"[86] that unsettled "'given' social positions and interrogate[d] the rules of inclusion, exclusion and domination which structured the social ensemble."[87] Antonia ultimately reaffirmed official norms by casting off her masculine dress, her liberty, and her Indian companion, and turning herself in to males: a saint, priests, inquisitors, Spaniards, and, ultimately, to masters, all of whom held the power to "heal" her bodily transgressions. They contrast with the devil, who, of course, was introduced to Antonia by an Indian who had already been "seduced."

Highs and Lows: The Politics of the "Grotesque" and the Active Pathic

In New Spain, Indians were the symbolic prism through which the grotesque body—the "low," the antithetical—came to be understood as corrupting the social order. Embodying the feminine, passive Indians were first acted on, including by the conquistadors whom theologians like Las Casas charged with morally corrupting as well as massacring them.[88] As receptors of a contagion discharged by the devil, among the most active of colonial subjects and the source of both witchcraft and sodomy, Indians went on to "actively" contaminate the colonial social body. Thus even as the "high" was threatened with the "ferocity" of the low,[89] the high informed the ways the low was both produced and undone, for the devil was a European invention.

Among the many facets of Antonia's story that are worth exploring, noteworthy is her devil, who offers her help once she is freed from enslavement by the Indian, who makes it possible for her "magical" male garments to work. This devil metamorphoses into San Antonio when she is ready to turn herself in. The resemblance between her own name and that of the saint should not go unremarked, and neither should the fact that San Antonio appears to her on a mountain bathed in light, much like a transfigured Christ. This association recalls what Alison Weber has written about the sixteenth-century Spanish nun Magdalena de La Cruz, who testified before the Inquisition about a beatific vision of Christ transmuting into a devil.[90] Antonia's juxtaposition of the devil and a Christ-like saint, the devil Mantelillos who took his name from an altar cloth, and the visions of another accused mulatto witch, who allegedly confused the figure of a priest with the figure of a demon she claimed was hiding behind an altar,[91] speak directly to the muddled heart of the low/high relationships that I am teasing out here.

Religious imagery often infused colonial Mexican tales of transgression, and witchcraft proceedings are full of references to sacrilegious prayers and whippings of Christ figures. In this respect, I would like to draw attention to blood, an ambiguous substance that was simultaneously holy and sacrilegious, neutral and polluted. Blood from a finger prick was solicited from a Spanish woman by a servant of a demon who identified an Indian woman as his daughter and who possessed a penis "as big as a club." "My master cries for you," the servant told the woman, threatening her with death if she did not comply. "Give me a bit of blood from your arm, I have to take it and give it [to him]."[92] Sometimes blood provided the ink with which the devil's words were inscribed in the "devil's books," which must have been as unintelligible to nonliterate people as the Bible that ecclesiastics used.[93] The lower parts—the "filth" and the "vulgar" through which the low was constituted and on which sexual transgressions were centered—were also the source of the menstrual blood with which innumerable colonial women of all castes adulterated the food and drink they used to tame their wayward lovers. Such blood was normally harmless, one doctor testified to the Inquisition. But it could also be a pathway to and incarnation of infection if the person whose body it came from was diseased or if that person had entered into a pact with the devil.[94]

Solicited by the devil, blood was synecdoche for kinship as well as a sign of loyalty. More generally, it symbolized the transference of the devil's potency to the body of the person who provided it. By the same token, so did the blood of Christ, which—along with his flesh—was said to nourish the souls of believers. In New Spain, where conversion was a principal goal of conquest and where monks and priests circulated widely, ecclesiastics taught their charges—including Indians and African slaves—to commune with Christ by drinking his blood.

Blood was not the only symbolic focal point at the core of the colonial Mexican imaginary, where the low and the high, the grotesque and the classical, the female and the male, and the profane and the sacred, met and mingled. As we have seen, clothing accommodated its own discordances, especially when it draped bodies and especially when it was coupled with heterodox sexualities, as it often seemed to be. Sartorial and bodily ambiguities were sometimes displayed through religious garb such as monks' tunics, which Garber identifies as special "invitations" to gender parody and gender crossover, and as therefore exceptionally challenging to the conventions of "sartorial gender" in Western history.[95] The witch and devil images with which we are familiar—which center on flowing tunics—in fact recall what a sixteenth-century monk might have worn. More startling still is a modern illustration of a Basque witch inspired by the writings of the early-seventeenth-century witch-hunter Pierre de Lancre; it depicts a young woman who is completely nude, but whose hair is shorn in the manner of a monk's tonsure.[96]

The bodily transgressions simultaneously hidden and signified by flowing garments could also be found among the clergy, who were bound by vows of celibacy but among whom "sodomy was widely practiced," at least according to the sixteenth-century Spanish Jesuit chaplain Pedro de León.[97] As Trexler has written, in the cloistered spaces of monasteries, male-male contact was the norm and young novices were subordinated to "father-monks and friars within a male ambiance, a subordination that often had a sexual component."[98] And even as the church itself became preoccupied with stifling sodomy and other sexual practices among the clergy,[99] the sexual atmosphere of monastery life might have influenced how the religious viewed the sexuality of the natives, blacks, mulattoes, and mestizos among whom they spread with conquest.[100] Indeed, we might ask in this respect whether the Indian Juan Zurrador, one of the men caught in the wave of repression that swept up the mulatto Juan de La Vega, had gathered together a number of men and boys for a simultaneous celebration of Saint Nicholas and pecados nefandos because he was confused or because his actions had a historically specific kind of clarity. And then, just what kind of companion was Miguel Tun to the Indian sacristan Pascual Couoh?

Bringing together an array of the "grotesque" with a range of actors, I have advanced an argument about the ways the bodily practices that indexed the low—from sodomy to cross-dressing and superstition—spoke to understandings of a lived world that was set ambiguously between violations of social norms and uncertainties encoded in official—in the main, religious—culture itself. In New Spain, the unsettled spaces where the devil reigned were most consistently suffused with religious imagery as a fertile array of fluid and burlesque symbols and acts spread with Spaniards throughout the territory. Thus if Catholic doctrine "shaped popular consciousness," as David Greenberg has observed of the European Middle Ages,[101] in New Spain it seems to have encouraged not just evolving ideas of what was respectable but also explosive displays of interconnected and "low" pursuits. Taken together, the associations that I have made suggest that those pursuits had in common not just their official condemnation as abominations, but also the similar ways they drew on images, discourses, and social relations that were simultaneously low and high.[102]

In the final analysis, the most virulent sexual and supernatural contagions in New Spain can be identified with the juxtaposed figures of religious elites and their devilish doppelgängers. All of these figures—sacred and profane—had special relationships to the neophyte Indians they subordinated to the requisites of their own goals. The "anxieties" provoked by the slipperiness of dress and other violative bodily practices in New Spain thus probably indexed not so much the "dissolution of boundaries" in times of social change, as Garber has argued for transvestism and its associated bodily states in early modern Europe,[103] as the desires of elites to contain and define slipperiness within the particular regimes of authority they directly maintained. As we see how such practices in New Spain mimicked the ambivalence encoded in dress, sexuality, and the supernatural as found in Catholic ritual, they appear to be not so much detached and challenging transgressions as a cluster of sublimated metaphors for "high" culture. That culture, which both protected Indians as legal "minors" under the dominion of the Spanish Crown[104] and imbued them with destabilizing devilish powers, reveals multiple suspicions around how and to what extent the pathic could in fact penetrate the colonial body politic. It also, not incidentally, suggests the existence of a hybrid colonial space that simultaneously disparaged and empowered the feminine.

Notes

This essay was originally prepared for "The Body and the Body Politic in Latin America," a conference at the Center for Historical Studies, University of Maryland, College Park, April 2003. I would like to thank Mary Kay Vaughn and Barbara Weinstein for the invitation, the conference participants for their comments, and Fletcher Linder, Howard Lubert, Pete Sigal, and the anonymous reviewers for *Ethnohistory* for theirs.

1 *Sodomy* generally referred to male-male anal penetration, though it could also refer to anal intercourse between a man and a woman, fellatio, and bestiality; Martin Nesvig, "The Complicated Terrain of Latin American Homosexuality," *Hispanic American Historical Review* 81 (2001): 693–94; Pete Sigal, "(Homo)Sexual Desire and Masculine Power in Colonial Latin America: Notes toward an Integrated Analysis," in *Infamous Desire: Male Homosexuality in Colonial Latin America*, ed. Pete Sigal (Chicago, 2003), 5.

2 This would have been a synonym for *mariquita* (lit. parakeet), an everyday term for a preening and effeminate man.

3 Archivo General de Indias, Seville (hereafter AGI), México, file 38, no. 57-B, 27 September 1658.

4 The deaths of these men were part of an unprecedented wave of repression of male same-sex practitioners that swept the capital that year. See Serge Gruzinski, "Las cenizas del deseo: Homosexuales novohispanos a mediados del siglo XVII," in *De la santidad a la perversión, o de porqué no se cumplía la ley de Dios en la sociedad novohispana*, ed. Sergio Ortéga (Mexico City, 1986), 255–90.

5 David F. Greenberg, *The Construction of Homosexuality* (Chicago, 1988), 311–12; see also John Boswell, *Christianity, Social Tolerance, and Homosexuality* (Chicago, 1980), 288–89.

6 William Monter, *Frontiers of Heresy: The Spanish Inquisition from the Basque Lands to Sicily* (Cambridge, 1990), 280; Greenberg, *Construction of Homosexuality*, 302; Nesvig, "Complicated Terrain," 699; Ward Stavig, "Political 'Abomination' and Private Reservation: The Nefarious Sin, Homosexuality, and Cultural Values in Colonial Peru," in Sigal, *Infamous Desire*, 142. Gruzinski ("Cenizas del deseo," 263) points out that while Jews were sent to the pyres, at least after the middle of the sixteenth century "[Indian] idolaters escaped burning in order to benefit from the clemency of the church." The fact that Jews were burned at the stake and "idolatrous" Indians in New Spain were not, suggests a categorical distinction between the two groups. Both were heterodox, but Jews were essentially different while Indians were only temporarily so.

7 Greenberg, *Construction of Homosexuality*, 311.

8 Monter, *Frontiers of Heresy*, 276–99.

9 Ibid., 296–99.

10 The feminized passive has long been condemned in the West. As Thomas Laqueur notes, for ancient Greeks "it was the weak, womanly male partner who was deeply flawed, medically and morally. His very countenance proclaimed his nature: *pathicus*, the one being penetrated; *cinaedus*, the one who engages in unnatural lust; *mollis*, the passive, effeminate one"; Laqueur, *Making*

Sex: Body and Gender from the Greeks to Freud (Cambridge, MA, 1990), 53. For Aristotle passivity was the least "normal" aspect of male homosexual behavior (Boswell, *Christianity*, 50). As for contemporary Latin America, Roger Lancaster notes, writing about the gendering of sex roles in Nicaragua, "Whoever is acted upon, dominated, or entered is feminine"; Lancaster, *Life Is Hard: Machismo, Danger, and the Intimacy of Power in Nicaragua* (Berkeley, CA, 1993), 242; see also Serena Nanda, *Gender Diversity: Crosscultural Variations* (Prospect Heights, IL, 2000), 43–56; and Octavio Paz, *The Labyrinth of Solitude* (New York, 1961), 39–40.

11 Nesvig, "Complicated Terrain," 699; Mary Elizabeth Perry, *Gender and Disorder in Early Modern Seville* (Princeton, NJ, 1990), 123; Richard Trexler, *Sex and Conquest: Gendered Violence, Political Order, and the European Conquest of the Americas* (Cambridge, 1995), 37, 45; Trexler, *Religion in Social Context in Europe and America: 1200–1700* (Tempe, AZ, 2002), 585n95; Pete Sigal, "Gendered Power, the Hybrid Self, and Homosexual Desire in Late Colonial Yucatán," in Sigal, *Infamous Desire*, 103; Stavig, "Political 'Abomination,'" 142.

12 Monter, *Frontiers of Heresy*, 296.

13 Nesvig's claim that fourteen "young men" were "roasted alive" in this incident is mistaken, for at least three of the men are described as "old" in the text: one was said to be seventy and another was said to be eighty. One should also note that the majority (more than 75 percent) of the defendants were not Spaniards, which might have put them more at risk for severe punishments; Nesvig, "Complicated Terrain," 700.

14 I am fully aware of the problems entailed in using the pseudoscientific term *homosexual*, which was not coined until the nineteenth century and fails to address the social relationships embedded in culturally specific same-sex systems; Gruzinski, "Cenizas del deseo," 256, 274; Lancaster, *Life Is Hard*, 270. As Gruzinski points out, however, the "silence" of male same-sex practitioners in the documentation from New Spain is reflected in the paucity and types of terms: all that exist are disparaging, like *puto* (fag), *somético* (submissive), and *sodomita* (sodomite), which circulated among officials and the populace alike. We are thus limited in the ways in which we can neutrally refer to male same-sex practices.

15 Gruzinski, "Cenizas del deseo," 256. On this point see also Nesvig, "Complicated Terrain," 690. For an English translation of Gruzinski's essay, see Serge Gruzinski, "The Ashes of Desire: Homosexuality in Mid-seventeenth-century New Spain," trans. Ignacio López-Calvo, in Sigal, *Infamous Desire*, 197–214.

16 One of the principal debates taking place around studies of early modern homosexuality is whether sexual acts were coupled with social identities and distinct communities as they are among modern homosexuals. I have nothing to add to the debate, but see the lucid discussion in Sigal, "(Homo)Sexual Desire," and the essays in Sigal, *Infamous Desire*.

17 Gruzinski, "Cenizas del deseo."

18 Trexler has been criticized for what some have understood to be his application of a Western model "feminizing" and thus degrading male same-sex practitioners and cross-dressers (berdaches) in indigenous American contexts (see Trexler, *Sex and Conquest*). Horswell, in contrast, argues for a space in at least

Andean culture for a "third sex" that drew on feminine imagery and quali-
ties without connoting degradation; Michael Horswell, "Toward an Andean
Theory of Ritual Same-Sex Sexuality and Third-Gender Subjectivity," in
Sigal, *Infamous Desire*, 25–69. For discussions of the controversy, see Nesvig,
"Complicated Terrain," 698–99; Sigal, "(Homo)Sexual Desire"; Horswell,
"Toward an Andean Theory"; Trexler, *Religion in Social Context*, 553–90.

19 Peter Stallybrass and Allon White, *The Politics and Poetics of Transgression*
(Ithaca, NY, 1986), 23, 56.

20 Ibid., 4.

21 Ibid., 5.

22 As Eric Van Young writes, such texts are where "private lives cross the public
record"; Van Young, "The New Cultural History Comes to Old Mexico,"
Hispanic American Historical Review 79 (1999): 238.

23 See, for example, Trexler, *Sex and Conquest*; Laura A. Lewis, "The 'Weakness'
of Women and the Feminization of the Indian in Early Colonial Mexico,"
Colonial Latin American Review 5 (1996): 73–94; Lewis, *Hall of Mirrors:
Power, Witchcraft, and Caste in Colonial Mexico* (Durham, NC, 2003);
James D. Fernández, "The Bonds of Patrimony: Cervantes and the New
World," *PMLA* 109 (1994): 969–81; Margarita Zamora, *Reading Columbus*
(Berkeley, CA, 1993); and Louis Montrose, "The Work of Gender in the
Discourse of Discovery," in *New World Encounters*, ed. Stephen Greenblatt
(Berkeley, CA, 1993), 177–217. For contemporary takes on the feminization
of Indians and the Indianization of women, see Marisol de La Cadena, "'Las
mujeres son más indias': Etnicidad y género en una comunidad del Cusco,"
Revista andina 9 (1991): 7–47; Carol Hendrickson, "Images of the Indian in
Guatemala: The Role of Indigenous Dress in Indian and Ladino Construc-
tions," in *Nation-States and Indians in Latin America*, ed. Greg Urban and
Joel Sherzer (Austin, TX, 1991), 286–306; and Lynn Stephen, "The Construction of Indigenous Subjects: Militarization and the Gendered and Ethnic
Dynamics of Human Rights Abuses in Southern Mexico," *American Ethnolo-
gist* 26 (1999): 822–42.

24 Similarly, women in Spain were Indianized and "primitivized"; Fernández,
"Bonds of Patrimony," 977.

25 By the sixteenth century, reason was the search for rational knowledge of God's
goodness. This idea was connected to Aristotelian ones linking reason to the
overcoming of passion, for all rested on "perfection," however defined, as the
pinnacle of creation (Arthur O. Lovejoy links the Platonic Idea of the Good to
the "God of Plato" as well as to the "God" of Aristotle; Lovejoy, *The Great
Chain of Being* [Cambridge, MA, 1936], 5, 42). During the Enlightenment,
"reason" came to counter rather than reinforce Christian faith and a "ratio-
nalist" was an unbeliever; Carl Becker, *The Heavenly City of the Eighteenth-
Century Philosophers* (New Haven, CT, 1932), 8. Genevieve Lloyd traces the
ways in which "reason" — however construed — has been defined as male and
valued, while "feminine traits" have been principally identified with nature
and understood as inferior; Lloyd, *The Man of Reason: "Male" and "Female"
in Western Philosophy* (Minneapolis, 1984). For sixteenth- and seventeenth-
century Spanish political thinkers, the authority of the monarch was ordained
by divine will. Thus religious reason was linked to a political imperative tying
Christianity to acceptance of the authority of Spanish monarchs.

26 Trexler, *Sex and Conquest.* For a summary of Western perspectives and disagreements on the role of the berdache in Native American culture, see Nanda, *Gender Diversity,* 11–13.

27 See Nesvig, "Complicated Terrain," 690.

28 Trexler, *Sex and Conquest,* 35–37, 44–45, 57.

29 Ibid., 146–47.

30 Gruzinski, "Cenizas del deseo," 261; see also AGI México, file 57–A.

31 Perry, *Gender and Disorder,* 123.

32 Sigal, "Gendered Power," 103; Stavig, "Political 'Abomination,'" 142; Nesvig, "Complicated Terrain," 699; Luiz Mott, "Crypto-sodomites in Colonial Brazil," trans. Salima Popat, in Sigal, *Infamous Desire,* 172–73.

33 Deborah Root, "Speaking Christian: Orthodoxy and Difference in Sixteenth-Century Spain," *Representations* 23 (Summer 1988): "The association of Moriscos with disease resurfaces in references to infection and vermin, and the need to 'cleanse' Spain and make it 'pure and clean from this people'" (131). See also Roger Boase, "The Morisco Expulsion and Diaspora: An Example of Racial and Religious Intolerance," in *Cultures in Contact in Medieval Spain,* ed. David Hook and Barry Taylor (London, 1990), 9–28.

34 AGI México, file 27, no. 52, 1608.

35 Archivo General de la Nación, Mexico City (hereafter AGN), Criminal, vol. 369, exp. 2, 1661; AGN General de Parte, vol. 11, exp. 367, 1663; AGN Reales Cédulas Duplicadas, vol. 3, exp. 7, 1587.

36 E.g., AGN Inquisición, vol. 360, exp. 31, 1627.

37 Anthony J. Cascardi, "The Subject of Control," in *Culture and Control in Counter-Reformation Spain,* ed. Anne J. Cruz and Mary Elizabeth Perry (Minneapolis, 1992), 237; Jean Franco, *Plotting Women: Gender and Representation in Mexico* (New York, 1989), xiv; Mary Elizabeth Perry, "Magdalens and Jezebels in Counter-Reformation Spain," in Cruz and Perry, *Culture and Control,* 7.

38 Asunción Lavrin, "Introduction: The Scenarios, the Actors, and the Issues," in *Sexuality and Marriage in Colonial Latin America,* ed. Asunción Lavrin (Lincoln, NE, 1989), 10.

39 María Helene Sánchez-Ortega, "Women as a Source of Evil in Counter-Reformation Spain," in Cruz and Perry, *Culture and Control,* 197; Perry, "Magdalens and Jezebels."

40 Heinrich Kramer and James Sprenger, *The Malleus Maleficarum,* trans. Montague Summers (New York, 1971 [1484]).

41 AGN Inquisición, vol. 619, exp. 1, 1672.

42 Kramer and Sprenger, *Malleus Maleficarum,* 42.

43 Trexler, *Sex and Conquest,* 146.

44 Lewis, *Hall of Mirrors;* Fernando Cervantes, *The Devil in the New World* (New Haven, CT, 1994).

45 Toribio Motolinía's account of Indian witchcraft follows his account of Indian polygamy, and he links the Spanish virtues of baptism and monogamy while describing Indian devotion to Christian friars: "Our fathers, why are you abandoning us now after baptizing us and marrying us? . . . If you leave us, to whom will we turn? The devils will try to deceive us again as they used to do, and return us to idolatry"; Motolinía, *Historia de los indios de la Nueva España*

(Barcelona, 1914 [1541]) 125, 135. One Augustinian claimed that Indians were "very carnal" and "incapable of self-restraint," while reserving his greatest condemnation for Indian women; Sergio Ortega Noriega, "Teología novohispana sobre el matrimonio y comportamientos sexuales, 1519–1570," in *De la santidad a la perversión, o de porqué no se cumplía la ley de Dios en la sociedad novohispana*, ed. Sergio Ortega (Mexico City, 1986), 38–39. Archbishop Alonso de Montúfar concerned himself with Indian incest and bigamy. Indians were not only "such loafers" that they did not even want to "work for themselves"; they also engaged in "unspeakable vices" (*bicios nefandos*) beyond incest and duplicate marriages. One of these was the pecado nefando, the "unspeakable sin"; Biblioteca Nacional de Antropología e Historia, Mexico City, Archivo Histórico, file 113, 418, 1554.

46 Gruzinski, "Cenizas del deseo," 262–63.

47 Trexler, *Sex and Conquest*, 103; Sigal, "(Homo)Sexual Desire," 9. The seventeenth-century Spanish lexicographer Sebastián de Covarrubias Orozco defined *puta* as a "whore" (*ramera*) or "base woman" (*ruín muger*) with an "evil odor"; Covarrubias Orozco, *Tesoro de la lengua castellana o española* (Madrid, 1984 [1611]), 889. On the other hand, he silenced *puto* with a Latin definition—*notae significationes et nefandae* or "marks of their shame and unspeakable sin."

48 For instance, two Indian messengers for the Holy Office were called putos by several mestizos and mulattoes who had robbed them (AGN Inquisición, vol. 316, exp. 40, 1617), and an Indian was called a puto by a Spaniard who assaulted him (AGN Criminal, vol. 645, exp. 29, 1578). In other instances, an Indian woman was called a puta by a Spaniard who came to her house looking for "black thieves and runaways" (AGN Criminal, vol. 132, exp. 2, 1647); an Indian woman was called a puta by an unidentified man who also grabbed her by the hair and punched her (AGN Bienes Nacionales, vol. 753, exp. 25, 1604); and an Indian woman was called an "old whore witch" (*puta vieja hechicera*) by the Spaniards who beat her (AGN Criminal, vol. 243, exp. 2, 1643). William B. Taylor identifies a variety of insults, including *joto* ("homosexual") and *cornudo* (cuckold) as part of the stock of sexual epithets employed as "fighting words" by Indian peasants in the late colonial period. Although *puta* is among the terms he references, *puto* is not; Taylor, *Drinking, Homicide, and Rebellions in Colonial Mexican Villages* (Stanford, CA, 1979), 81.

49 Indian women were particularly susceptible to rape and other abuses of power, but Indian men could also be subjected to sexually tinged violence. For instance, when two mulattoes assaulted the Indian Domingo de La Cruz, whom they believed to be a witch, they beat him about the genitals; AGN Inquisición, vol. 517, exp. 13, 1674. And when two mulattoes attacked and attempted to rob an Indian couple, they removed the trousers of the man in an act of symbolic emasculation; AGN Criminal, vol. 109, exp. 20, 1683. Indian men were otherwise portrayed as poor protectors of their own women, and vulnerable even to the female black slaves that slaveholders might send to harass and coerce them; AGN Criminal, vol. 34, exp. 13, 1639; Lewis, *Hall of Mirrors*.

50 Nesvig's contention that the penetrators gave such names to their passive part-

ners might not be entirely accurate, for the original text states that "old men and young boys . . . called each other girls and gave themselves the names of beautiful women from this city"; Nesvig, "Complicated Terrain," 701.

51 Gustav Henningsen, *The Witches' Advocate: Basque Witchcraft and the Spanish Inquisition (1609–1614)* (Reno, NV, 1980), 22.

52 Solange Alberro, *La actividad del Santo Oficio de la Inquisición en Nueva España, 1571–1700* (Mexico City, 1981), 86; Alberro, "Herejes, brujas y beatas: Mujeres ante el tribunal del Santo Oficio de la Inquisición en la Nueva España," in *Presencia y transparencia: La mujer en la historia de México*, ed. Carmen Ramos-Escandón (Mexico City, 1987); Alberro, *Inquisición y sociedad en México, 1571–1700* (Mexico City, 1988), 192; Ruth Behar, "Sex and Sin, Witchcraft and the Devil in Late-Colonial Mexico," *American Ethnologist* 14 (1987): 42; Cervantes, *Devil in the New World*, chap. 5.

53 One early punishment consisted of "two hundred lashes" (AGN Inquisición, vol. 38, exp. 5, 1537, Mexico City). This was common for many offenses, but it was likely formulaic, since such excess would certainly kill the offender; see also AGN Inquisición, vol. 206, exps. 4, 5, 6, 7, 1593, Mexico City; AGN Inquisición, vol. 523, exp. 3, 1686, Querétaro. On the Inquisition's treatment of women, see Lewis, *Hall of Mirrors*, esp. chaps. 2 and 5; Alberro, "Herejes, brujas y beatas"; Behar, "Sex and Sin"; and Cervantes, *Devil in the New World*, chap. 5.

54 Cited in J. Jorge Klor de Alva, "Colonizing Souls: The Failure of the Indian Inquisition and the Rise of Penitential Discipline," in *Cultural Encounters: The Impact of the Inquisition in Spain and the New World*, ed. Mary Elizabeth Perry and Anne J. Cruz (Berkeley, CA, 1991), 14; see also Alberro, *Actividad del Santo Oficio*, 100. Klor de Alva argues that the shift away from inquisitorial punishment for Indians was due to the recognition that its selective methods were ineffective in eliminating the "minute illegalities" that were the stuff of Indian deviance from Spanish social norms. Required instead was a system of indoctrination and retraining led by priests and secular officials. In Peru such a system produced large-scale and violent extirpation campaigns; Kenneth Mills, *An Evil Lost to View? An Investigation of Post-evangelisation Andean Religion in Mid-colonial Peru* (Liverpool, 1994), 26–27. In Mexico, perceived links between Indians and the devil actually strengthened during the seventeenth century; Fernando Cervantes, *The Idea of the Devil and the Problem of the Indian: The Case of Mexico in the Sixteenth Century* (London, 1991); Cervantes, *Devil in the New World*, chap. 1.

55 AGN Inquisición, vol. 498, exp. 16, 1691. Gruzinski's contention that homosexuality was an urban phenomenon confined to large cities, a contention echoed with some caveats by Nesvig ("Complicated Terrain," 700), is belied by this case, which occurred in a provincial town (Mérida).

56 Monter (*Frontiers of Heresy*, 287–88) writes in this respect that "even the tribunal of Mexico had to be warned in 1580 that Rome would never permit them to judge either sodomy or incest." Alberro's statistical compilation of sixteenth- and seventeenth-century Inquisition cases indicates that the most common "sexual" sins were bigamy, polygamy, and fornication outside the sanctity of marriage; Alberro, *Actividad del Santo Oficio*.

57 Interestingly, Las Casas describes a Mayan spirit named Chan who was said to have introduced sodomy to the natives; Trexler, *Sex and Conquest*, 93.

58 It is worth noting that the verb *jugar*, to play, was the same word used to describe Juan de La Vega's activities with another man.

59 For an extended discussion of caste meanings and relationships in colonial society, see Lewis, *Hall of Mirrors*. There I argue that *casta* (caste) was a concept distinct from what we today call "race." It was a network of hierarchical connections between the different social segments of colonial society—principally Indians, Spaniards, mulattoes (black/Indian and black/Spanish mixtures), mestizos (Spanish/Indian mixtures), and blacks. "Caste" was defined by genealogy (both symbolic and real), degrees and different sorts of power, notions of temperament, and behavioral attributes. Spaniards and Indians formed the two extremes of the caste system while mestizos, mulattoes, and blacks mediated these poles in a variety of ways.

60 Lewis, *Hall of Mirrors*, chap. 3.

61 The term *weakness*, or variations thereon, is repeatedly associated with women and Indians in colonial texts. Franco (*Plotting Women*, xiii) writes in this regard that "the 'natural' weakness of women was the ideological pin that rotated the axis of power" in New Spain; see also Irene Silverblatt, *Moon, Sun, and Witches: Gender Ideologies and Class in Inca and Colonial Peru* (Princeton, NJ, 1987), 161. I extend the implications of this observation to Indians.

62 Trexler, *Sex and Conquest*, 134–35.

63 Greenberg, *Construction of Homosexuality*, 295; Perry, *Gender and Disorder*, 124, 133.

64 Marjorie Garber, *Vested Interests: Cross-Dressing and Cultural Anxiety* (New York, 1992), 223.

65 Trexler, *Sex and Conquest*, 142.

66 Perry (*Gender and Disorder*, 136) writes that few such women can be found in the Spanish records because women were less free than men to express themselves through dress, controlled, as they were, through "the home, the convent, the brothel, the confessional, and a system of charity." This might be true for Spanish records, but I have found as many transvested women in the Mexican records as I have found men.

67 Ibid.; Nanda, *Gender Diversity*.

68 Greenberg, *Construction of Homosexuality*, 306, 310–11; Perry, *Gender and Disorder*, 123; Nanda, *Gender Diversity*, 87–88.

69 As Bishop Juan de Zumárraga wrote, "Sodomy is a very abominable placing of the virile member in the dirtiest and ugliest part of the body of the person who receives the man; that part is delegated to the expulsion of feces"; cited in Nesvig, "Complicated Terrain," 694, which also notes that Zumárraga did not consider sodomy performed on a woman by a man to be as sinful as the male-male variation.

70 Perry, *Gender and Disorder*, 127–36. It might be worth noting in this regard that contemporary Euro-American society tolerates women who dress like men—attested by the ubiquity of trousers—to a much higher degree than it tolerates men who dress like women. For who, society says, would want to be a woman?

71 Ibid., 133–34.

72 The reference in the text to Lent suggests that Las Vírgenes might have been given more leeway had she chosen to wear this garb at some other time, for the authorities probably interpreted her actions as mocking the clergy, as was

the case with an incident I discuss below. Stallybrass and White (*Politics and Poetics*, 184) discuss how Carnival precedes Lent in a kind of a battle between the classical and the grotesque—the thin, deprived, clean body and the meaty, excessive, promiscuous one—and Lent invariably triumphs.

73 AGN Bienes Nacionales, vol. 596, exp. 20, 1684.
74 Garber, *Vested Interests*, 25.
75 Horswell, "Toward an Andean Theory," 37–40.
76 Trexler, *Religion in Social Context*, 392, 399, 399n97.
77 Garber, *Vested Interests*, 220.
78 Gruzinski, "Cenizas del deseo," 272–73.
79 AGN Bienes Nacionales, vol. 732, exp. 2, 1605.
80 AGN Inquisición, vol. 276, exp. 2, 1605.
81 Trexler (*Religion in Social Context*, 380) draws connections in fifteenth-century Europe between the clothes worn by clergy, those worn by statues of the Virgin, and altar cloths, all of which were interchangeable.
82 For more on this trial, see Lewis, *Hall of Mirrors*, 138–42.
83 AGN Inquisición, vol. 147, exp. 6, 1595.
84 Lewis, *Hall of Mirrors*, chap. 7; see also Susan M. Deeds, "Brujería, género e inquisición en Nueva Vizcaya," *Desacatos: Revista de antropología social* (Fall/Winter 2002): 30–47, for a discussion of this case.
85 AGN Inquisición, vol. 525, exp. 48, 1691.
86 Stallybrass and White, *Politics and Poetics*, 182.
87 Ibid., 44.
88 Bartolomé de Las Casas, *The Devastation of the Indies*, trans. Herman Briffault (Baltimore, 1992 [1552]).
89 Stallybrass and White, *Politics and Poetics*, 147.
90 Alison Weber, "Saint Teresa, Demonologist," in Cruz and Perry, *Culture and Control*, 173, 176.
91 AGN Inquisición, vol. 439, exp. 14, 1656.
92 AGN Inquisición, vol. 218, exp. 4, 1598.
93 See also Michael Taussig, *Shamanism, Colonialism, and the Wild Man: A Study in Terror and Healing* (Chicago, 1987), 259, 264.
94 AGN Inquisición, vol. 442 exp. 33, 1652.
95 Garber, *Vested Interests*, 212.
96 Rossell Hope Robbins, *The Encyclopedia of Witchcraft and Demonology* (New York, 1959), 41.
97 Boswell, *Christianity*, 188; Greenberg, *Construction of Homosexuality*, 285–86, 290.
98 Trexler, *Sex and Conquest*, 3; see also Sigal, "(Homo)Sexual Desire," 15.
99 Greenberg, *Construction of Homosexuality*, 312.
100 Trexler, *Sex and Conquest*, 3.
101 Greenberg, *Construction of Homosexuality*, 291.
102 Indeed, in a number of European social arenas contagions were thought to "trickle down" from elites to ordinary people; Trexler, *Sex and Conquest*, 146–47. Thus Greenberg (*Construction of Homosexuality*, 294–95) writes of Italian and French class antagonisms that linked "sodomy" and other excessive "indulgences" to fourteenth-century ruling elites, while Marjorie Garber (*Vested Interests*, 26–28) notes that England's Elizabeth I was a famous cross-dresser, whose reign was "the apogee of a movement to regulate dress" among

the masses quick to follow the lead of their transvested monarch. In 1597, the British authorities even closed theaters because of the "verie great disorders" that the "lewd matters" of plays encouraged; Stallybrass and White, *Politics and Poetics*, 62. Stallybrass and White also analyze the later processes by which the bourgeois co-opted the messiness of Carnival dress through masquerade, while simultaneously subjecting public spaces to increasing regulation.

103 Garber, *Vested Interests*, 24–25.
104 Lewis, *Hall of Mirrors*, 18–19, 52–53.

"That Monster of Nature": Gender, Sexuality, and the Medicalization of a "Hermaphrodite" in Late Colonial Guatemala

Martha Few, *University of Arizona*

Abstract. In Guatemala City in 1803, the court of the Royal Protomedicato requested that the physician Narciso Esparragosa examine Juana Aguilar, called by the court a "suspected hermaphrodite," as part of the legal proceedings against her for double concubinage with men and women. This essay considers Esparragosa's report on Aguilar's sexual ambiguity and his efforts to classify her. The first section analyzes the scope and purpose of the report and places Esparragosa's anatomical and physiological assertions within the context of Enlightenment-era understandings of sexuality and sexual difference. The second section traces how Esparragosa built the argument that led him to classify Aguilar and her ambiguous sexuality into a separate category of "neither man nor woman." Throughout his medical report, Esparragosa appropriated the language of monstrosity to underpin his characterization of Aguilar's sexual and physical difference, recast in gendered and racialized terms. He used these assertions to make certain claims of categorization that attempted to naturalize the female genitalia and to argue that female anatomical and physiological ambiguity led to sexual deviance.

In Guatemala City in 1803, the criminal court began prosecuting Juana Aguilar for the crime of double concubinage with men and women. As the court pursued the case against Aguilar, whose sexual ambiguity quickly came to the fore, the judge referred the matter to the court of the Royal Protomedicato, the bureaucracy that regulated medical and health issues in the colonies. The Protomedicato requested that the physician Narciso Esparragosa examine Juana Aguilar, called by the court "a suspected hermaphrodite," and present his findings.[1]

Esparragosa, in a meticulously written medical report, noted that at first glance Aguilar's external genitalia appeared "the same as in every

Ethnohistory 54:1 (Winter 2007) DOI 10.1215/00141801-2006-042

woman," except for what he described as an enlarged clitoris that he mea-sured to be an inch and a half long. A further physical examination of Aguilar revealed that the skin of the vaginal area was "stuck together." And, to his expressed surprise, Esparragosa discovered near the clitoris what he called "two glandular bodies, with an oval shape, of the size of a cacao bean." He judged these to be either misplaced ovaries or incom-pletely formed testicles. Esparragosa submitted his report on Aguilar to the Protomedicato court. The *Gazeta de Guatemala*, a colonial-era news-paper, published it over two issues under the headline "Hermaphrodites" (*Hermafroditas*).

The Audiencia of Guatemala, which in the colonial period stretched from what is today the Mexican state of Chiapas through much of Central America, is an important but largely overlooked site to analyze the material and ideological interactions surrounding medicine and healing in colo-nial Latin America. At the time of Juana Aguilar's legal case, the capital, Nueva Guatemala, had a medical school, public health board, medical court, hospitals, and active formal and popular medical cultures. The com-munity of physicians, healers, and scientists practicing in colonial Guate-mala, in which Esparragosa played a major role, was neither insular nor parochial. Its members engaged with broader issues facing health policy and medical practice, not only in Central America, but also in the Spanish Empire and Europe. The case of Juana Aguilar and Esparragosa's proposed framework to define sexual difference drew on his medical experiences in Guatemala, while at the same time he placed his findings within the con-text of the larger intellectual debates about sex difference and sexuality of the Enlightenment era and its aftermath.[2]

This essay in two parts considers Esparragosa's report on Juana Agui-lar's sexual ambiguity and his efforts to classify her. The first section analyzes the scope and purpose of Esparragosa's report and places his anatomical and physiological assertions within the context of Enlightenment-era understandings of sexuality and sexual difference. In the report, Esparra-gosa asserted not only that Juana Aguilar was not a hermaphrodite, but that the hermaphrodite, what he called "that monster of nature," was a fiction perpetuated by certain mistaken learned physicians, anatomists, and philosophers, as well as an example of the ignorance of "the common people."[3] Through his report debunking the hermaphrodite and its pub-lication in the *Gazeta de Guatemala*, Esparragosa strove to establish his place among other Western medical physicians in what he called "this new century of learning," based on his experience in healing cultures of colonial Central America.

The second section traces how Esparragosa built the argument that led him to classify Juana Aguilar and her ambiguous sexuality in a separate category, not as "man and woman" (which is how he defined a hermaphrodite) but as "neither man nor woman." Esparragosa's categorization relied on the juxtaposition of the anatomy and physiology of the female genitalia, and particularly the clitoris, in what he called its "natural state." He contrasted this with a description of Aguilar's ambiguous genitalia and her enlarged clitoris.

Throughout his medical report to the Royal Protomedicato, Esparragosa appropriated the language of monstrosity to underpin his characterization of Aguilar's sexual and physical difference, recast in gendered terms to make certain claims of categorization. This new categorization hinged on an attempt to naturalize the female genitalia, and in particular the clitoris, that could then be used as a contrast to other women's "deformed" and "excessive" physical bodies and body parts, and to make claims about the potential for sexual deviance based on women's anatomy and physiology. Esparragosa's reconfiguration of ideas of monstrosity to depict anatomical and physiological ambiguity and outline its tendency to sexual deviance, placed within the context of scientific frameworks and language of sexuality, worked to legitimize medicine's authority, and his own as a medical practitioner, to judge cases of sexual ambiguity.

In the process, the medical description of Aguilar and her anatomy became a way to circulate explicit information about male and female genitalia and their physical functions. It also became a means to circulate information about Aguilar's exotic, exceptional body, both to the legal court and to the broader public. The representation of Aguilar and her body for the cause of medicine and scientific inquiry effectively put her on public display, in a way that informed readers about scientific and medical analytic processes and at the same time entertained them with anatomical details of women's bodies and racialized claims about certain women's sexual proclivities.

Debunking the Monstrous Hermaphrodite

Hermaphroditism and other physical expressions of sexual ambiguity are today known as intersexuality and can be attributed to genetic or hormonal anomalies.[4] In historical analyses of cases of intersexuality, the use of gendered pronouns proves a difficult issue. This is especially the case here, as so far I have not found any legal testimony or other information that recorded Juana Aguilar's own words. For purposes of this essay, I will refer to Aguilar as "she." Aguilar's given name, as recorded in Esparragosa's medical report, is feminine, and he refers to her as "La Juana" and "she." Aguilar is also briefly described as wearing female clothing.[5] In addition, Esparragosa referred to Aguilar in the report as "Juana La Larga," which appears to be in reference to the size of her clitoris, as this nickname roughly translates into "Long Juana."[6] She was commonly known as "Juana La Larga," as rumors of her sexual ambiguity had spread throughout the capital city, presumably also fueled by the publication in the newspaper of Esparragosa's medical report. The documents do not record Aguilar's age, race or ethnicity, genealogy, or family life; nor do they shed light on the resolution of the legal case.

Esparragosa was a rising star in medicine who eventually became head physician of the Protomedicato, the medical court of colonial Central America. Born in Venezuela, he emigrated to Guatemala in 1785. He studied medicine under the premier late-eighteenth-century physician José Flores at the University of San Carlos in the capital city of Santiago (now Antigua).[7] Esparragosa came to hold a chair in the medical school at the university and performed new surgeries such as the first successful cataract operation in Central America. He also invented new medical tools and instruments including the *asa elástica*, rubber forceps designed to aid in the delivery of healthy infants in difficult births. He also helped manage the anti-smallpox campaigns of the late eighteenth and early nineteenth centuries. He published on his research in Guatemala and Europe. At the height of his career, Esparragosa was arguably one of the leading physicians in Central America with a growing international reputation.

Esparragosa began his medical report on Juana Aguilar's sexual ambiguity by telling the reader that she was not a hermaphrodite. This assertion contradicted the claims of those who had previously examined her. It also contradicted public speculation about Aguilar that was rampant in the capital. Esparragosa wrote:

> Naturally, the present case of Juana La Larga, object of my investigations and of this report, has been cited previously as something certain, [as] irrefutable proof of hermaphroditism for future ages. If it had not been for the criminal excesses that have been attributed to her, she would not have been subject to the judgment of the Tribunal [of the Royal Protomedicato] and had [the issue] resolved by the most prudent and only means [necessary] to unmask that phenomenon.

Esparragosa also argued that the legal arena of the Protomedicato court of the Audiencia of Guatemala was the appropriate place to definitively judge Aguilar's "suspected" hermaphroditism.

To bolster his assertion that Aguilar was not a hermaphrodite, Esparragosa challenged the findings of female midwives (*parteras*) and surgeons (*cirujanos*) who had previously examined her body and categorized her. "As a result," Esparragosa wrote,

> there remains to be dissipated [by] the brilliant light of my experi-
> ence the darkness of whim and the ignorance with which it has been
> concluded [that Aguilar was a hermaphrodite], as those who have
> charged that she consummated the carnal act as a man, such as the
> midwives and surgeons who, by recognizing what they believed and
> asserted to be a hermaphrodite, gave weight to such an error, so that
> the unhappy one [Aguilar] should suffer at the very least some same
> punishment as the Athenians and Romans have agreed to for sup-
> posed hermaphrodites, the result of their ignorant superstition, and
> by their false philosophy.

Here Esparragosa attacked three kinds of medical practitioners and creators of medical knowledge: female midwives, lay healers (such as empiric surgeons), and ancient philosophers whose scholarship had under-pinned conceptions of illness, healing, and the body into the medieval and early modern periods. Between the seventeenth and the early nineteenth centuries, the cultural authority and power to interpret illness was gradu-ally transferred to licensed male medical physicians, as part of the profes-sionalization of medicine. This transformation broke down the authority of the midwives, lay healers, and ancient scholars who previously had structured cultural understandings and scientific practices of health and healing.[8] Esparragosa was conscious of his place in this new era. Through this medical report he sought establish a place for himself as part of the Enlightenment, what he called the *siglo de más ilustración*, the "century of great learning." He also disseminated his findings to the broader public by publishing his report in the *Gazeta de Guatemala*.[9]

Within this intellectual and historical context, Esparragosa depicted himself as a heroic physician using the weapons of reason and observation to slay the misguided belief in the "fantastic being" (*ente quimérico*) of the hermaphrodite: "[The hermaphrodite] is opposed to [what we know from] experience, claimed by the invariable laws of nature. And, with the weapons so invincible of the learned . . . of this century that is about to end, [who] fight against that monster [*monstruo*] between a multitude of physiques and anatomies, [and] whose profound knowledge and respected authority, erected above the insurmountable throne of observation and of the most decisive reasoning, obliges me to follow in their footsteps."

Here, what is monstrous to Esparragosa is the figure of the hermaph-rodite, as a relic of the ignorance of ancient scholars, and as an example of the tendency of the common people to "easily give their credulity to all that is presented with a mysterious air and outside of nature's scope." The classification of the hermaphrodite as a monster drew on familiar medieval and early modern tropes used to represent beings that Europeans speculated about or expected to find outside of Europe, and that were written about and represented in maps, travel accounts, artwork, and other sources. For Esparragosa, in this "new century of learning," the monstrous hermaphrodite needed to be debunked, using the newfound tools of reason and observation, to leave behind the previous era of ignorance.

Esparragosa linked his depiction of Aguilar to historical traditions of the monstrous and marvelous, reconfigured in late colonial Guatemala. At the time of European colonization of the New World, the monstrous and marvelous together were components of late medieval and early modern conceptions of "wonder," and were often invoked to distinguish between the known and the unknown, the civilized and the barbaric, in European intellectual thought and the popular imagination.[10] Scholars have analyzed the role that the monstrous and marvelous played in discovery accounts as a key literary strategy that shaped written descriptions of encounters between Old and New World peoples and landscapes.[11]

These discourses also played a central role in everyday conceptions of health and illness in southern New Spain as European wonder interacted with Mesoamerican ideologies of monstrous and marvelous exceptionalism. Physicians, popular healers, and colonial peoples appropriated and used descriptions of monsters and marvels in the context of physical expressions of health, illness, and pain in daily life throughout the colonial period. While Esparragosa used what can be seen as a traditional rhetoric of monsters to talk about exceptionalism, here and as we will see below, he is commenting instead on Aguilar's genital anatomy.

Esparragosa was not exceptional in his intellectual curiosity and medical investigations regarding hermaphrodites. Hermaphrodites were a key preoccupation of the early modern and modern eras, and the hermaphrodite frequently appeared in medical, legal, and popular works.[12] Lorraine Daston and Katharine Park argue that a wide range of interpretations of hermaphrodites existed in the early modern period, as did distinctive differences among the various European national medical traditions.[13] At stake were competing ideas regarding generation, sexual difference, and their social implications. The mid-nineteenth to the early twentieth centuries again saw a preoccupation with defining sexual identity and sexual difference through the lens of the hermaphrodite, as Western medical and scientific men sought to establish the categories of "true" male and female, and link them to emerging ideologies that naturalized heterosexuality.[14]

Esparragosa's analysis of Aguilar and his arguments about how to classify her sexuality bridges early modern writings on the topic with emerging modern approaches to sexual identity and sexual difference from the mid-nineteenth century on, such as the famous case of Abel/Alexina Barbin of France, who, after committing suicide in Paris in 1868, was "discovered" to be a hermaphrodite during a postmortem exam.[15] Esparragosa's writings show that he was familiar with a larger literature on hermaphrodites, as well as anatomy and other medical writings on the human body. He also anticipated issues that become key to late-nineteenth- and early-twentieth-century writings on the topic, as we will see below, as he strove to establish a definition of "natural" female genitalia, and juxtapose that with what he found during his examinations of Aguilar's body to construct the category "neither man nor woman."

Medicine, Monstrosity, and Categories of Sexual Difference

As Esparragosa proceeded, he developed the argument that sexual categorization was not defined by gendered social roles—what economic activity one performed, whether one took care of children and the elderly or gathered and prepared food for the family. Nor did sexual categorization depend on the clothing one wore or how an individual self-identified. Instead, according to Esparragosa's model, sexual categorization turned on whether or not the person had male or female sexual organs: "But how such a deceptive understanding can be so capable of being mistaken! And such outlandishness can support ignorance! Juana La Larga not only does not join [together] the two sexes, she is lacking the male [sexual] organs, and also nature has denied her the necessary [sexual organs] to constitute a woman. Rare phenomenon!"

Esparragosa began to build his argument to categorize Aguilar as "neither man nor woman," explaining just what he meant by sexual organs, and what parts of those mattered for his assessment. To support his assertions, Esparragosa told his readers that he would first describe female genitalia in what he called their natural state, and then compare them with what he found during his physical examinations of Aguilar's body. This, he believed, would lay the ground work for him to expose the false idea that the natural world included the hermaphrodite:

> To demonstrate this truth to [the Royal Protomedicato], daughter of the most scrupulous and loyal observation, it appears to me absolutely necessary to briefly describe the external sexual organs that one observes in women by simple sight, in their natural state, [and from

there] provide an analysis of those of La Juana, [that] one observes by
an exact result of [the] comparison [of] the differences between them,
and the original deformity of the last, so, with regard to the excess
and the defect.

This "deformity" and "defect" in Aguilar's genitalia was the clitoris: "The
labia, which are separated, [are] joined together in their uppermost part
by a somewhat prominent small body, very similar to a [male] member
[*miembro*], called a clitoris, whose circumstances it seems to me are necessary to describe, in particular because it is the organ that in this scene
assumes a distinguished and admirable role." Here it is the clitoris that
stands in for female genitalia as the important factor for Esparragosa in
determining just where Aguilar fit in.

There are two strands of historiographical argument about how
medical writers and others characterized sexual difference from the early
modern to the modern era. Thomas Laqueur has argued for a premodern
one-sex model (before the 1800s), that is, medical writers theorized that
only one sex existed, the male.[16] Women, according this model, had male
genitalia inside their bodies, but this genitalia stayed inside because women
had colder bodies than men did. If women's bodies at some point became
unnaturally hot, due to inappropriate work, exercise, and so on, the male
genitalia could suddenly emerge, transforming them. This was the explanation given in 1573 by Ambroise Paré, a French medical writer who analyzed the case of Germain Garnie. She lived the first part of her life as a
female, but then when she was fifteen years old, she ran and jumped over a
ditch, causing a penis to appear on her body. Around the turn of the nineteenth century, Laqueur argues, the two-sex model for sexual difference
emerged in Western medical literature, a new medical idea that saw male
and female sexes as distinct.

Other writers, including Joan Cadden, Lorraine Daston, and
Katharine Park, argue that the one-sex model never dominated Western
medical thought about sex difference. Instead, the Middle Ages and the
early modern era saw two distinct models, the Hippocratic and the Aristotelian.[17] The Hippocratic model viewed sex difference as a spectrum
between male and female on either end with possibilities for intermediate
sex lying in between.[18] The Aristotelian model saw sex difference as either
male or female, with no intermediate possibilities. In the Aristotelian
model, the sex of a hermaphrodite was determined not by the genitals he
or she possessed but by "the heat of the heart, which in turn determined
the complexion of the body as a whole."[19] From these models, two con-
trasting views of hermaphroditism emerged, each with different sexual
and social implications. The Aristotelian model maintained sex difference

as either/or with no intermediate possibilities. The Hippocratic model, however, allowed for a range of categories of sexual difference. The stances occupied by these two schools of thought created the conditions for a lively debate about hermaphrodites and sex difference in the early modern medical literature.[20]

Esparragosa conceptualized the differences between male and female via the genitalia. He focused specifically on the clitoris and penis as the key aspects of Aguilar's genitalia that would reveal which category Aguilar fit into. Esparragosa first considered whether or not Aguilar's clitoris was in fact a male penis in less developed form. His description of the clitoris linked its physiology and function to a penis: "Not only is the exterior configuration of the clitoris very similar to the virile member, but also its internal structure, in the way that according to the uniform consent of the most famous anatomists, it only lacks the urethra or the duct through which urine leaves [the body], for which one can not establish any difference whatsoever between the sexes."

While Greek medical and surgical authors had identified the clitoris as a distinct part of the female genitalia, European medical authors had lost that knowledge, only to rediscover it in the mid-sixteenth century.[21] In early modern European medical literature, Renaldo Colombo, in his treatise *De re anatomica* (*On Anatomy*), published in 1559, was the first to "rediscover" the clitoris and link it to female sexual pleasure.[22] Colombo remarked, "since no one has discerned these projections and their workings, if it is permissible to give names to things discovered by me, it should be called the love or sweetness of Venus."[23]

Esparragosa clearly was aware of this literature when he linked the clitoris to female sexual pleasure in his report on Aguilar: "The organ that I have just described [the clitoris] physiologists have conceded has the property of exciting lustfulness [*concupiscencia*], because during intercourse no other part receives more delight." For Esparragosa's analysis, then, the clitoris was a key part of the female anatomy because of its "lustful" properties, an important element not only in classifying male and female, but also in trying to explain Aguilar's reported sexual behavior.

Esparragosa next focused on size, what he described as Aguilar's overly large clitoris: "At first glance, I observe in La Juana the large labia, the same as in every woman, with the difference that [her] clitoris sticks out from between them a little more than half an inch. That is not very strange, since in some women one observes the same prominence. [And] separating the labia and locating the clitoris one observes it to be an inch and a half from its root to its tip."

As Esparragosa's interest was in whether or not Aguilar was capable of performing the sexual act as a man, he quickly added that even though the clitoris had a similar anatomical appearance to the penis, Aguilar's clitoris was not, in fact, a penis. "Its exterior configuration exactly resembl[es] that of the virile member with its head, gland and foreskin, but it lacks the urine duct that longitudinally perforates the man's member."

In some ways Esparragosa's focus on anatomy, especially the question of whether or not Aguilar had a clitoris or a penis, anticipated the focus on anatomy in analyses of sexual difference developed in the field of teratology some three decades later, in the 1830s.[24] This highly influential field portrayed sexual difference as a continuum in which sexually ambiguous, "effeminate men" and "masculine women" occupied a gray area between the ideal "types" of man and woman. Katharine Park and Robert Nye point out that for Isidore Geoffroy Saint-Hilaire, "a large clitoris was an 'arrested penis' and a small penis a 'hypertrophied clitoris' and both inclined their bearers away from the 'type' of their sex."[25]

Esparragosa argued that Aguilar's genital anatomy, specifically her enlarged clitoris, was key to placing her in the correct sexual category. But as is apparent here, anatomy and anatomical depictions as reported in medical literature are not fixed but instead vary by historical and cultural context, playing a significant role in the production and maintenance of sexual difference.[26] Lisa Jean Moore and Adele Clark argue that anatomies, while seemingly stable and "known," are "socially constructed and diverse not only across historical time but within particular eras."[27] By labeling the clitoris as the site of women's lustful behavior, and connecting that lust to size, Esparragosa made a medical claim that tied Aguilar's sexuality to the size of her clitoris.

Anatomical labels were important for the establishment and maintenance of what is normal for women's bodies, and by extension their sexual behavior.[28] Sixteenth-century representations of the clitoris by Renaldo Colombo and Gabriele Falloppia both describe it as a "female penis."[29] Within the renewed medical interest in the clitoris, French medical authors Ambroise Paré (1573) and Jean Riolan (1614) were the first postclassical medical authors to extend the connection between the clitoris and female sexual pleasure to the possibilities of sexual desire and sexual activity between women. Park argued that the larger implications for the rediscovery of the clitoris in the medical writing of early modern Europe and the clitoris's function as the locus of female pleasure "proved explosive, triggering a host of contemporary cultural concerns about female sexuality."[30]

Esparragosa pointed out the possibilities and dangers that an enlarged clitoris might pose to Aguilar's sexual activity in particular, and women's sexual activity in general. For Esparragosa, this possibility turned on whether Aguilar's clitoris could become erect and thus make vaginal penetration possible. He asserted that Aguilar's clitoris could not become erect, even though he tried "many" times to stimulate it: "The consistency of the clitoris is so flaccid that it falls from its own weight beneath the rest of the parts, and despite many different examinations and handlings, I have not noted even a weak erection [of the clitoris]."

Whether Aguilar's clitoris could become erect was an important question, since this would allow her to take the active sexual role in relations with other women, as the charge of having sex with men and women accused her of doing. The question then is how to interpret the meaning of "double concubinage" in Aguilar's case.[31] The crime/sin of concubinage in colonial Latin America referred to the cohabitation of persons not legally married, but this usually referred to a man and a woman. The "double" here appears to have charged that Aguilar cohabitated with men and women, and Esparragosa's detailed analysis of the clitoris and its physiology focuses on this possibility.[32] Esparragosa never used the phrase "double concubinage" in his report. Because Aguilar's clitoris was not a penis and could not become erect, Esparragosa concluded that she was not capable of the sexual act as a man because "even if one concedes that in the act of coitus it was possible for it [the clitoris] to acquire some kind of erection, that pleasure would be little more than that which obscene friction [*la obscena confricación*] would provide, that one is aware of between women, but [such an act] lacks the seminal pollution." The question remained, however, whether Aguilar could participate in other kinds of sexual acts with women, what Esparragosa referred to as sodomy (*pecado nefando*), here raising the possibility of identifying female sexual deviance based on the size of female body parts.

Daston and Park have shown that early modern medical writers often linked hermaphrodites to transgressive sexual behavior of sodomy, transvestism, and sexual transformation.[33] Esparragosa also used this connection in his own analysis. The meaning of sodomy in this historical context included both sexual acts between men and sexual acts between women. Esparragosa was eager to spell out the social implications and dangers that an enlarged clitoris posed: sodomy and masturbation. Even though Esparragosa did not consider Aguilar a hermaphrodite, he continued to associate sexual ambiguity, and what he depicted as a large clitoris, with transgressive female sexual behavior.

In contrast to the present case, most of the work on pecado nefando and sodomy in colonial Latin America has dealt with sexual relations between men. The pecado nefando, or the abominable or unmentionable sin, referred to the sexual act between members of the same sex. In colonial documents, this was often used with the phrase "against nature" (*contra natura*) and "of sodomy" (*de sodomía*).[34] This act could also be referred to simply as "sodomy." Esparragosa used both terms in his report. The policing of sodomy increased after the Council of Trent reforms (1545–63), when the policing of sexuality became an especially important part of Catholic ideology in colonial Latin America and elsewhere.[35]

Amid the analysis of the link between an enlarged clitoris and the tendency toward sodomy, Esparragosa took the opportunity to argue that this same enlarged clitoris had led the midwives, surgeons, and others to mistakenly declare Aguilar to be a hermaphrodite. He noted that it was not uncommon to see women with large clitorises such as Aguilar's, particularly among "Egyptian women" and other women of the "East":

> One has observed with excessive frequency the extraordinary size [of the clitoris], as have testified various anatomists and surgeons. That excess that is most familiar to us is the excess [found] among Egyptians and the rest of the nations of the East, where it is necessary that their women suffer burning or amputation for the purpose that they remain suitable for marriage; this kind of surgery being very common in those nations, as much for necessity as for honor [and decorum].

Aguilar fell into this category of women who tended toward transgressive sexual behavior due to an overly large clitoris. Esparragosa continued to use the language of monstrosity. The focus shifted, however, from hermaphrodites ("that monster of nature") to the monstrous female bodies of women like Aguilar, whose enlarged clitoris supposedly resembled those of exoticized women of the "East," whose threat had to be tamed through clitoridectomy by burning or amputation.[36] Implicit in Esparragosa's use of the terms "Egyptian" and "nations of the East" is the association with "blackness," applied in sexualized terms to layer racial and gender stereotypes onto his medical interpretation of Aguilar. The theme of non-Christian Egyptians, Ethiopians, and other North African and Middle Eastern peoples as monstrous races dates from antiquity to early modern Europe.[37]

For Esparragosa and, I would argue, for colonial Guatemalan society in general, what was dangerous about monstrous female bodies and body parts was the possibility that this would lead to transgressive female sexual behavior of the kind that Juana Aguilar was charged with engaging in. This included the possibility of women's masturbation, but also sexual interactions between women, both seen as transgressive acts that challenged gendered social roles of colonial society, and the heterosexual relations that structured it legally, religiously, and socially. Esparragosa wrote: "The excess size [of the clitoris] has contributed much to the reprehensible abuse that some women have committed to capriciously sate their lasciviousness, cheating men of that which nature has granted them."

The possibility of female-female sexual acts also threatened the construction and subsequent naturalization of male sexual roles as the providers of female sexual pleasure. This framework as a biolegal discourse had serious implications. In addition to establishing what is natural in terms of physical bodies, Esparragosa also extended this to make claims as to what is natural in terms of sexual relations—heterosexual sexual relations in which "nature" gives men the active role.

The Medicalization of Sexuality in Late Colonial Guatemala

Esparragosa's medical findings regarding Aguilar, his claims of categories of sexual difference and characterizations of sexual transgression, were given broad authority by their production in the legal context of the Protomedicato court, and by their publication for the broader public in the *Gazeta de Guatemala*. Esparragosa's medical report shows his focus on whether or not Aguilar was physically capable of carrying out the sexual acts of which the court accused her. To do so he analyzed the anatomy and physiology of the clitoris and whether or not Aguilar was physically capable of reproduction, acting as either a man or a woman in sexual relations.

For Esparragosa, the urge for what he called unnatural female sexual activity was located in the monstrous body part of an overly large clitoris. By establishing what was considered a "natural" clitoris, given authority by the weight of professional medical knowledge, these kinds of medical writings worked to establish what was "natural" in terms of sexual activity, in the process marking some women as unnatural or at the very least as having the potential for transgressive sexual behavior. In this case, discourses of monstrosity continued to operate as key signifiers of difference in late colonial society, reconfigured through medical writings and legitimized through a legal system that established the criteria for what constituted a natural female body.

The case of Juana Aguilar suggests that by the late eighteenth and early nineteenth century, medical frameworks of sexual difference were not uniform. Nor did medical practitioners in colonial Latin America simply follow European writers on the subject. In his report Esparragosa argued that his examinations of Aguilar's body did not allow him to declare her as either male or female. Nor did she fall into the category of "hermaphrodite," what Esparragosa stridently declared to be a "fiction" of ancient scholars, surgeons, midwives, and common people, as he staked a claim for himself as part of the Enlightenment. Instead he constructed a new category of "neither man nor woman" and carefully worked through his analysis his medical assessment of Juana Aguilar to draw the contours of this new category.

Through medical writings such as Esparragosa's report, one can identify the development and maintenance of ideologies of sexual difference and the construction of the boundaries of natural sexual behavior in late colonial Latin America. Esparragosa's report, his integration of both traditional languages of monstrosities and the larger European medical literature on hermaphrodites and sexual difference, show him to be connected to an Atlantic World circulation of medical theories and writings. This included medical works that addressed the creation and maintenance of medical definitions of sexual difference, as well as the categorization of specific individuals, especially hermaphrodites, in those frameworks, often working in tandem with legal efforts to do the same.

Notes

The medical report that is the basis of this essay was also published in Carlos Martínez Durán, *Las ciencias médicas en Guatemala: Origen y evolución* (Guatemala City, 1941), 267–77. Martínez Durán also included some background information, discussed below, but did not include any citations for this information. Part of his report was printed under the title "Hermafroditas: Informe del Cirujano honorario de Cámera Doctor D. Narciso Esparragosa, hecho a la Real Audiencia en el 3 de febrero de [1803], por orden del Protomedicato, sobre una supuesta hermafrodita," as the lead article in an 1803 edition of the *Gazeta de Guatemala*. A copy of this issue of the *Gazeta* is held at the Archivo General de Centro América, Guatemala City (hereafter AGCA), A1–6083–55038, 1803. All the translations are mine. Previous versions of this essay were presented at the Women's Studies Colloquium at the University of Arizona, October 2004; the American Association for the History of Medicine meetings, Madison, WI, May 2004; "New Directions in Latin American History: A Conference Celebrating New Research on Latin America," Center for Latin American Studies and Department of History, University of Miami, April 2004; and the American Historical Association (cross-listed with the Committee on Latin American History), Washington, DC, January 2004. I thank Guido Ruggiero and Laura Giannetti for their helpful discussions about the history of sexuality and the literature on this topic for early modern Europe. I thank Lisa Vollendorf, who generously shared her research on hermaphroditism, sexuality, and the Inquisition in early modern Spain, part of her book *The Lives of Women: A New History of Inquisitional Spain* (Nashville, TN, 2005). I also thank Pete Sigal and the two anonymous reviewers for their helpful comments.

1 Martínez Durán, in setting up the medical report, noted that a previous criminal case pursued against Aguilar, which began in September 1792 in Cojutepeque, located in what is now El Salvador, charged her with "violat[ing] and tak[ing]" a woman named Feliciana María Mejía. He wrote that the case continued (most likely on and off) for nine years (ending in 1801). During this time period, Aguilar was ordered to submit to at least three physical examinations, by two female midwives (*parteras*) and one male court official (*maestro*). In the end, however, the court does not appear to have made a ruling.

Martínez Durán also noted that, sometime later, Aguilar traveled to Guatemala City and set up an alchemist's shop just off the city's central plaza, the capital's most high-profile, expensive location for businesses and residences. Someone, presumably from Cojutepeque, recognized Aguilar and denounced her to Guatemalan officials. It appears from this background information provided by Martínez Durán that he had access to the original court records and other documents, and that he may have even selectively quoted from them. However, because he provided no footnotes for this information, and because I have not yet been able to locate these documents despite a fairly thorough search at the AGCA in Guatemala City, I will not, at this time, include this information in my analysis.

2 The relatively recent development and application of Atlantic World analytic frameworks to colonial history in the Americas has reinvigorated the analysis of key issues of European colonialism, and this study takes advantage of its strengths. The Atlantic World framework places the circulation of ideas, political culture, and economic exchange within the wider comparative geographic context of North and South America, Europe, and Africa, seeing the region as an interactive whole.

3 Here I draw on Ruggiero's argument that a key issue at stake in the transition to modern medical understandings and practices involved excising what he calls the "everyday cultural" understandings of illness, healing, and the body of the early modern world; Guido Ruggiero, "The Strange Death of Margarita Marcellini: *Male*, Signs, and the Everyday World of Pre-modern Medicine," *American Historical Review* 106 (2002): 1–41.

4 See Alice Domurat Dreger, *Hermaphrodites and the Medical Invention of Sex* (Cambridge, MA, 1998); and Suzanne J. Kessler, *Lessons from the Intersexed* (New Brunswick, NJ, 1998). For a comparative case of hermaphroditism investigated through the Inquisition court in early modern Spain, and an analysis of it in relation to contemporary explanatory frameworks for sexual ambiguity, see Vollendorf, *Lives of Women*.

5 Vollendorf, analyzing the Inquisition case of the hermaphrodite Eleno/a Céspedes, refers to Céspedes as "he" since that was how he identified himself in the testimony. Mary Beth Hall, in her discussion of Thomas/ine Hall in colonial America, uses the gender-neutral "T"; Hall, *Founding Mothers and Fathers: Gendered Power and the Forming of American Society* (New York, 1996). An analysis of the Hall case can also be found in Kathleen M. Brown, *Good Wives, Nasty Wenches, and Anxious Patriarchs: Gender, Race, and Power in Colonial Virginia* (Chapel Hill, NC, 1996), esp. 75–80.

6 This may not be the only possible intention of the nickname, as the word *larga* can have multiple meanings depending on context.

7 Santiago de Guatemala, now Antigua, was the capital of colonial Central

America from 1541 to 1773. After a severe earthquake in 1773 destroyed much of the city, the capital moved to Nueva Guatemala, today known as Guatemala City.

8 Ruggiero argues that the transition to modern medical practice transformed everyday understandings and practices of illness and healing in early modern Italy: "*The program of knowledge* that we label science developed not just from intellectual changes in the high tradition of ideas, not just from new social structures of knowing, but also in crucial and little understood ways by breaking away from everyday ways of knowing and strategies for dealing with the world—the breaking away, that is, from everyday culture" (Ruggiero, "Strange Death," 7; original emphasis).

9 *La Ilustración* is the Spanish term for the Enlightenment.

10 For an analysis of the role of wonder and wonders in Europe from the Middle Ages to the Enlightenment, see Lorraine Daston and Katharine Park, *Wonder and the Order of Nature, 1150–1750* (New York, 1998). And for an analysis of how tropes of wonder and the marvelous operated in discovery narratives of the New World, see Stephen Greenblatt, *Marvelous Possessions: The Wonder of the New World* (Chicago, 1991). On monsters, see, e.g., Park and Daston, "Unnatural Conceptions: The Study of Monsters in Sixteenth- and Seventeenth-Century France and England," *Past and Present* 92 (1981): 20–54; Zakiya Hanafi, *The Monster in the Machine: Magic, Medicine, and the Marvelous in the Time of the Scientific Revolution* (Durham, NC, 2000); and Jeffrey Jerome Cohen, ed., *Monster Theory: Reading Culture* (Minneapolis, 1996).

11 See esp. Greenblatt, *Marvelous Possessions*.

12 An important work that identifies the hermaphrodite as a central object of intense medical, legal, and popular interest in early modern Europe is Lorraine Daston and Katharine Park, "The Hermaphrodite and the Orders of Nature," *Gay and Lesbian Quarterly* 1 (1995): 419–38.

13 Daston and Park, "Hermaphrodite," 419–20. Daston and Park cite the following examples of medical writers concerned with hermaphrodites: Ambroise Paré, *On Monsters and Prodigies* (1573); Jacques Duval, *Treatise on Hermaphrodites* (1612); Jean Riolan, *Discourse on Hermaphrodites* (1614); and Gaspard Bauhin, *On the Nature of Births of Hermaphrodites and Monsters* (1614).

14 Alice Domurat Dreger, *Hermaphrodites and the Medical Invention of Sex* (Cambridge, MA, 1998), 10, 15. See esp. chap. 4, "Hermaphrodites in Love."

15 Barbin's memoirs, dating from 1864, were discovered after his death and published in 1874. For more on this case see Dreger, *Hermaphrodites*, 21–23; and Herculine Barbin, *Herculine Barbin: Being the Recently Discovered Memoirs of a Nineteenth-Century French Hermaphrodite*, intro. Michel Foucault, trans. Richard McDougall (New York, 1980).

16 Thomas Laqueur, *Making Sex: Body and Gender from the Greeks to Freud* (Cambridge, MA, 1990).

17 Much of this discussion is taken from Daston and Park, "Hermaphrodite," 420–24. See also Joan Cadden, *The Meaning of Sex Difference in the Middle Ages: Medicine, Science, and Culture* (Cambridge, MA, 1993).

18 This model is associated with Hippocratic writers and with Galen.

19 Daston and Park, "Hermaphrodite," 421. For more on these two traditions that continued to frame sex difference into the early modern period, see Cadden, *Meaning of Sex Difference*, 15–37.

20 Katharine Park and Robert Nye, "Destiny Is Anatomy," *New Republic*, 18 February 1991, 54.

21 Katharine Park, "The Rediscovery of the Clitoris," in *The Body in Parts: Fantasies of Corporeality in Early Modern Europe*, ed. David Hillman and Carla Mazzio (New York, 1997), outlines this process in early modern French medical writing. Park writes (188n10) that lay healers presumably never lost the knowledge regarding the clitoris and its functions, and they used this knowledge in treating certain female ailments with clitoral stimulation.

22 Ibid., 177. According to Park, Gabriele Falloppia, an Italian medical author and professor of anatomy at Pisa and Padua, wrote about the clitoris around 1550, but he did not publish this work until 1561.

23 Quoted in Laqueur, *Making Sex*, 64.

24 See Isidore Geoffroy Saint-Hilaire, *Histoire générale et particulière des anomalies de l'organisation chez l'homme et les animaux, . . . ou Traité de tératologie (Treatise on Teratology)*, 4 vols. (Paris, 1832–37).

25 Park and Nye, "Anatomy Is Destiny," 56.

26 See Lisa Jean Moore and Adele E. Clark, "Clitoral Conventions and Transgressions: Graphic Representations in Anatomy Texts, c1900-1991," *Feminist Studies* 21 (1995): 255–301.

27 Ibid., 257.

28 Ibid., 292.

29 Ibid., 265; see also Laqueur, *Making Sex*, 64–66.

30 Park, "Rediscovery of the Clitoris," 173.

31 The crime of "double concubinage with men and women" is ascribed by Martínez Durán, *Ciencias médicas*, 267. He did not explain the meaning of this crime.

32 For good overview of sexuality in colonial Latin America, see the essays in Asunción Lavrin, ed., *Sexuality and Marriage in Colonial Latin America* (Lincoln, NE, 1989), esp. Lavrin, "Sexuality in Colonial Mexico: A Church Dilemma," 47–95.

33 Daston and Park, "Hermaphrodite," 423.

34 For more on this topic, see, e.g., Pete Sigal, ed., *Infamous Desire: Male Homosexuality in Colonial Latin America* (Chicago, 2003); Geoffrey Spurling, "Honor, Sexuality, and the Colonial Church: The Sins of Dr. González, Cathedral Canon," in *The Faces of Honor: Sex, Shame, and Violence in Colonial Latin America*, ed. Lyman Johnson and Sonya Lipsett-Rivera (Albuquerque, NM, 1998), 45–67; and Richard C. Trexler, *Sex and Conquest: Gendered Violence, Political Order, and the European Conquest of the Americas* (Ithaca, NY, 1999).

35 The Council of Trent reforms responded to the Protestant Reformation; Geoffrey Spurling, "Under Investigation for the Abominable Sin: Damien de Morales Stands Accused of Attempting to Seduce Antón de Tierra de Congo (Charcas, 1611)," in *Colonial Lives: Documents on Latin American History, 1550-1850*, ed. Richard Boyer and Geoffrey Spurling (New York, 2000), 112–29.

36 Park notes this Orientalist trope in early modern European medical literature of Egyptian women and other women from the "East" with large clitorises as having a tendency toward sexual deviance in "Rediscovery of the Clitoris." Jorge Cañizares-Esguerra, *How to Write a History of the New World* (Stanford, CA, 2001), 14, briefly notes that a kind of crude Orientalism began to be used in Enlightenment-era analogies of pre-Columbian Amerindian cultures, a shift

from earlier assertions that pre-Columbian Amerindian cultures were analogous to ancient Roman and Greek polities.

37 For more on this, see Valeria Finucci, "Maternal Imagination and Monstrous Births: Tasso's *Gerusalemme liberata*," in *Generation and Degeneration: Tropes of Reproduction in Literature and History from Antiquity to Early Modern Europe*, ed. Valeria Finucci and Kevin Brownlee (Durham, NC, 2001), 41–80.

It Happened on the Way to the *Temascal* and Other Stories: Desiring the Illicit in Colonial Spanish America

Kimberly Gauderman, *University of New Mexico*

Spaniards had a lot on their minds in early Latin America: constructing cities, organizing tribute, and becoming wealthy in lands where native populations were already doing the same was complicated. Spaniards had to compete with indigenous forms of community, prescribed obligations between peoples and their rulers, and traditional economic practices. The Spaniards' unrelenting pursuit of authority over the economic and political relations of indigenous communities has been the subject of a great deal of historiography, but, as the essays in this collection demonstrate, Spaniards also thought about sex. Here, too, Spaniards faced competition; labeling particular acts as sinful and criminal was no more successful at controlling sexuality in indigenous America than it had been in Europe. As all these authors agree, the "sexual conquest" is connected to other relations of authority in Spanish America and, like other colonial projects, the "colonization of the intimate" was, at best incomplete, at worst a failure.

The five essays in this issue, geographically focusing on Mesoamerica (here, Mexico and Guatemala), explore an array of situations in which official discourse that sought to contain sexual identity and practices was misunderstood, challenged, manipulated, or just ignored by indigenous peoples, blacks, Spaniards, and even colonial officials themselves. The essays span almost the entire colonial period and include research on urban and rural areas. The authors' use of diverse sources, their methodological approaches, and their conclusions about the nature of colonial authority all demonstrate, if more proof is necessary, the importance of sexuality as an emerging subfield of Latin American history. In this commentary, I would

Ethnohistory 54:1 (Winter 2007) DOI 10.1215/00141801-2006-043
Copyright 2007 by American Society for Ethnohistory

like to explore how the authors approach their sources and their views of colonial culture and its connection to sexuality.

"You, Tezcatlipoca, are a faggot." With this shocking statement about a major Nahua deity, Pete Sigal abruptly brings us to the dark core of all historical research, the problem of translation. How can we avoid modern biases in ascribing meaning to historical texts that were produced in ambiguous circumstances? As Sigal reminds us, all translation is political, and the historical truths we tend to build and rely on only mask the contingency of our narratives. Sigal proposes that, to avoid asserting transcultural and transhistorical meanings to our texts, historians pay more attention to the writing process itself by examining the historical conditions in which the text was produced. This shift to a discursive analysis also impacts our historical inquiries. Rather than asking what a text reveals about a particular behavior, in this case homosexuality, the analysis focuses on how a word or concept functions in a text as part of a symbolic system. As Sigal notes, his essay is more about text than sex.

Sigal uses a Foucauldian genealogical approach to explore how the term *puto* and the Nahuatl words it glosses operate in both text and image in the *Florentine Codex*. This twelve-volume text was produced by Franciscan-trained indigenous scribes working under the direction of Bernardino de Sahagún, using aged nobles recommended by the Tlatelolco city council as informants. The work itself was structured with a text in Nahuatl and a corresponding text or translation in Spanish. Produced over many years with multiple authors and influences, the *Florentine Codex* is an obviously hybrid text for which an analysis that seeks to understand the authorial filter can be seen as particularly useful. While Sigal's focus is on a single statement in a single document, he does not treat the *Florentine Codex* as a closed text. He teases out the multiple meanings of words and concepts by tracing their European and indigenous influences back through time and across texts.

Sigal's genealogical approach frames history as a conflict between discursive regimes. It is possible to reconstruct discursive systems by reading backward and placing them in their historical period. Sigal successfully uses this approach in his analysis of the Spanish *puto* and the Nahuatl *xochihua*, *cuiloni*, and *patlachuia* to illuminate dissonance and convergence in Spanish and Nahuatl sexual symbolic systems as they operate simultaneously in a text, image, or even a single utterance. By tracing the historical etymologies of *puto* (translated into English as "faggot") and the texts and images of Tezcatlipoca, the statement "You, Tezcatlipoca, are a faggot" becomes more than just a Spanish attempt to feminize the Indian by denigrating this omnipotent deity. Indeed, in this analysis a third figure emerges, that of the lesser god Titlacauan, who represented one of Tezca-tlipoca's many identities. In the Nahuatl text, it is this deity who is referred to as a *cuiloni*, a Nahuatl term that came to signify *puto*. The presence of this sexually ambiguous being and his close affiliation to Tezcatlipoca provided an ambiguous moment that the Spanish interpreter filled by replacing Tezcatlipoca with Titlacauan. Tezcatlipoca becomes a puto in a statement in which two symbolic regimes approached each other but did not meet. For Sigal, this textual dissonance suggests that the spiritual conquest was failing.

By carefully analyzing individual Spanish and Nahuatl texts, revealing the authorial filters in the texts' production, and historically contextualizing language and images, Sigal reminds us that the very concept of a sexual identity is a cultural creation, and a modern one at that. While the Nahua continued to describe sexual behavior that conflicted with Sahagún's sexual norms in the *Florentine Codex*, Sigal would argue that it was not possible in Nahua culture to articulate a homosexual identity. For the Nahua, sexuality was performance and not linked to an individual's core identity. Nahua sexuality would alter over time, but like other cultural changes in indigenous society, this was due not to the conscious efforts of Spaniards but to increasing contact with Hispanized individuals.

Zeb Tortorici's essay focuses on just such a network of thirteen indigenous men accused of committing sodomy in and around the Spanish center of Valladolid in early seventeenth-century Mexico. While all the men came from the less Hispanized sectors of indigenous society, they varied in marital status, age, and sexual experience. Tortorici analyzes the testimonies of these men and witnesses to argue that the active/passive paradigm is inadequate for understanding male-male sexual relations. For this reason, he suggests, indigenous sexuality remained distinct from the highly gendered ways that Spaniards conceptualized sodomy. His research also finds evidence of a sodomitical culture that seemed generally tolerated by local society.

Tortorici, like Sigal, analyzes a single document, albeit a remarkable criminal case that grows from a single accusation against two indigenous men found committing sex in a *temascal* to a criminal investigation of the sexual activities of thirteen men. The case provides a wealth of details, which Tortorici enthusiastically includes in his essay, about these men's sexual encounters. Because the men's testimonies were translated into Spanish, it is not possible to analyze indigenous categories of sexuality through language use. However, Tortorici argues, it is possible to gain an understanding of indigenous sexuality through the physical descriptions of sexual acts, other information about the men in the records, and the testimonies of Spanish witnesses. Tortorici asks the provocative question, does it matter whose on top and, if so, to whom? His answers to this question complicate the active/passive model traditionally used to understand sexual behavior.

Spaniards who inadvertently wandered across male-male sexual encounters and the Spanish officials who pronounced judgments on such acts had the tendency to describe the participants as men who were acting "as if they were man and woman." The indigenous defendants themselves drew on this model to describe the physical details of their encounters, noting who "served as a woman." Understanding what this model meant to those who used it is the focus of Tortorici's analysis. In their encounters with other men, the defendants usually showed preferences for top or bottom sexual positions but not always; some men engaged in both positions. Importantly, the particular sexual position that men chose did not seem to be influenced by their age, prior sexual relations with men or women, or whether or not they had initiated the encounter. These indigenous men performed their sexuality outside of the active/passive model.

What is less clear in this essay is what Spaniards meant when they used the man/woman model of sexual behavior. As Tortorici notes, this model for understanding sexual acts is usually associated with notions of dominance and submission. A question one might ask here is, by whom? By Spaniards in the colonial period? Or by modern scholars? The assumption seems to be that Spaniards found sodomy to be a particularly vile crime because it violated the binary logic of their own culture that naturalized relations of domination and subordination through gender norms. Men who allowed themselves to be penetrated like women were an affront to a societal order based on a clear hierarchy of political authority (absolutism) and social authority (patriarchy). There is substantial scholarship on colonial governance that suggests that throughout the Hapsburg period and up until at least the 1760s, authority was not centralized but dispersed, generated in a network that structurally enabled local officials to ignore Crown dictates. Society was marked by contingent, rather than fixed binary relations of authority. Officials shared overlapping legal jurisdictions and their conflicts with each other prevented the emergence of a clear center of authority.

Tortorici's description of the 1604 sodomy case seems to suggest that sexuality, like other social relations, emerged in a network of competing claims to authority, struggles over the organization of political power, and conflicting ideological justifications for rule. Rather than being seen as a violation of a fixed gendered norm, sodomy was ignored, tolerated, or prosecuted as a crime by Spaniards based largely on local strategic interests. Research suggests that, indeed, the Spanish treatment of sodomy was inconsistent and varied by region. Tortorici's research shows that in Valladolid, men's sexual activities with each other were tolerated or ignored for long periods. Local tolerance allowed indigenous men in this rural community to build a sodomitical subculture where men could seek out sex with each other. Officials only moved to prosecute when charges of sodomy aggravated other crimes, such as in the case of El Caltzontzin, who was also accused of murder, or when sodomy was particularly "público y notorio," as the activities of the accused seem to have become. Even church officials, as Tortorici shows, were less concerned with sodomy than they were in the opportunity that the criminal case gave them to exert authority over local civil officials.

Punishment for the crime of sodomy, as for other crimes in the early modern period, was brutal and public. While there is a historiographical debate over whether the top or bottom sexual partner in sodomy cases was punished more harshly, the research seems to show that communities varied in the significance they attached to men's specific sexual positions. In Valladolid, both participants, if prosecuted, were aggressively punished. Spaniards in the early modern period, like their indigenous contemporaries, did not fix sexuality into polarized gendered positions of dominance and subordination; there was, using Tortorici's terminology, "penetrational ambiguity." The continued use of the active/passive paradigm by modern researchers masks more than it reveals about desire and power not only for indigenous peoples but, I would argue, for early modern Spaniards as well.

Tortorici's research shows that official prohibitions of sodomy did not destroy local sodomitical subcultures, largely because of local tolerance. His research also suggests that the prosecution of illicit sexual activities allowed local officials to fight over social and political authority. The essay by John F. Chuchiak IV demonstrates that the Yucatec Maya understood these terms of engagement as well and charged priests with illicit sexual conduct as a strategy to limit the authority of Spanish priests in their communities. Chuchiak uses a creative array of sources to establish Spanish priests' contradictory attitudes toward morality and sexuality. Chuchiak argues that the Maya were generally successful in limiting the authority of priests in their communities but that, over time, the Maya became more sexually promiscuous because of their exposure to libertine European sexual mores.

Chuchiak uses confession manuals to suggest that, though the church connected sex with sin, the detailed descriptions of prohibited sexual behavior in the manuals, far from containing sexuality, could instead sexualize the act of confession itself. The church's emphasis on sexual morality could indeed have allowed individual priests to vicariously experience their indigenous parishioners' sexual activities or even, as Chuchiak argues, have excited clerical sexual depravity. It is difficult to be certain, however, what impact these manuals had on the local priests who used them or on their parishioners without knowing how often individual priests confessed their parishioners, how much time they spent with them, or what sections of the generally large confession manuals they chose to use.

Indigenous and Spanish chronicles are also uncertain sources for understanding sexual practices at the local level. While the indigenous and Spanish authors of these documents seem to agree that the Maya, especially Maya women, were more chaste before contact with Spaniards, it is unlikely that their commentaries were unbiased descriptions of local practice. It would be understandable, for example, if indigenous writers chose to idealize traditional Maya society to critique the Spanish conquest more fully. In these accounts the arrival of the Spaniards coincided with economic and political turmoil, as well as sexual violence and promiscuity. This could be evidence that indigenous communities traditionally viewed a loss of sexual control as a symptom of decreased political and economic authority, a connection that Chuchiak shows indigenous groups continued to make in their legal battles against priests. Spaniards, on the other hand, unabashedly used reports as political tools. Fray Diego de Landa, for example, consistently wrote about the horrors committed by nonreligious personnel, such as the commentary on Captain Alonso López de Avila that Chuchiak includes, to justify the edifying presence of clerics and to increase their authority vis-à-vis civilian officials in the region. In the seventeenth century, throughout Spanish America, clerics lamented the lack of morality in indigenous communities. By this time, many regions were flooded with Spaniards. Increased daily contact among groups made cultural differences more evident, which brought great disillusionment to many clerics who had believed that indigenous communities had understood and embraced their moral teachings. The increased population of Spaniards also meant greater conflicts over resources, and these writings were used to condemn other Spaniards and justify control over a particular region. While it is important to recognize that sexual violence occurred during the conquest, these documents tell us more about the writers' need to use sexuality to morally legitimate their political and economic programs than about the impact of sexual violence on community standards of morality.

One gets a better understanding of the sexual dynamics between priests and indigenous communities at the local level by examining the Maya petitions accusing their priests of the serious crime of solicitation. The Maya accused clerics of sexual violence, including the rape of both women and men. While it is likely that some priests did abuse their authority, Chuchiak shows that these cases are not simply evidence of indigenous victimization by clerics. Indigenous men and women found that accusing priests of solicitation was an effective strategy for removing them from the community. Charges of sexual immorality against priests were often connected to, if not motivated by, other complaints against the same priests, such as interference in communities' traditional political and economic relations. In addition to being a tool to rid the community of troublesome outsiders, charges of sexual abuse could also be made against other community members as leverage in conflicts between commoners and elites and, likely, in traditional rivalries between dynastic families. Indeed, other scholars have shown that indigenous peoples used the Spanish legal system to protect their communities from encroachments by Spaniards and other indigenous groups and used litigation to resolve internal community disputes. Chuchiak extends this research by showing that indigenous peoples understood sexual politics as well.

While Sigal, Tortorici, and Chuchiak focus on the impact of Spanish sexual morality on indigenous peoples in rural, largely indigenous communities, both Laura Lewis and Martha Few focus on large Spanish urban centers. Lewis argues that the construction of distinct racial groups in seventeenth-century Mexico City was gendered; the Spanish conquest produced feminized Indians. Assuming a particular form of gender construction in colonial Spanish America, she argues, however, that this feminization of the "other" did not successfully disempower indigenous peoples. Because of their non-Christian religious practices, indigenous peoples were connected to superstition and thus, like women, gained a kind of illegitimate power through sorcery and witchcraft. The contradiction that Spaniards faced in constructing feminized Indians becomes even more apparent in criminal prosecutions of sodomy, the main subject of this essay. Here, she argues that Spaniards viewed indigenous sexuality as passive and feminized yet, contrarily, as uncontrollable and thus active. Like Tortorici, then, she finds that indigenous sexuality exceeded the active/passive model of sexual behavior that, also like him, she argues Spaniards sought to impose.

Arguments that indigenous peoples were feminized by the Spanish conquest and colonial legal and economic practices depend on the Spanish construction of female gender norms. If indigenous peoples were treated like women, what did being a woman mean? There is a substantial bibliography on women and gender in Spain and Spanish America. This historical scholarship shows that women there were never legally considered minors, and that they exercised substantial economic and legal rights. Women were not under the tutelage of men but retained separate juridical and economic identities even after marriage. The historical evidence that women of all racial backgrounds actively participated in their communities' economic and legal life complicates the theory that Spain traditionally defined women as passive, and it further problematizes theorists' use of a gendered active/passive binary as a conceptual framework for understanding Spanish colonial society.

Lewis uses two Inquisition sodomy trials to demonstrate that indigenous people were, indeed, constructed as weak and feminine. She argues that because the indigenous men were in the bottom position, they were viewed as even more feminized than the mulattoes who mounted them, despite witnesses' descriptions of the mulattoes as having feminine characteristics, because of their style of dress and/or domestic activities. This might not be a contradiction, because, as Tortorici's research suggests, men's positions in their sexual encounters did not necessarily indicate passivity or aggression, femininity or masculinity. While there is little information on the indigenous participant in the first sodomy case, in the second case the indigenous man testifies that the mulatto sexually victimized him. Lewis suggests that this could be a strategizing discourse that appealed to colonial society's gendering of Indians as passive and mulattoes as aggressive. The Indian's depiction of himself as a victim, in addition to his bottom position in the sexual encounter, were important in the case because, Lewis argues, colonial authorities punished the top person more severely. However, as Lewis notes in her analysis of the first sodomy case, which apparently led to charges against a number of men, in Mexico City men in either position could be condemned to death. Finally, it is unclear that the Indian's strategy worked. Lewis seems certain that the Indian, because of his racial gendering as weak and dependent, was released. It could also be that, because the Inquisition did not have jurisdiction over Indians, his case was transferred to civil authorities who, as Tortorici also shows, prosecuted indigenous men for sodomy with full rigor.

While I am skeptical of some of Lewis's conclusions, she does make remarkable use of a number of theoretical models to examine the limited number of documents at her disposal. Her analysis of the significance of clothing, which is based on a greater number of cases, illuminates its use to both fix and confound sexual identity. Clothing was particularly important in the colonial period for marking racial identity and social status. Authorities attempted to limit individuals' ability to use clothing as a means of migrating between racial identities and social distinctions through largely unenforced laws that dictated apparel. It is interesting that there were not comparable laws regulating dress by gender. This may be because although cross-dressing, by men at least, could have marked cross-dressers as potentially deviant, their clothing style did not confuse the social order; that is, the men seemed to have added feminine flourishes to their wardrobe but were not attempting to convince others that they were actually women. This does not seem to have been the case for most female cross-dressers who chose to mask their gendered identities completely and appear as men. Authorities may not have viewed these women as a threat to the social order, however, since, as Lewis argues, the women's choice to appear as men may have been more comprehensible to male authorities and, because same-sex practices were not associated with women, their male clothing did not violate heterosexual norms.

As Lewis's work suggests, and the research of the essays I have already discussed supports, male sexuality was viewed as aggressive and potentially deviant by colonial authorities. Both church and civil authorities considered men's sexual relations with each other as a particularly vile crime that, when brought to their attention, should be rigorously prosecuted and harshly punished. For most of the colonial period, contrarily, women's sexual relations with each other were rarely prosecuted and perhaps not recognized by colonial society. Toward the end of the colonial period, perceptions of female sexuality began to change. In Guatemala City, at the beginning of the nineteenth century, as Martha Few demonstrates, the female body and its potential for violating heterosexual norms initiated a criminal prosecution for sexual deviancy, a campaign to educate the public about the female body, and the erasure of bodies that did not conform to medically established sexual norms.

Few analyzes the 1803 report of a court-ordered medical examination of Juana Aguilar in an Atlantic World framework, placing the findings of the examining physician, Narciso Esparragosa, in the context of Enlightenment theories about the body. Few's research into Esparragosa's background and training, shows that he and others considered him part of this new "century of great learning." Consciously drawing on new scientific and medical knowledge, he strove to create categories of precisely sexed bodies based on sexual organs. As Few points out, this view represents an ideological shift from earlier perceptions that masculinity and femininity were culturally variable. The new logic sought to eliminate the possibility of sexual ambiguity by imposing a male/female sexual binary grounded in scientifically approved distinctions between male and female bodies.

Few suggests that this new emphasis on a sexual binary explains Esparragosa's preoccupation with scientifically demonstrating to the public that Juana was not a hermaphrodite. In public perception, a hermaphrodite's body had elements of both male and female sexual organs. For Esparragosa, such a body defied the binary model of sexual distinction and therefore could not exist. The coexistence of two sexualities in the same being would produce a monster and only the ignorant and irrational (a group that in his mind included midwives, surgeons, and the general public) could believe in the existence of a creature that defied scientific logic. In his examination of Juana's body, then, Esparragosa sought to show that Juana's sexual organs were neither male nor female; rather than sharing elements of both, he created a new category to contain her body.

By situating her analysis of this late colonial Guatemalan document in an Atlantic World framework, Few sheds light on the Esparragosa's ideological motivations for rejecting the description of Juana as a hermaphrodite in order to recategorize her body as "neither man nor woman." What remains less clear is why he chose to focus almost exclusively on the female body to do so. The emphasis in his examination and his later publications seems to have been on defining "normal" female genitalia, especially the clitoris, and then on describing how Juana's sexual organs were different and thus not female. His preoccupation with the size of Juana's clitoris seems to have even led to her being publicly recognized as "Juana La Larga." Connecting sexual behavior to the body, he compared her to foreign women whose extraordinary clitorises caused them to become sexually deviant. In the end, it appears that Juana became a special kind of woman for Esparragosa. It might be interesting to further explore why his intellectual commitment to defining sexual difference collapsed around the female body.

For some, reading these essays will be an exciting foray into a new subfield of Latin American history, as it has been for me. Each of these authors makes important contributions to our knowledge of how the control and production of sexuality was used to enforce mechanisms of colonial authority in Spanish America. This work is encouraging in that it shows that reconstructing sexuality, although difficult, is still possible for the colonial period. The essays also show the limitations that the study of sexuality in early Latin America faces; as in any new field, there is not a large documentary base and little prior research to build on. The lack of information on sexuality, indeed, has led some researchers to allow conceptual frameworks to dominate their research. The present scholarship shows great promise, however, allowing us to hope, with Tortorici, that it will inspire further research for "more systematic and conclusive evidence."

Alternative Sex and Gender in Early Latin America

Caterina Pizzigoni, *Columbia University*

The five essays presented here are varied and each worthy of separate analysis on its own terms, but they are also part of a united effort, and their approaches contain unifying threads. They range widely over New Spain and Guatemala, including both central and more peripheral areas. Their protagonists lived and acted between the sixteenth and the late eighteenth century, and in several of the articles were predominantly indigenous, either Nahua, Maya, or Purépecha. Mulattoes play a key role in the article by Laura A. Lewis, while in the study by Martha Few no one appears to be indigenous.

This special issue invites us to reflect on the evolution of the field of colonial Latin American gender history since its beginnings in the 1970s. Starting as primarily women's history, it has gradually broadened to encompass gender in society generally, diversifying its sources and cooperating with other subfields, including social history and ethnohistory. Within this picture it can be said that sexuality, though no one would deny that it is crucial to gender, has not been widely or deeply studied until very recently. The reason is not lack of interest on the part of those doing gender history but the fact that their sources overall seem to contain relatively little explicit material on sexual activity. In my own research in eighteenth-century litigation from the Toluca Valley relating to formal and informal woman-man relationships, I found only hints of such material. In a large body of Nahuatl wills from that time and place, rich though it was for gender studies, I found even less.[1] The articles presented here show a concerted effort to study sexuality directly. This subdiscipline can surely be

Ethnohistory 54:1 (Winter 2007)   DOI 10.1215/00141801-2006-044

included in gender studies as it has been taking shape in Latin American history, but at the same time it acts like a distinct new field. I will formulate some general points to put the case studies in a broader frame.

To begin with, a thread that links all the articles is their attention to what I would call alternative sexualities, meaning sexual behaviors beyond those officially sanctioned and occurring within the limits of marriage and procreation. Most of the pieces here deal with topics outside hetero-sexuality; one treats sexuality where chastity was prescribed, among the clergy. The explicitness of the discourse about sex is striking; one wonders if the material on these formally disapproved relationships, though relatively rare, delivers an important kind of information mainly lacking in the records of relationships of other types.

Alternative sexualities in colonial Latin America have been investigated for a few decades now, but the focus has been mainly on extramarital relations, such as those that were considered concubinage (informal relations between women and men), bigamy, or adultery. Those studies have emphasized the legal and social aspects and have said little about sexuality specifically and directly. An approach that underlines the existence of diverse alternative sexualities, treating them in the same way as the more studied man-woman relations as well as integrating more physical sexual realities, is therefore very welcome. It is also a significant contribution that attention is paid to sexuality in the indigenous world, so often left at the margins of the study of sexuality in the colonial period and confined to discussions of the precontact period.

Yet one must ask if indigenous and Spanish sexualities were so different. The existence of important distinctions cannot be doubted, but we also glimpse some similar patterns in a colonial world whose diverse societies and cultures shared more attributes than one might expect. For example, formal indigenous sources (usually with a precontact flavor but produced much later) stress the importance of moderation and decorum in sexual behavior, maintaining a strict prohibition of adultery, very much in line with Spanish preaching of the time. Of course these were public norms and prescriptions, while social reality was another story; but that is equally true of indigenous and Spanish sectors. Although rigorous punishment was imposed for deviant sexual behavior, it may have been more exemplary than standard. It is still a challenge to understand how much of indigenous sexuality comes from preconquest times, how much is influenced by contact with Spaniards, and how much was common to the two cultures from the beginning. The articles here and the sources they are based on abound in suggestive passages, but a definitive approach to these questions is still to be found.

Surely the Indians had a rather different view than the Spaniards did on what was called concubinage and polygamy, as is already well known. Here we see, with John F. Chuchiak IV, that celibacy for indigenous priests existed, but that it was ritual and therefore temporary; also, indigenous minds did not conceive of sex as inherently linked to sin, which was typical of morality as proclaimed by the Catholic Church. Nor was it obvious to them that sexual behavior would condemn them to hell, for it is likely that many were not fully indoctrinated in the concept of hell itself. As late as the eighteenth century we find reference among the Nahua to *mictlan* as the general land of the dead of their ancestors, not as the Christian hell in a dichotomy of hell and heaven.[2] Also, more than one author here stresses that indigenous societies acknowledged an almost institutionalized role for cross-dressing figures; they could be despised at times, but even the powerful god Tezcatlipoca had a counterpart with female behavior, something inconceivable in Spanish theology.

Zeb Tortorici's piece reveals the existence of social networks for alternative sexualities, in this case related to same-sex sexual practices among men. Pedro Quini and his mates knew where and how to find partners; clearly they could rely on links connecting and supporting individuals who shared their sexual preferences. This reminds us of social networks bonding other people who occupied a delicate or weak position in colonial society, such as women, and suggests a need for further research on the various kinds of social networks operating in postcontact Latin America.

Such connections show individuals following their own impulses and being active in society instead of passively accepting restraints placed on them. And more broadly, this special issue provides plenty of examples of indigenous (and nonindigenous) people trying to manipulate the colonial system of rules and values. Indian agency has been at the core of much scholarly production in recent decades; it is interesting to see it applied in a variety of ways to the realm of alternative sexualities. For example, in Chuchiak's article, Francisco Ek was just one of many Maya men and women who accused Father Cristóbal de Valencia of unsanctioned sexual acts, claiming a violation of Spanish sexual morality in order to provoke the authorities to intervene against a priest whom the Maya opposed. As the author shows, whether Valencia was abusive, as they claimed, or how abusive, is hard to determine behind the language of petitions. It turns out that Valencia had previously punished some of these Indians for drunkenness or idolatry, so that the accusation of sexual abuse could have been a way to take revenge by using precisely the sexual morality that the Spanish tried to impose.

A similar case, in the article by Tortorici, is that of Joaquín Ziziqui and other Purépecha men who emphasized their Christianity along with their youth and supposed naïveté in order to mitigate their culpability in "sodomy." Or again the case of Andrés Chan discussed by Lewis, who vividly introduces the factor of caste in the discourse around alternative sexualities. Chan, an Indian from Valladolid who lived in Mérida, was caught having sex with a free mulatto, Juan Ramírez, and in front of the Inquisition insisted on being a victim, playing on the fact that usually mulattoes were considered more aggressive than indigenous people. That Juan was reported as carrying out activities usually associated with women (preparing chocolate or doing the shopping) did not help his position. As Lewis reminds us, same-sex relationships may at times open an additional dimension, that of cross-dressing, and discrepancies between sex, social behavior, and clothing exposed individuals to more rigorous consideration by colonial authorities.

In these cases the Indians insisted on characteristics that Spanish authorities often recognized in subjects they looked on as minors and thus meriting less severe punishment. Such behavior reminds us of indigenous women who, when arrested for concubinage, presented themselves before Spanish authorities as weak, exactly the way judges were inclined to see them, hoping to be pardoned or at least treated with leniency.[3] For some women this strategy worked.

No information is given about the fate of Andrés Chan, but what is sure is that at least one of the Purépecha men tried for sodomy, Simpliciano Cuyne, managed to escape capital punishment by playing on his connections with the local church, where he was a sacristan and whose priest portrayed him as a good Christian. Also, the Maya men and women played the system very successfully, since following their accusations the abusive or simply bothersome priests were often removed. These cases do differ in that it was not the indigenous people who engaged in alternative sexualities; instead they attacked Spaniards for supposedly violating the code.

The great loser in indigenous (and nonindigenous) manipulation of the formally sanctioned system of morality was the set of rules and norms that the Spanish authorities tried to impose. They transferred from the homeland to the New World the mechanisms and mental constructions used to organize and control society. In their view, women and now Indians were weak, almost children to be guided and controlled.[4] The same can be said to a certain extent of those inclined to homosexual activity, especially those who took the so-called passive role; they are sometimes interestingly depicted as initiating the sexual transaction, just as women were often considered the initiators of illicit relationships. But the fact that some were condemned to death for sodomy, independently of the role they took in sexual intercourse, leaves doubt about Spanish willingness to apply the leniency so often granted to minors.

Laws and regulations concerning social behavior multiplied in the late colonial period (in the eighteenth century and particularly with the late Bourbon reforms) to the same extent that the reality of social practices escaped Spanish control and became more complex. In the end, Spanish attempts to control the sexual desires of women and men, force obedience to church dictates, and restrict miscegenation were overcome by practices of daily life in which both genders mixed freely and loosely, exactly as ethnic groups did. Accepting the dichotomy in legal and ecclesiastical discourse between the order sought by Spanish authorities and the frequent disorder in actual society, I would add another more socially oriented view. Colonial Mexico saw a juxtaposition of rules and tangible behaviors where the latter are not always to be seen as disorder and especially were not so seen by the protagonists, but simply as facts of real life. They had their purpose, their pattern, their order, as strong as any declared system of rules.

Along these lines, the five articles presented here support a reading of the colonial world in which social and religious tolerance had more weight than we might have expected. As long as individual behavior was kept private and discreet, authorities were willing to refrain from intervention and punishment. Thus frequently the problem was not the practice itself, no matter how deviant it was from the rules, but some situation in which this practice became too overt and scandalous. Tolerance of behavior deviant from formal rules already has been recognized for cases such as those of informal relationships between men and women.[5] It is significant to find the same applied to alternative sexualities and particularly to same-sex sexual relations, which have so often been conceived as taboo for the Spanish and colonial mindset.

During the late eighteenth and early nineteenth centuries, new elements entered the discourse around sexuality in colonial Mexico, and not only there; partly for this reason Few's article takes place in a quite different framework than the rest of the essays. The influence of the Enlightenment and the advance of medical science fostered an approach in which medical practitioners tried to explain as well as heal what was considered sexual deviance. Instead of attacking alternative sexualities with judicial instruments, doctors were called on to deal with the phenomena first through reason and observation. It was a more scientific approach, at least for many people of the time, since sexual categorization was now based essentially on the physical characteristics of sexual organs and far less on social roles or clothing. And yet, as in the case of ecclesiastical or civil judges, it was a world dominated by men; medical practitioners were all men, and no space was left, at least in the sanctioned domain, for female healers. Men were the ones who had the power to discipline behaviors considered outside the norm. Moreover, the so-called scientific approach did not necessarily mean better treatment of the individuals involved; perhaps she was not garroted or burned at the stake, but the cruel scrutiny to which Juana Aguilar was subjected may not have been more pleasant.

Any field, and especially a new one, must concern itself with methodological issues. We can start with the nature of the sources available to study alternative sexualities in colonial Latin America. It is as encouraging as it is rare, to date, to have such a source as the one employed by Tortorici, so rich in details about sexual behavior in a whole circle, with considerable information about the participants' social and other positions. Lewis's sources have most of the same characteristics. Specific litigation of this kind remains the type of document that most closely portrays human actions in real life. If historians can dig more of this kind of material out of the archives, it matters little whether the sources are Inquisition records, secular criminal records, or similar documents created under other auspices.

Due to the scarcity of such documents relating to sexuality, at least until now, it is necessary to employ a different type of source that, on the one hand, is further removed from social and cultural reality as lived by individuals in a particular setting but, on the other, often contains more in the way of general statements about and vocabulary for sexuality. Such is the *Florentine Codex* of Bernardino de Sahagún—a rich world in itself, quite isolated from all else, infinitely complex and difficult in its double or triple "authorship" and its simultaneous reference to precontact and postcontact epochs—or the Mayan chronicles, so posterior but so full of precontact knowledge. Then there are the public statements of ecclesiastics, more contemporary usually although also inclined to pronounce on preconquest matters. All of these are generally highly normative and to a certain extent removed from social reality; yet if analyzed critically (as the contributors to this special issue do) for the motivation of the authors and the implications of the vocabulary, they can provide significant and unique insight into conceptual frameworks affecting the sexual behaviors of actual individuals.

A critical approach is also linked (here specifically by Pete Sigal) to another issue, the filters that can affect the content of a text. The importance of this aspect is evident particularly for sources that report events and thoughts originally expressed in another language, that involve translation in the most obvious way. But filters can operate in any context; after all, the people who produced written documents in colonial times were not usually the protagonists of the events described or even the original authors of the statements made, as in wills. We face the classic problem of mediation in text production, further complicated by the fact that the statements of indigenous people often were translated into Spanish, a language far more distant from their own than any two European languages would be from each other. Thus translation may even become a "political act," in Sigal's words. I would only add that even beyond—or, better, prior to—the intentions of informants, writers, or translators, the encounter of two different vocabularies and traditions creates involuntary filters, as I would call them. Each language possesses many categories without a close equivalent in another; this would be true even between Nahuatl and Purépecha or Maya, and it is far more marked between Spanish and any one of them.

Thus a critical approach should not just transcribe and translate original texts but consider the context of the statement, as well as all the possible influences operating on the process of text production. With this I fully agree; I do believe, however, that most of the people who have been translating older indigenous texts have already been considering context, and also going beyond "mere" translation in other ways. When dealing with an indigenous language it is essential to study relevant terms in their actual original textual context, as opposed to translating them in a vacuum or straight from the dictionary (and Sigal gives valuable examples of this) as well as comparing them with their use in other texts.[6] Through systematic compilation of many instances we can get very close to the meaning of terms for the people who used them. It is also crucial to pay attention to idiosyncratic vocabulary in texts and not too quickly identify it with some apparent English or Spanish parallel. This is what Sigal is doing with *cuiloni* and *patlache*, and the same has been done with a great deal of Nahuatl sociopolitical and economic vocabulary.

This special issue should stimulate research on colonial sexualities toward a twofold contextual analysis. First, the sources need to be analyzed in the full context of their production, with attention to voluntary as well as involuntary filters, textual traditions of localities or genres, time of production compared to other texts and to the time of the subject matter, and many other factors. Second, sexual behaviors need to be considered in their chronological, geographical, and above all social context, trying to place the protagonists in their full reality and going beyond contemporary dichotomies and stereotyped categories. Through such studies, of which the present set is a strong anticipation, colonial society can stand out as a vibrant world capable of challenging our modern preconceptions.

Notes

1 For some analysis of the research in Spanish-language litigation, see Caterina Pizzigoni, "Between Resistance and Assimilation: Rural Nahua Women in the Valley of Toluca in the Early Eighteenth Century," PhD diss., King's College, London, 2002, chap. 3; for testaments in Nahuatl, see Pizzigoni, *Testaments of Toluca* (Stanford, CA, forthcoming).

2 Pizzigoni, *Testaments of Toluca*, testament of Melchora María, no. 24, 96–97.

3 Here I refer to cases presented in Caterina Pizzigoni, "'Como frágil y miserable': Las mujeres nahuas del Valle de Toluca," in *Historia de la vida cotidiana en México*, vol. 3, *El siglo XVIII: Entre tradición y cambio*, ed. Pilar Gonzalbo Aizpuru (Mexico City, 2005), 501–30. For a more general statement, see Laura A. Lewis, "The 'Weakness' of Women and the Feminization of the Indian in Colonial Mexico," *Colonial Latin American Review* 5 (June 1996): 84–85.

4 On women considered as weak rather than simply minor, see Silvia M. Arrom, *The Women of Mexico City, 1790-1857* (Stanford, CA, 1985), 53–81.

5 See, for example, Ann Twinam, *Public Lives, Private Secrets: Gender, Honor, Sexuality, and Illegitimacy in Colonial Spanish America* (Stanford, CA, 1999), esp. 59–88; and Susan Midgen Socolow, *The Women of Colonial Latin America* (Cambridge, 2000), 61–77.

6 For large-scale application of this method, see Pizzigoni, *Testaments of Toluca*; and Pizzigoni, "Region and Subregion in Central Mexican Ethnohistory: The Toluca Valley, 1650-1760," *Colonial Latin American Review* (forthcoming).

Book Reviews

The Americas That Might Have Been: Native American Social Systems through Time. By Julian Granberry. (Tuscaloosa: University of Alabama Press, 2005. xiii + 204 pp., maps, references, bibliography, index. $29.95 paper.)

1491: New Revelations of the Americas before Columbus. By Charles C. Mann. (New York: Alfred A. Knopf, 2005. xii + 465 pp., maps, illustrations, appendixes, notes, bibliography, index. $30.00 cloth.)

Colin G. Calloway, *Dartmouth College*

Each of these books attempts to peel back the layers of European contact and colonialism and offer a different view of the Americas. Charles C. Mann tries to reconstruct the Americas before European invasion; Julian Granberry imagines how the Americas might have evolved without European invasion.

Granberry, a linguist, focuses on kinship systems and divides human societies into three types: unitary, dualistic, and trinary. Unitary societies see only one solution for any situation; dualistic societies see two, polarized solutions, one good, one bad; and trinary societies see good and bad solutions but prefer to pursue a third, compromise solution. Granberry draws examples from all over the world to slot peoples into these categories (in China, a unitary society, for instance, concepts of good and bad, right and wrong "do not exist, as they do with us, as simple, clear universal polar opposites" [50]), and he finds evidence from historic and contemporary events to support his case. He then identifies half a dozen Native

Ethnohistory 54:1 (Winter 2007)
Copyright 2007 by American Society for Ethnohistory

American polities (his "Big Six") that exemplify these characteristics. He deliberately selects societies that at the end of the fifteenth century were "similar in structure to the emerging nation states of Europe" (69). The Inca and Aztec empires represent unitary societies; the Maya kingdoms of Central America and the Mississippian city-states were dualistic; and the Pueblo of the Southwest and the Taino of the Greater Antilles fit the trinary model, their social systems explaining why they reacted to Europeans in the way they did.

Granberry insists that his depictions are fact-based but sometimes the factual bases seem a bit shaky. Apparently, the trinary Pueblo received the Spaniards with "open arms," and the 1680 revolt was their "only known instance of out-and-out violence against others" (125–26). A map of Pueblo towns in 1492 (118) shows about thirty, with Pecos, Piro, and Tano already extinct, although the text points out that more than 120 Pueblo towns existed when the Spaniards arrived in 1540. According to a map of major Native American societies (35), the Creek Confederacy was already in existence in 1492.

Working from the premise that "no major alterations" have occurred in Inca, Aztec, Maya, and Pueblo social systems over the past five hundred years (142), and "forecasting on the basis of verified data" (139), Granberry then speculates about what America, indeed the world, would be like today if Europeans had not set foot in the Americas. Readers of *Ethnohistory* will doubtless conjure up alternative but equally plausible scenarios and Granberry acknowledges that his is but one of many possibilities, which prompts one to wonder what the point is. In Granberry's "future cast" (139), unhampered by European invasion, Native American societies sharing similar social characteristics would have come together in large confederations (an Inuit alliance, an Algonquian alliance, an Andean alliance, etc.), although it is not exactly clear why. Indians would have discovered Europe, engaged in extensive commerce with the Old World, and affected the balance of powers today as trinary societies reduced the dominance of dualistic Euro-American states and generated more tolerant ways of conducting international relationships. Interesting speculations, but this fact-based future-cast ignores what is surely the most obvious fact of all: that epidemic diseases would have caused massive depopulation in the Americas whether brought by European invaders or brought home by Native American traders. Diseases may not "disabuse one of the soul" (27), but they would surely have rendered improbable the developments Granberry imagines.

1491 is more useful. Rather than employ social models and post-processual approaches, Mann has waded through the literature, walked the ground, flown over the sites, and interviewed the experts. He actually has little to say about 1491 per se—the title is an attention grabber, to help convey to a general readership a sense of the richness, diversity, and sophistication of Native America before Columbus. Readers more often learn about the work and controversies of archaeologists or the impact of European expeditions in Indian country, but the overall impression is of an American hemisphere that was heavily populated, rich in linguistic and cultural diversity, with urban centers that matched or dwarfed those of Europe, where impressive civilizations had already risen and fallen, and where people developed crops and ideas that spread to the world. Focusing attention on new archaeological evidence from Monte Verde and relating the debate over the Bering Straits and how long humans have inhabited the Americas, Mann confounds old stereotypes and suggests the possibility that "people were thriving from Alaska to Chile while much of northern Europe was still empty of mankind and its works" (173). Focusing on the "numbers from nowhere" debate, he leaves no doubt that pre-Columbian America was a world shaped by many, many Indian people, and that post-Columbian America was a world shaped by European diseases.

Specialists will learn nothing new about their own areas of expertise, but the purpose and achievement of 1491 is to synthesize the work done over the last thirty years or so and to lay before the general public a bird's-eye view of Native America, North and South. 1491 has received plenty of publicity—several colleagues in the sciences told me they read it before I did—and ethnohistorians who have spent their lives dealing with the issues it covers may wonder what all the fuss is about. But Mann has produced a wide-ranging and readable book that will push readers to rethink assumptions about America before Columbus, and about American history after Columbus. The fact that such a book is getting a lot of attention is surely a positive sign.

DOI 10.1215/00141801-2006-045

Shades of Hiawatha: Staging Indians, Making Americans, 1880–1930. By Alan Trachtenberg. (New York: Hill and Wang, 2004. xxv + 369 pp., preface, introduction, illustrations, notes, bibliography, index. $30.00 cloth.)

John W. Troutman, *University of Louisiana, Lafayette*

At the same time that images of American Indians saturated early twentieth-century U.S. popular culture, many prominent writers, entrepreneurs, and artists, heavily invested in their Anglo-Saxon racial stock, grew increasingly alarmed by the influx of tens of millions of Eastern and Southern Europeans. Their worries prompted them to consider a series of questions: What does it mean to be an American? Who qualifies as an American? How would you know who or what an "American" is? Is Americanness an inherently inclusive or exclusive, biological or cultural, learned or inherited trait? Alan Trachtenberg considers their questions in his latest book, *Shades of Hiawatha*, in order to answer some of his own queries: Why were American Indians universally bestowed U.S. citizenship in 1924 after they had vehemently resisted the federal government's forty-year-old assimilation (and thus Americanization) campaign? Why were they given citizenship at the same time (indeed the same year) that the National Origins Act shut the door to millions of Europeans clamoring for that opportunity? And, most important, what is the relationship between Indianness and immigration—what can we make of a Yiddish translation of Longfellow's "Hiawatha," for example, or business mogul Rodman Wanamaker's attempt to create a gargantuan memorial statue of an American Indian, the "first Citizen," to *welcome* hoards of European immigrants on their arrival in New York harbor? Trachtenberg illuminates remarkable relationships between images and ideas of Indianness and immigration in the period 1880–1930, and suggests that an East Coast fascination with Indianness served as a "powerful nationalizing force" to remedy an American identity crisis (xii).

The historical and literary vignettes that shape this monograph reveal that the meanings of Americanness and citizenship were no less contested (or ambiguous) in the past than they are today. Trachtenberg's distinction between cultural and political nationality—that immigrants and American Indians in this period both faced certain assumed cultural requirements to become "American" and to obtain the political rights implicated in U.S. citizenship—exposes important comparative terrain between immigrant and Indian experiences. For example, Henry Pratt, founder of the Carlisle Indian School, certainly deemed similar the educational needs necessary for the cultural "uplift" and Americanization of Indian and immigrant children; indeed, both groups of children participated in the popular American pageants of the time. As Trachtenberg ably demonstrates, performances of "Hiawatha" pageants transformed the children into actors of a story that had nothing to do with Hiawatha, the Mohawk founder of the Iroquois Confederacy, and everything to do with the creation of a new, singular American mythology. The Europeans' historical slate of greed, theft, murder, and rampant destruction of Native America was wiped clean as Hiawatha, reminted as an American literary figure, was transformed into a forgiving founder of all that was noble and just in the new country.

While Trachtenberg devotes some attention to Indian people as actors in such plays and in the bewildering Wanamaker citizenship ceremonies conducted on reservations across the country, his analysis is most realized, compelling, and creative in his literary exploration of "Hiawatha" and in the literature on immigration, such as Henry James's *The American Scene* (1907). In another chapter, Trachtenberg explores the well-known work of photographer Edward Curtis, who, he argues, attempted to portray "pure" Indians in a country that was perceived by many as becoming increasingly diluted and mongrelized. Finally, Trachtenberg posits the work of Luther Standing Bear as a model for a better, more inclusive conception of what it means to be an American. As interesting as his subjects are, the chapters would gain strength if they were tied together in a more engaged dialogue with the comprehensive themes that eloquently frame his introduction—because the subjects and the relationships he exposes among them are so rich, a concluding chapter would also greatly enhance their power. In *Shades of Hiawatha*, Trachtenberg has rendered a palette of extraordinary juxtapositions, but he only partially succeeds in reconciling their contradictions.

DOI 10.1215/00141801-2006-046

Leslie A. White: Evolution and Revolution in Anthropology. By William J. Peace. (Lincoln: University of Nebraska Press, 2004, xviii + 282 pp., acknowledgments, illustrations, notes, bibliography, index. $55.00 paper.)

Sergei Kan, *Dartmouth College*

A major strength of this first full-scale biography of Leslie White is the author's detailed documentation of the political influences that affected White's career and anthropological thinking. One cannot but agree with William J. Peace that a historian of anthropology has to address the issue of the "conjunction between a scholar's political beliefs and anthropological theory" (xv). The author utilizes rich archival sources, such as White's correspondence and the journals he kept for much of his life. He also draws on White's field notes and unpublished manuscripts as well as his own interviews with individuals who knew White well. Peace does a good job of sketching out White's biography to explain why he came to embrace a particular brand of anthropology, which seemed so much in conflict with the prevailing paradigm of the 1920s–1930s. White served in the navy in World War I and that experience made him a foe of war and the social ills of his own society. As a result, during his undergraduate years at Columbia and the New School he embraced "revolutionism" and the social sciences. Despite having been strongly influenced by Alexander Goldenweiser during those years, White eventually turned against Franz Boas and the Boasians. As a graduate student at the University of Chicago he conducted ethnographic research among the Keresan Pueblo, some of the most secretive of the southwestern Indians. He continued his periodic (and usually short) research trips to the Southwest for the next thirty years. Despite White's subsequent attack on the "Boas school," his field methods followed it, particularly as exemplified by his mentor, E. C. Parsons. While by modern standards his methods, involving clandestine meetings with a relatively small number of willing informants, "were unethical or, at best, questionable" (63) and while he observed very few Keresan ceremonies, he was able to penetrate the inner workings of Pueblo culture rather success-fully. Still, with the exception of his unpublished dissertation on medicine societies, White's books and articles on the Pueblo tended to be descrip-tive, rather than theoretical, and fit well within the Boasian tradition. At the same time, some passages in these works did contain interesting theo-rizing on the nature of class and power differences within Pueblo societies and on the major threat to their way of life posed by "acculturation" pres-sure from the U.S. government.

One of Peace's important discoveries is that between 1931 and 1945 White published a lot of short pieces in the official organ of the Socialist Labor Party (SLP) under a pseudonym. These writings shed new light on White's early Marxism and on his use of anthropological analysis to cri-tique the capitalist society and argue that it would inevitably give way to a socialist/communist one. Peace's argument that it was White's political commitment to the SLP that shaped the corpus of his evolutionary work makes good sense (69). One of the early manifestations of this enthu-siasm for socialism and left-wing evolutionism was White's trip to the USSR in 1929, sponsored by an organization fronting for the Communist Party. Sympathy for White's politics and a lack of familiarity with Soviet history result in Peace's glossing over the fact that in 1929 Soviet society was already in the grips of early Stalinism, with the academic intelligent-sia among the first victims of ideological harassment, purges, and arrests. What White saw in that country was largely staged for naive foreign visi-tors badly needed as allies by the regime. As a result, his controversial 1931 address to the American Association for the Advancement of Science, "An Anthropological Appraisal of the Russian Revolution," which interpreted the Bolshevik coup and Russia's transition to socialism as evolutionary and inevitable, was factually inaccurate and did not stand the test of time.

Although White eventually tempered his admiration for the Soviet system and parted company with the SLP, he remained a committed evolutionist who seemed to relish attacking the American anthropological establishment, particularly the "atheoretical Boasians." Even those of us who do not share his evolutionism should give White some credit for rediscovering Lewis Henry Morgan, appealing to fellow anthropologists to produce more theoretically driven work, maintaining courageous public anticlericalism, and training a cohort of major figures in American anthropology at the University of Michigan. However, a closer examination of his evolutionism shows that it was much more materialist-utilitarian and technology-focused than Morganian or Marxist. Moreover, as Richard Barrett demonstrates in a 1989 article ("The Paradoxical Anthropology of Leslie White," *American Anthropologist* 91: 986–99), White's "culturological" writings of the 1940s–1970s were much more Boasian than evolutionist. Peace's book does not explain why his subject's evolutionist theorizing had such a limited effect on his other writing. He also downplays somewhat the degree to which White exaggerated his differences with the Boasians and the viciousness with which he attacked them. Was this wrath motivated by White's personality, a feeling of being a lonely native son from the heartland whom the East and West Coast anthropologists (many of them Jewish and/or foreign-born) kept outside their circle, or a desire to establish himself as a major alternative voice in American anthropology? Regardless of the answer, this stand made White the darling of Soviet anthropologists, who reprinted his early attack on the Boasians in a 1932 issue of their leading journal and praised his "progressive" critique of "bourgeois empiricism," while criticizing him for not being a true dialectical materialist. This positive Soviet view of White's anthropology persisted and at the 1964 international anthropological congress, held in Moscow, he played a major role in a plenary session on Morgan and, according to other American delegates, was much too accommodating to his rather dogmatic hosts. At the same time, as Peace demonstrates, during the Cold War White had to protect his job by not discussing Marx in his published works. Surprisingly, he eventually developed a critical view of the American Left and kept a low profile during the turbulent 1960s. We will never know whether this represented a change in his ideology or resulted from fear. In any event, the latter might have been behind White's purging of many of his letters and journals. Thanks to Peace's painstaking research we know a lot more about White's life and scholarly career. Despite the

author's overly generous view of White's early politics, this biography is
well written, interesting, and useful.

DOI 10.1215/00141801-2006-047

Montana 1911: A Professor and His Wife among the Blackfeet. Edited
by Mary Eggermont-Molenaar with contributions by Alice Kehoe, Inge
Genee, and Klaus van Berkel. (Lincoln: University of Nebraska Press,
2005. xii + 417 pp., preface and acknowledgments, introduction, illustrations, appendixes, references, notes. $45.00 paper.)

William E. Farr, *University of Montana*

This is a big, attractive book, adorned with a clutch of previously unpublished historical photographs, yet the title does not sufficiently reveal the
gold of its contents. Yes, it locates the place, Montana, and time, 1911, and
gives some tantalizing clues about its contents, namely the existence of a
professor and his wife among the Blackfeet. But the contents, including
the editorial comments, are far richer than the title led me to expect. In
her preface, editor and translator Mary Eggermont-Molenaar tells us that
the book began as the idea of publishing the summer diary of Wilhel-
mina Maria ("Willy") Uhlenbeck-Melchior, composed as her husband,
the Dutch linguist C. C. Uhlenbeck, pursued his fieldwork in 1911 on the
Blackfeet Indian Reservation adjacent to Glacier National Park in Montana.
Eggermont-Molenaar quickly decided that introductions were in order.
After all, who were the Uhlenbecks? From there the project took on a life
of its own, one element requiring another, the parts multiplying, almost
threatening the initial project. Not only did the two Uhlenbecks require
a biographical introduction, so did the Blackfeet, and so too did C. C.
Uhlenbeck's published linguistic and narrative production. Having gone
that far, the next step was to include C. C. Uhlenbeck's long-out-of-print
1911 and 1912 Blackfoot texts (without their parallel English translations)
along with a series of other supporting appendices and articles, including
some by J. P. B. de Josselin de Jong, Uhlenbeck's capable graduate student.
The resulting "collage" dovetails nicely with Uhlenbeck-Melchior's diary
and the insightful introductions, producing a rewarding and mutually but-
tressing congruence. The whole is truly greater than the sum of its many
parts, and this is the strength of this collaborative publishing effort.

It is, however, Uhlenbeck-Melchior's previously unpublished diary
that captivates and engages—I read entry after entry in a single wintry,

gray afternoon and evening. The appeal of being transported to another time, among names and places that I know from photographs and other contexts, was enormous. It rested in the close intimate details of camp life that the Uhlenbecks shared with their interpreter and hosts, Joseph and Annie Tatsey and so many of the other "southsiders," those south of the Great Northern Railroad that divided the communities of the reservation Blackfeet. There were wonderfully honest physical descriptions of individuals, of the pervasive dust and grit, the sweet reality of canned peaches, the wet boots and cold feet of an unusually rainy summer, the lack of privacy, the unannounced visits, and the welcome closeness of eleven people crowded into the small, walled tent on a cold day. But it is the people who are most engaging—not just the "teachers," the endearing term C. C. Uhlenbeck employed for his paid informants, however frustrating they may also have been, but their wives, the numerous children to whom both of the Uhlenbecks paid such close attention, and the crowds of visitors who delighted in candy kisses or small gifts of tobacco. All drift in and out of Uhlenbeck-Melchior's warm vision. The Blackfeet liked to be around the convivial Uhlenbeck-Melchior, and she clearly liked being with them. Included as well are her offhand but insightful remarks about her husband's research methods and the conditions under which many of the narratives were collected and corrected.

Montana 1911 with Uhlenbeck-Melchior's diary and the introductions adds a wonderful new layer of information to the instructive Blackfoot narratives, enriching, and, one can hope, reviving new interest in the old classics of C. C. Uhlenbeck.

DOI 10.1215/00141801-2006-048

"Bringing Them under Subjection": California's Tejón Indian Reservation and Beyond, 1852-1864. By George Harwood Phillips. (Lincoln: University of Nebraska Press, 2004. xv + 369 pp., acknowledgments, preface, illustrations, maps, tables, bibliography, index. $59.95 cloth.)

Quincy D. Newell, *University of Wyoming*

With this book, George Harwood Phillips completes the examination of Indian history in California's San Joaquin Valley that he began in *Indians and Intruders in Central California, 1769-1849* (1993) and continued in *Indians and Indian Agents: The Origins of the Reservation System in California, 1849-1852* (1997). Drawing on a wealth of sources ranging from nineteenth-century newspapers and government documents to letters and oral histories, Phillips chronicles Anglo-Americans' attempts to bring the California Indians "under subjection" in the 1850s and 1860s. Phillips borrows the term *subjection* from the nineteenth-century Anglo-Americans who used it "to describe the process of rounding up Indians and placing them on reservations" (xvi). While he recognizes the potentially oppressive aspects of this policy, Phillips makes it clear that subjection was a far cry from the genocide that some have claimed California Indians experienced. The goal of subjection, he writes, was "domination, not extermination" (xvi). According to Phillips, subjection also represented a major innovation in U.S. Indian policy. Instead of removing the Indians beyond California's borders, the course that had been pursued in the eastern United States, Indian Commissioners (and later Agents) Redick McKee, George Barbour, and O. M. Wozencraft sought to "confin[e] Indians within the state where they resided," thus "plant[ing] the reservation system in [California]" (259).

Phillips traces the foundation and dissolution of the Sebastian Military Reserve, also known as the Tejón Reservation, in the San Joaquin Valley. He argues that "the federal government introduced at Tejón a benign form of subjection," because "Indians were encouraged, not coerced, to settle on the reservation. . . , to learn new skills and values," and to provide the labor that allowed the reservation to run (262). However, when Indians faced starvation due to Anglo-American destruction of traditional food resources, when they were threatened with physical harm by white settlers and with economic competition from white and Chinese immigrants, the distinction between encouragement and coercion must have seemed very slight indeed.

Indians' experiences of state and federal Indian policy, however, are not the main concern in this account. Instead, Phillips pays close attention to the political and economic factors involved in the creation and eventual demise of the Tejón Reservation as well as several "Indian farms"—private land leased by the government and cultivated by California Indians. One of the major figures in the creation and implementation of Indian policy in California was Edward F. Beale, the first superintendent of Indian affairs in California and later the man who hastened the Tejón Reservation's dissolution by claiming the land on which it was located. Because of Beale's pivotal role, Phillips singles him out for heightened scrutiny. In his conclusion, Phillips argues that Beale was not as benevolent a figure as many historians have made him out to be. Beale did not single-handedly craft the innovative Indian policy implemented in California, Phillips writes, nor was he responsible for that policy's initial success. Though Beale claimed credit for these achievements, it was his predecessors—men like McKee, Barbour, and Wozencraft—as well as the Indians themselves, who deserved the accolades. Nevertheless, Phillips concludes that, though Beale engaged in questionable financial activities during and after his tenure as superintendent, he acted in good faith while he occupied that post.

This book is too dense for most students, and some scholars may fault it for including too much detail and not enough analysis. However, this exhaustively researched volume will prove a valuable resource for scholars of California and Indian history, and will provide raw material for other scholars to do further analytical and comparative work on U.S. Indian policy.

DOI 10.1215/00141801-2006-049

A Colonial Complex: South Carolina's Frontiers in the Era of the Yamasee War, 1680-1730. By Steven J. Oatis. (Lincoln: University of Nebraska Press, 2004. ix + 399 pp., acknowledgments, introduction, notes, bibliography, index. $65.00 cloth.)

Patricia Barker Lerch, *University of North Carolina, Wilmington*

The entire story of the Yamasee War may never be known, but Steven J. Oatis provides as complete an examination as may be possible. His in-depth research gives an exhaustive account of the era before and after the war. By detailing the causes of the war, the perspective of the different Indian societies, and the views of the South Carolinians, Oatis takes us deep into the subject, showing how the war set off a string of events from South Carolina to the Mississippi River. Scholars interested in the Southeast will find this book a valuable addition to their libraries.

On Good Friday 1715 the Yamasee of Pocotaligo village, located close to the colonial settlement at Port Royal Sound, South Carolina, burst into the home of trader Thomas Nairne to capture, torture, and kill him. The death of Nairne, a long-time trader and "friend" of the Yamasee, stands symbolically for the death of the old relationship between South Carolina, the Yamasee, and most of the colony's other Indian allies and trading partners. The Yamasee War transformed colonial relationships and the fates and fortunes of all involved. Oatis places the Yamasee War in historical context and fits it into the "colonial complex," which was essentially a series of "frontiers" involving the "interaction of distinct cultures in a context of undefined power relations" (6). He investigates three closely related themes—trade, combat, and diplomacy (9). In tracing them, Oatis not only offers insight into European viewpoints but also allows us to glimpse those of Indian leaders who tried to balance the demands of potential European trading partners with those of their own societies. Indian leaders carefully considered their decisions, weighing them against their impact on internal factional struggles and external demands of their various European trading partners. The book's portrayal of the dilemmas faced by these leaders is one of its strengths.

Oatis concludes that the Yamasee War transformed the physical and human geography of the region as well as European military and mercantile policy. It shocked South Carolinians out of their confident complacency and forced Indian leaders to deal with the intertribal conflicts it sparked. No one was spared. Oatis offers evidence that the Yamasee War, while involving many different Indian societies, did not represent a coordinated pan-Indian "conspiracy" against South Carolina (306). This lack of coordination and cooperation likely allowed the South Carolinians to survive.

DOI 10.1215/00141801-2006-050

Los siete mitos de la conquista española. By Matthew Restall. (Barcelona: Paidós, 2004. 307 pp., acknowledgments, introduction, illustrations, notes, bibliography, index. €19.00 paper.)

Paul E. Hoffman, *Louisiana State University*

The "seven myths" of the Spanish conquest of the Americas appeared contemporaneously with that long, complex process as Spanish authors (and some other Europeans) used their participation in it to seek favors from the Crown or simply recorded it as news worthy of publication. Later generations of European and Euro-American writers refined that material so that it became accepted fact for the uninformed public and for the producers of the movie *1492: The Conquest of Paradise*. That film, Kirkpatrick Sale's book that lay behind it, and an awareness of scholarship that showed the errors of some of the myths led Matthew Restall to conduct a graduate seminar and then write this book, here reviewed in its Spanish translation.

A summary of Restall's argument is this: It is not true that a few exceptional men carried out the conquest. It is not true that the conquistadors were mostly former soldiers in the king's army and in the king's employ at the time of the conquest. It is not true that only Europeans carried out the conquest (Native Americans were in every case critical to Spaniards' military success). It is not true that the conquest was completed quickly; in some respects it is still going on. There is considerable doubt about how well Spaniards and Native Americans understood each other, even when there were alleged interpreters like La Malinche. It is not true that because of diseases and the disruptions of the conquest that Native Americans and their cultures died out and were devastated, respectively. And finally, it is not true that Native Americans were nonhuman, inferior beings ("apes").

Restall's method is to lay out these myths in their various expressions, as well as their original sources and more recent repetitions, then refute them. For example, in chapter 7 ("Monkeys and Men: The Myth of Superiority") he notes that contemporaries of the conquest claimed divine and saintly intervention in support of Christianization, an interpretation that transmitted the idea of Spain's election for this task and the superiority of its language, religion, organization, civilization, weapons, and so on. Restall then discusses three factors that he thinks were the real reasons for Spanish success: disease, lack of Native American unity, and weapons and war animals (only the steel sword was really decisive, he says).

No short review can do justice to the richness of this book. While many of the ideas in it will be familiar to scholars of the conquest period, the contextualization and deconstruction of the texts that started the myths is a useful addition to modern ethnohistorical literature. Restall's evidence against the myths comes largely from that literature. In combating the myths, however, Restall sometimes resorts to his own distortions. The most notable is the definition of "completion" in chapter 4's discussion of this myth. His implicit definition is the full Hispanization and social integration of Native Americans (who would then be Native Americans only in a biological sense). It is doubtful that sixteenth-century Spaniards thought that. For them establishing political control and an end to the combat phase of conquest meant it was finished. Restall is right that claims of "mission accomplished" arose from the nature of conquistadors' contracts with the Crown and other political considerations, but that does not mean that the sixteenth-century definition of "completion" was wrong.

In sum, this is a useful book for anyone who has some knowledge of the Spanish conquest but needs to understand it in the light of modern scholarship.

DOI 10.1215/00141801-2006-051

Enfermedad y muerte en América y Andalucía (siglos XVII–XX). José Jesús Hernández Palomo, coord. (Seville: Consejo Superior de Investigaciones Científicas, Escuela de Estudios Hispano-Americanos, 2004. 546 pp., introduction, maps, illustrations, tables. €38.95 paper.)

Murdo J. MacLeod, *University of Florida, Emeritus*

This strange collection of twenty essays by seventeen authors, the result of a summer institute held at La Rábida some years ago, has few threads connecting the essays on Andalusia and the Americas, and not much in common among those on the New World.

Perhaps strangest of all is one of the essays that attempts to link the two sides of the Atlantic. The author, Antonio Orozco Acuaviva, writes of the brutality of the ancient Europeans and the pre-Columbian Indoamericans, but then, what to make, in this day and age, of a statement such as "cuando los europeos llegaron al Nuevo Mundo habían ya olvidado estos horrores. Llevaban mil quinientos años de una cultura cristiana, que aunque no exenta de algunos casos de comportamientos concretos fanáticos y crueles, era puro amor, mansedumbre y caridad ante estas costumbres crueles primitivas" (20)? The Taino and the inhabitants of Tenochtitlán, among others, would have found this view astonishing. The author also asserts that Native Americans, unlike Europeans, had no science. As for the builders of Sacsahuaman, the chinampas, Maya astronomy, and so on, "ninguno de ellos . . . poseía conceptos científicos, porque sus conocimientos eran aún de nivel mágico" (21). What then to make of such European beliefs as those in pacts with the devil and witchcraft?

Some essays simply recapitulate or summarize the authors' previously published work and, given space constraints, will not be reviewed here. Perhaps a dozen essays contain new analysis or fresh findings.

Four essays, by Angelines Pisón Casares, José Jesús Hernández Palomo, Gregorio García-Baquero López, and Manuel Jesús Fernández Naranjo, discuss the arrival of cholera in the small towns of southern Andalusia around 1834. Skilled uses of parish registers and town council papers provide much of the data. Circumstances such as geography, proximity to cities, and climate vary, but there are common findings. Unknown in Spain before the 1830s, cholera caused great fear and dispersal because of its rapid onset, horrifying symptoms, and high mortality. But the brief duration of each epidemic meant that few preventative measures had much chance of success. Other conclusions are that cholera was seasonal—occurring during the hottest months—most common in humid climates, and struck adults disproportionately. Hernández Palomo goes beyond the other three essayists, claiming that the cholera epidemic of 1834 ushered in an era of new epidemiology that lasted until the influenza epidemic of 1918. Social and economic change was rapid, but the author also asserts, paradoxically, that the cholera century in some areas delayed the end of the ancien regime (254–55).

The studies of the Americas are a more mixed bag. In the first of his two essays, Manuel Salvador Vázquez examines the 1833 cholera epidemic in Cuba, where rural mortality rates, especially among slaves and blacks, were much higher than in Havana. Deaths were especially rare among soldiers. Elsa Malvido and María Elena Morales compare the 1833 cholera outbreaks in Mexico with those of 1991. While admitting that comparative death rates have declined, they stress that rural poverty, governmental corruption, and related underreporting add to present-day problems.

In his other essay, Salvador Vázquez discusses the Mutis scientific expedition, its advocacy of new sources of quinine, and the various personal, political, and professional rivalries that frustrated José Celestino Mutis and others.

Gunter Vollmer (writing about Puebla) and Nadine Béligand (writing about Calimaya, near Toluca), in two of the best essays in the book, skeptically look at sources and conclude, in Vollmer's case, that epidemics account for only about half of the native colonial population decline, making necessary more research into "las condiciones de la vida cotidiana de los indígenas mexicanos" (64), and, in Béligand's, that subsistence crises were more closely linked to Indian death rates than to those of mestizos or Spaniards. Béligand also finds that the years 1727–37 were the most catastrophic of the seventeenth and eighteenth centuries.

The remaining essays on the Americas are more related to institutional and cultural history than to demography and epidemics. Ricardo González Leandri explores the politics of and political strife over public hygiene and epidemics in Buenos Aires in the 1880s. Elsa Malvido tells the history of the establishment, after independence, of hospitals in Mexico by the Spanish Sisters of Charity (1844–76), a Vicentian order. (Mexican sisters continued the work after the expulsion.) Béligand, continuing her studies of Calimaya, tries to deduce the evolution of forms of piety in another fine essay based on confraternity records and 223 Nahuatl wills.

In a second study of Buenos Aires, focusing in this case on the years 1785–1816, Sandra Olivero attempts to understand how this society faced death collectively, using data from church death registers. "Conocer cómo moría la gente es una forma de conocer como vivía," is one of the propositions she advances.

Another outlying essay concludes the book. Francisco Javier Rodríguez Barberán attempts to compare funerary art and architecture in Andalusia and Ibero-America. New fashions reach the colonies after some delay. Modern evolution has followed the same general course in both areas.

In sum, the book is an uneven, disparate collection with some nuggets among the dross.

DOI 10.1215/00141801-2006-052

The School of the Americas: Military Training and Political Violence in the Americas. By Lesley Gill. (Durham, NC: Duke University Press, 2004. xviii + 281 pp., preface, introduction, illustrations, bibliography, index. $19.95 paper.)

Peter M. Beattie, *Michigan State University*

The infamous School of the Americas (SOA), recently recast as the Western Hemisphere Institute for Security Cooperation, trained some sixty thousand military and police officers and enlisted men from across the Americas from World War II to 1993 and since then has trained hundreds more each year. Many Latin American SOA graduates went on to become top officers in their armed forces, and a disturbingly large number of them have been accused of gross human rights abuses against their own citizens. There are many prominent examples, but perhaps most egregious is that of the ten Salvadoran SOA graduates who participated in the El Mazote massacre of some one thousand villagers. Lesley Gill explores how the SOA is linked to broader U.S. imperial power and argues that it is an important part of the "dense networks of economic, cultural, social, and military control" essential to U.S. hegemony in the hemisphere (3). More specifically, she sees the SOA as a conduit through which the U.S. military made Latin American militaries into "foot soldiers of U.S. Empire."

The author conducted extensive interviews with SOA staff officers, graduates from Honduras, Colombia, and Bolivia, as well as U.S. activists who since 1990 have led protests against the SOA. Through this triangulated ethnographic approach, Gill seeks to untangle the webs of politics, influence, power, and impunity that characterize so much of the transhemispheric relations between armed forces, governments, and citizenries. This is an important study that, like Martha Huggins's *Political Policing: The United States and Latin America* (1998), shows us how U.S. military training facilities were used to win allies and influence in Latin American security forces. Gill adds to this perspective an analysis of mostly American activists who have created SOA Watch. These protestors had succeeded in calling public attention to the SOA's abysmal record, and they led a political drive that nearly succeeded in cutting funding to the institution before September 11, 2001. As Gill demonstrates, public scrutiny and protest has thus far only succeeded in forcing minor curricular modifications that have not changed the SOA's essential character.

This admirable study sometimes leans on sweeping statements that exceed its scope. For instance, "Impunity reinforces a particular kind of 'order'—political, economic, social—that is necessary for the expansion of free market capitalism in Latin America" (166). Was there a golden age when impunity did not characterize the actions of military officers and police acting at the behest of the political elite in Latin America, or elsewhere for that matter? This hypothesis may fit the recent case studies of Honduras, Bolivia, and Colombia that the author features, but applying it across the region seems dubious. Brazil's military government, supported by the United States from 1964 to 1985, surely operated with greater impunity than the civilian governments that came after and before it. Ultimately Brazil's authoritarian military government embraced nationalist development that expanded the state-owned sector of the economy in no small part as a check on the influence of multinational corporations. As in Argentina, center-left elected civilian presidents implemented the bulk of Brazil's neoliberal policies, to the chagrin of many military nationalists.

These comments do not impeach in any way the author's overall point that U.S. military and police training is an important factor in maintaining U.S. power in the region, but that power needs to be understood in the broad context of other local and transhemispheric relationships. This book should be read with interest by all Latin Americanists, and I know it will enliven my own lectures on contemporary U.S.–Latin American relations. This is a timely publication that will also be useful for seminars that treat issues of peace and justice on a global scale.

DOI 10.1215/00141801-2006-053

El urbanismo en Mesoamérica/Urbanism in Mesoamerica, vol. 1. Edited by William T. Sanders, Alba Guadalupe Mastache, and Robert H. Cobean. (University Park: Department of Anthropology, Pennsylvania State University; Mexico City: Instituto Nacional de Antropología e Historia, 2003. xiv + 513 pp., preliminary note, introduction, illustrations. $35.00 paper.)

Thomas H. Charlton, *University of Iowa*

The first cities were founded about five thousand years ago in a small number of widely spread primary civilizations. Today, though varying in form and function, cities have become the most common settlement type in all areas of the world. The comparative history of their development is the focus of this volume.

These essays are revised presentations from the first two seminar meetings in a project organized by William T. Sanders of the Pennsylvania State University and Alba Guadalupe Mastache of the Instituto Nacional de Antropología e Historia in Mexico City. The goal is to investigate the nature of Mesoamerican urbanism through a series of six seminars, two a year, one in Mexico City, one in University Park. The six projected meetings have been held, the most recent in University Park in August 2006. We should expect another two volumes in this bilingual series.

As set out, the goals of the project are (1) to focus on basic concepts such as urbanism and urbanization, (2) to look at thirty-five examples (Sanders, xi) of Mesoamerican central places (a neutral term for what might be called cities) over two and a half millennia, (3) to develop a synthesis of our current knowledge of processes involved in Mesoamerican urbanization, and (4) to outline necessary future research to address the urban phenomena. The sixth and final meeting was projected to cover goals 3 and 4. The volume under review addresses goals 1 and 2.

Participants in these meetings include Mesoamerican archaeologists, archaeologists with specialties in other areas, and scholars from non-archaeological disciplines whose interests include urbanism. The inclusion of the last is important since archaeologists borrow and use theories from a wide range of disciplines.

Given space constraints I can only briefly note each essay. The essays and participants reflect the orientations and goals noted above. The first five chapters focus on goal 1, basic ideas about urbanism. George Cowgill presents a broad survey of studies of cities around the world, including views of cities as cosmograms, as inventions, and as situated within regional site hierarchies. The urban geographer Jérôme Monnet discusses the dynamics of urban forms and functions in archaeological and contemporary examples. The social anthropologist Aidan Southall's essay is a partial version of chapter 1 in his book *The City in Time and Space* (1998) and discusses Marxist-based approaches to urban development. Kenneth G. Hirth's essay and that of Gerardo Gutiérrez Mendoza attempt to construct an indigenous view of Mesoamerican urbanism including ethnohistorical data.

There are twelve case studies, ten on Mesoamerican sites, one on urbanism in medieval France (Joëlle Burnouf), and one on sites in sub-Saharan West Africa (Jean Polet).

Of the Mesoamerican studies five are on sites in or adjacent to the

Basin of Mexico: Xochicalco (K. G. Hirth), Tula (Alba G. Mastache and Robert H. Cobean), Tenochtitlán (Eduardo Matos Moctezuma), and Tenochtitlán-Tlatelolco (one by Edward Calnek and one by W. T. Sanders). Cantona to the east of the basin (Angel García Cook) and several sites in the core of the Tarascan state to the west (Helen P. Pollard) complement the highland sites.

The lowland sites studied include Cerro de las Mesas on the Gulf Coast (Barbara L. Stark), Chichén Itzá (Rafael Cobos), and Piedras Negras (David Webster and Stephen Houston).

This volume could have been improved with a listing of times, places, and participants for each meeting, as well as a general synthesis of the essays. Nevertheless, the directors of the project have produced an important study of Mesoamerican urbanism. Future volumes are eagerly awaited.

Requiescat in pace Alba Guadalupe Mastache.

DOI 10.1215/00141801-2006-054

Cartographic Mexico: A History of State Fixations and Fugitive Landscapes. By Raymond B. Craib. (Durham, NC: Duke University Press, 2004. xviii + 300 pp., introduction, illustrations, maps, bibliography, index. $79.95 cloth; $22.95 paper.)

Jordana Dym, *Skidmore College*

Raymond Craib presents a thought-provoking study of the ways late nineteenth-century leaders, state agents, and residents mapped and thereby contested sovereignty and power over the spaces and places of Mexico. He draws on and analyzes an impressive array of archival sources, including Mexican cartographer Antonio García Cubas's 1858 *General Map of Mexico* (the first in the thirty-five-year-old country), the *Boletín* of Mexico's Society of Geography and History, sixteenth- through twentieth-century maps produced to define territories and jurisdictions, and private and official correspondence of city councils, surveyors, and landowners.

The principal strength of the analysis is its application of sources and methods of historical cartography, agrarian history, and studies of "everyday forms of state formation" to look at the top-down theories and bottom-up practices of surveying and mapping that defined, appropriated, and apportioned Mexico's internal spaces in Porfirian and revolutionary Mexico (ca. 1850–1940). In engaging prose, Craib shows that map production in the service of the state, the attempt to "fix" space, is only half the story; the reception and application of maps in "fugitive" ways that resist state control is the equally important other half. Craib focuses on the work undertaken in the state of Veracruz by the Geographic Exploration Commission (CGE), an agency Porfirio Díaz established to create a general map of Mexico to serve military, political, and economic ends. Over four chapters, a sensitive exploration emerges of the contingency of CGE mapping on local resources and knowledge. En route, we learn how a diverse audience including national and state agencies, scientists, peasants, city councils, and miners acquired and used CGE maps as a source of authority when making competing claims about the naming of and jurisdiction over community and "vacant" land and waterways. These chapters are bookended by discussions of how García Cubas's map and illustrations sought to define Mexico through history as well as territory, and of how cartographic practices influenced land reform policy and the titling of *ejidos* under Lázaro Cárdenas.

Craib is not the first Latin Americanist to follow J. B. Harley's lead and explore maps as objects of power. However, his training in agrarian studies allows him to do a particularly fine job of highlighting the human agency that undermines maps' totemic value and of emphasizing how the interaction of national figures and surveyors with local authorities and regional powerbrokers can constrain as well as support federal and state government initiatives. There is thus substantial material here for those interested in the human agency and contingency of state projects. Perhaps because of this interest in human agency, however, there are silences that may make some aspects of the work opaque to nonspecialists, particularly the lack of a clear description of the nineteenth-century Mexican state and explanation of the complex political history of the period under study. The essays may stand alone, as the author intended, but the decision to append revolutionary Mexico's policies to what is essentially a study of the Porfirian era is puzzling. Finally, the text does not assess continuities and disruptions between colonial, imperial, and national mapping practices and jurisdictional processes, leaving open the question of how much individuals and institutions were adapting or abandoning existing strategies and methods. Still, Craib's theoretically informed and readable text will be a welcome addition to scholarly libraries and university classrooms of those interested in debating how national governments, specialized institutions, businessmen, and local authorities participated in processes of state formation, boundary demarcation, and national representation in the nineteenth and early twentieth centuries.

DOI 10.1215/00141801-2006-055

The Culture of Migration in Southern Mexico. By Jeffrey H. Cohen. (Austin: University of Texas Press, 2004. 207 pp., 20 black-and-white illustrations. $50.00 cloth; $21.95 paper.)

Rosana Barbosa, *Saint Mary's University*

This book is a significant contribution to the better understanding of migration patterns. Jeffrey H. Cohen's anthropological study takes place in the region of Oaxaca in southern Mexico. In comparison to other Mexican regions, Oaxaca has contributed little to the total flow of migrants. Cohen shows that the impacts of migration in that area are nonetheless profound.

The book is divided into five chapters. Chapter 1, "The Household and Migration," introduces the reader to the household in rural Oaxaca and the influence of family concerns on the decision to migrate. Chapter 2, "History, Trajectory, and Process in Oaxacan Migration," discusses the history and geography of the region in relation to migration. Chapter 3, "Contemporary Migration," analyses the outcomes of contemporary movements, in relation not only to emigration to the United States but to migration in general. Chapter 4, "Migration, Socioeconomic Change, and Development," discusses the costs and benefits of migration by looking at socioeconomic and cultural outcomes. Here Cohen examines migrants' continued interest in their culture and community and the impact of remittances. Chapter 5, "Nonimmigrant Households," describes those who chose not to migrate. The question of why some stay while others migrate is an important one that is ignored by many migration studies.

One major contribution of Cohen's book is its demonstration that migration theories cannot explain why people move without looking at several factors. For instance, there is no doubt that Mexicans migrate because they see a possibility of economic improvement. Yet, despite similar economic circumstances, not all Mexicans migrate. As Cohen points out, people do not blindly follow others and do not move in response to some biological impulse. Individuals migrate because they can and "in response to desires, lifestyles, resources and needs" (19).

Cohen also considers that migration cannot be understood without looking at the influence of families and communities. Finally, he highlights that migration is a pervasive force in the region, one that goes back generations. In addition, Cohen illustrates the impact of kinship on migration. Scholars have shown that a network of family and friends shapes and sustains migration. Cohen gives us examples of this kind of influence.

One weakness of the book is repetitiveness. Although this makes his arguments clear, it is a bit tedious to read. Moreover, the impact of neoliberal policies in creating a new wave of Mexican migrants, only mentioned in one paragraph in the conclusion (149), could have been further explored. The impact of these policies in impoverishing Mexicans and pushing them to seek jobs elsewhere should have been better addressed. Cohen concludes that the Oaxacan migrant contrasts with counterparts from other regions of Mexico (143). He considers other Mexican migrants to be "loner[s]," focused on self and uninterested or unable to think about households and communities," whereas "the Oaxacan migrant thinks about his or her family and is deeply concerned for the future and the changes that are ongoing in the region." I believe this to be a generalization. Throughout history we have seen concern for their community and family expressed by migrants from different parts of the world, not just Oaxaca.

DOI 10.1215/00141801-2006-056

Silence on the Mountain: Stories of Terror, Betrayal, and Forgetting in Guatemala. By Daniel Wilkinson. (Durham, NC: Duke University Press, 2004. x + 375 pp., contents, author's notes, list of names, note on sources, selected bibliography, acknowledgments, index. $19.95 paper.)

Ana Yolanda Contreras, *University of North Florida*

Since the colonial times of Spanish rule, and especially during the thirty-six years of civil war and state-sponsored terrorism, silence has been the most common way to preserve one's life in Guatemala. The overthrow of the democratically elected government of Jacobo Arbenz Guzmán in 1954 resulted in successive despotic governments that terrorized and repressed the populace. These tactics were intended to undermine social and political change and to maintain the dominance of a very small but powerful and wealthy class over the poor majority. This past and the social phenomenon of mass amnesia regarding events in the coffee-growing region of San Marcos is the subject of Daniel Wilkinson's book, *Silence on the Mountain: Stories of Terror, Betrayal, and Forgetting in Guatemala*.

During his years of research in Guatemala as a human-rights activist, Wilkinson discovered what at first appeared to be a peculiar lack of recall and denial among the populace of significant historical events. Through patient, investigative work, years of interviews, and, of course, due to recent changes in the political climate, Wilkinson finally began to uncover truths. His book unravels a considerable amount of heretofore undocumented detail on the history of San Marcos coffee plantations.

As a foreigner and independent researcher, he had access to various sides and voices in the conflict. He had the opportunity to interview victims and perpetrators, the coffee oligarchy and their workers, the military as well as former guerrilla combatants. He collected stories that otherwise might never have been told.

Wilkinson creates what could be called a North American rendition of magical realism, blurring boundaries between reality and fantasy to create a unique perception of reality for the characters in the story. Through investigative journalism and concerned and impartial observation, he has created a compelling story that is part adventure travel log, part ethnocultural dialogue, and part academic history lesson. Though the risk of losing objectivity is clearly present, he makes no claim that his work is purely academic. He manages to tell a believable and compelling story without falling into propaganda.

Wilkinson narrates his stories as an ethnographer, in an easily accessible manner and style reminiscent of *National Geographic* magazine and the ethnocultural TV docudramas of the 1970s and 1980s. His literary technique is a journey to uncover a mystery, interspersed with frequent "back stories," flashbacks and entertaining descriptions of the geography and ecology. He is an excellent observer of Guatemalan reality and gives the reader a sense of what Guatemalan life is all about. His observations of daily life, both rural and urban, are so accurate that even a native Guatemalan would have a hard time disputing them.

Yet this book offers something more significant than simply a good travel story. The mere writing of this book allows survivors of massacres the opportunity to overcome years of struggle with fear and silence to speak the truth about their experiences. The eloquent and dignified presentation of their voices touches an intimate fiber in the reader, raising social consciousness for the suffering and pain caused by the ruthless pursuit of material and political interests.

Wilkinson's recounting of major historical events and their consequences include the early twentieth-century dictatorships, the liberal governments and the decade of democracy, the overthrow of Arbenz, the thirty-six years of civil war, and the signing of the peace accords in December 1996. Even for Guatemalan scholars this book is an excellent source of historical information and an unusually detailed account of worldviews from the oligarchy.

For those unfamiliar with Guatemala this book is a fine acquisition. It is of great value to introduce students to Guatemalan and Central American history, anthropology, and political science. More than that, it is a good leisure read for the socially conscious travel enthusiast.

DOI 10.1215/00141801-2006-057

The Jesuit and the Incas: The Extraordinary Life of Padre Blas Valera, S.J. By Sabine Hyland. (Ann Arbor: University of Michigan Press, 2003. xii + 269 pp., contents, illustrations, introduction, appendixes, references, index. $30.00 cloth.)

Isabel Yaya, *University of New South Wales*

The mestizo Father Blas Valera was a major figure in Jesuit policy and mission in the late sixteenth-century Viceroyalty of Peru. His thought is inscribed in the seminal debates of the time, most notably in discussions about Indian nature and status in relation to law and the consequent question of the Spanish Crown's dominion over America. Sabine Hyland's biography, *The Jesuit and the Incas*, frames Valera's story through an incisive description of his historical and political context. The account of the Jesuit's life and an understanding of his sources are enriched by Hyland's historical analysis and archival research. She underlines the original influence of Northern traditions on Valera's work and other late chroniclers like Fernando de Montesinos. In her concern over historiographical reconstructions, the author offers a rigorous study of Valera's final controversy; beyond the degenerating turmoil caused by the Naples Documents, Hyland's book demonstrates the influence of Valera's thought on his seventeenth- and eighteenth-century followers. She also gives a valuable analysis of the work of classical author Varro, used by the Jesuit as an alternative perspective to the Augustinian view on paganism.

However, while *The Jesuit and the Incas* effectively focuses on important individuals and their historical setting, some important themes are not treated with sufficient depth. Little is said about the influence of Jesuit social ideals over Valera's reconstruction of Inca society. At that time, some members of the Society of Jesus developed a utopian image of Amerindian societies, comparable to religious communities governed by Jesuit spiritual virtues. Three such principles—respect for hierarchy, praise for communal work, and, above all, temperance—govern Valera's description of the Inca Empire. These themes, specific to Ignatius of Loyola's teaching, appeared early on in the *Annuae Litterae* of the Society's consignment in Mexico. The widely spread—and controlled—diffusion of these reports in religious and lay circles likely influenced distant members of the Society like Valera, and fostered a utopian vision of the Indian's natural leaning toward pious actions.

Valera's conception of the Quechua language is related to the idea of *civilitas*. Not only does this concept sustain his description of the Inca Empire as akin to classical societies, as Hyland indicates, it also supports the providential nature of its civilization. For Valera the Roman civilization was the social paradigm and fertile soil in which Christianity originally sprouted. Thus, comparing Cuzco to Rome implied the former's predisposition to receive and spread the true religion. The almost obsessive importance Valera gave to Inca legislation derives from this same parallel. His picture of pre-Hispanic laws offers a seductive precedent to the Christian constitution, just as the Justinian code anticipated the Common Law constituting the legal foundation of Christian nations during the Renaissance. Furthermore, the main preoccupation of humanist thought was to reach a more accurate understanding of Christian fundaments through the study of the *humanitas* that included grammar. By associating Quechua to the languages of the Book, Valera audaciously suggested the equal nature of the Revelation in all civilized places. Eventually, by appealing to Varro's typology to describe Inca religion, Valera directly challenged Augustine's condemnation of Varro's proposition, deemed heretical, that gods were historically instituted by political society. These arguments inevitably led to theological conflict and may partly explain the later charges brought against Valera and his final condemnation to never again teach grammar.

The Jesuit and the Incas is the richest analysis of Valera to date, particularly in addressing the significant problems involved in understanding his context. The issues raised above reveal the extent of the complexity that remains. The extended discussion that this invites is due in no small part to the value of Hyland's contribution.

DOI 10.1215/00141801-2006-058

Cañar: A Year in the Highlands of Ecuador. By Judy Blankenship. (Austin: University of Texas Press, 2005. ix + 209 pp., maps, 41 black-and-white photographs. $21.95 paper.)

George M. Lauderbaugh, *Jacksonville State University*

The indigenous peoples of highland Ecuador have fascinated travelers for centuries. From the sixteenth-century chronicles of Pedro Cieza de León to the writings of the U.S. diplomat Friedrich Hassaurek in *Four Years among the Ecuadorians* (1966 [1867]) to Blair Niles's *Casual Wanderings in Ecuador* (1923), descriptions of native communities in the Andes abound. Countless coffee-table books of photo collections have provided striking images of life in the Ecuadorian Andes. However, these works are those of the passerby, often providing a plastic image of highland people and reducing them to mere curiosities for the tourist in search of an exotic setting. Judy Blankenship, an independent journalist and photographer, first visited the southern highlands of Ecuador in 1993 and like so many before her was captivated by the indigenous population. Blankenship is no passerby, however, having devoted over a decade to documenting the life of the indigenous people of Cañar, a province in the southern Ecuadorian Andes, and the challenges they face in the twenty-first century.

Blankenship's objective was to create a still photographic record of the cycle of life in Cañar and to augment it with oral histories as well as tape and video recordings. This was not an easy task: the Cañari viewed cameras as intrusive instruments and photographers as unwelcome interlopers. Blankenship overcame these obstacles by adopting a protocol that included permission of the subject, reciprocity, and ultimately collaboration. By being patient, offering color photos to her subjects, and training Cañari photographers, she was eventually invited to document some of the most intimate of events, including a midwife-attended birth, funerals, weddings, and even family disputes.

This book is unpretentious: the author admits it is not an academic project, even though the Cañari first referred to her and her husband, Michael Jenkins, as "los académicos." However, as an astute observer, Blankenship provides a window into the life of the Cañari that could not be achieved through conventional research methods. Her account of the immediate effect of Ecuador's decision to use the U.S. dollar as its currency is one example. The Cañari were initially bewildered by the new money, refused to trust the banks, and suffered from a sudden rise in prices that saw the cost of cooking gas double and bus fares rise even higher. The resulting protest included blockading the Pan-American Highway with huge boulders and burning tires, but it was for the most part nonviolent. In the end the government made modest adjustments to the price increases and the crisis passed. The impact of globalization on Ecuador is best reflected not by dry statistics but by the absence in Cañar of young men who have migrated to the United States and by the requests of their families to deliver to them messages and videotapes of family events. The blending of traditional folkways with modern medicine is richly presented in the account of a birth that included herbal remedies, incantations, and a UNICEF medical kit. In the same anecdotal manner the author presents the problems of alcoholism, underemployment, and family violence. She also includes the richness and joys of family life at festivals, weddings, and other rituals.

In addition to being an enjoyable read about a South American adventure, *Cañar* offers a wealth of material useful for academics. Accounts of the blending of indigenous beliefs with Roman Catholicism, the effects of television, relations with the state, as well as family and environmental issues, would enhance lectures in a multitude of disciplines. In the end, Blankenship's greatest achievement is presenting the humanity of her subjects in both photographs and words.

DOI 10.1215/00141801-2006-059

I Die with My Country: Perspectives on the Paraguayan War, 1864–1870. Edited by Hendrik Kraay and Thomas L. Whigham. Studies in War, Society, and the Military. (Lincoln: University of Nebraska Press, 2004. 257 pp., preface, introduction, contributors, index, 3 maps, 18 illustrations. $69.95 cloth.)

Emily Story, *Georgetown University*

This volume brings together nine original essays that explore various aspects of the Paraguayan War (also known as the War of the Triple Alliance), the bloodiest intrastate conflict in modern South American history. For four years the ill-equipped allied forces struggled to defeat the tenacious defense mounted by the Paraguayans. The war had profound and lasting implications for each the four nations involved—Argentina, Brazil, Paraguay, and Uruguay—forcing all of them, in different ways, to confront modernity.

Editors Hendrik Kraay and Thomas L. Whigham provide a lucid introduction to the subject, helpfully accompanied by three maps. They present a useful overview of historiography of the conflict and examine how the war has been remembered in different countries. Kraay and Whigham take a clear and controversial position on the demographic consequences for Paraguay by accepting the legitimacy of a recently uncovered census from 1870–71, which shows that nation's population declined by more than 60 percent as a direct consequence of the war. If accurate, this figure means that Paraguay suffered a human loss unparalleled in the history of modern warfare. Barbara Potthast shows that, because the prolonged conflict literally consumed the nation's male population, the burden of managing the economy and supplying the troops shifted to the women of Paraguay. Most interesting, Potthast explores how President Francisco López Solano used the nation's women in a propaganda campaign aimed at generating and maintaining popular support for the war effort.

While Paraguay experienced the most immediate and devastating effects of war, the allies did not emerge unchanged. Ariel de La Fuente shows popular resistance to the war in La Rioja as an example of political action undertaken by the lower classes as part of a broader challenge to the central authority of Buenos Aires. Three essays on the Brazilian side offer fascinating examples of how the conflict brought to the surface various conflicts within the empire—racial, political, and regional—and contributed to the transformation of Brazilian society in the late nineteenth century, as slavery was abolished and a republic was created. Renato Lemos uses the correspondence of Benjamin Constant, a young Brazilian officer, to show how dissatisfaction with the prolonged Paraguayan War fed growing republicanism among the imperial forces. Kraay explores the complex political repercussions of the organization of several companies comprised solely of Afro-Brazilian volunteers.

The book is dedicated to the late Miguel Angel Cuarterelo, who contributed an essay on images of the war. Cuarterelo analyzes the ways in which both sides of the conflict used visual images to generate support at home. His essay includes rarely seen photographs that starkly illustrate the war's brutality and the suffering endured by the people of Paraguay. In his concluding chapter, coeditor Whigham argues that the war profoundly marked the four nations involved. Paraguay was nearly destroyed, but the war precipitated fundamental change in the victorious states as well, serving as a "catalyst for nationalism" in all four. Taking the long view, the war finally put to rest a territorial conflict inherited from the colonial era, allowing the countries to move toward regional cooperation. This collection makes a valuable contribution to existing scholarship on the Paraguayan War. I highly recommend it.

DOI 10.1215/00141801-2006-060

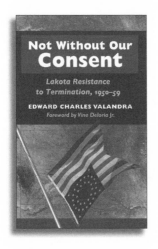

Not Without Our Consent

Lakota Resistance to Termination, 1950–59

EDWARD CHARLES VALANDRA

Foreword by Vine Deloria Jr.

Documents the tenacious and formidable Lakota resistance to attempts at applying Public Law 83-280, which allowed states to apply their criminal and civil laws to Native American country. The various congressional bills discussed are reproduced in five appendices.

Cloth $35.00

Benjamin Franklin, Pennsylvania, and the First Nations

The Treaties of 1736–62

Edited by SUSAN KALTER

A carefully researched edition of the treaties between the British colonies and Indian nations, originally printed and sold by Benjamin Franklin. Last published in 1938, the new edition features a simpler, easier-to-read format, extensive explanatory notes, and maps.

Illus. Cloth $45.00

Lost and Found

Reclaiming the Japanese American Incarceration

KAREN L. ISHIZUKA

Forewords by John Kuo Wei Tchen and Roger Daniels

Details the strategy that invited visitors to become part of the groundbreaking exhibition, "America's Concentration Camp: Remembering the Japanese American Experience," at the Japanese American National Museum.

The Asian American Experience

Illus. Cloth $70.00; Paper $24.95

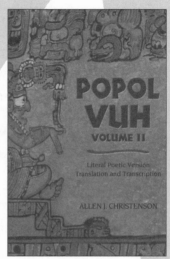